如何撰寫文獻探討

給社會暨行為科學學生指南

Jose L. Galvan 著

吳德邦、馬秀蘭 譯

Writing Literature Reviews

A Guide for Students of the Social and Behavioral Sciences

THIRD EDITION

Jose L. Galvan

California State University, Los Angeles

Concents
目　　錄

Writing Literature Reviews: A Guide for Students of the Social and Behavioral Sciences

譯者簡介

吳德邦

現任 國立台中教育大學教育學系兼任教授

曾任 國小教師

師專、師範學院助教、講師

教育大學副教授、教授

學歷 國立台中教育大學教育測驗統計研究所博士（Ph. D., 2010）

美國北科羅拉多大學教育數學博士（Ph. D., 1994）

國立台灣師範大學理學碩士（M. S.）

國立台灣師範大學理學學士（B. S.）

省立台中師範專科學校畢業

e-mail wudb@hotmail.com

著作 學術論文（含 SCI, SSCI, EI 雜誌）數百餘篇

專書數十餘冊，包括：

統計學——以 Microsoft Excel 為例（第八版，新文京出版社，2016）

統計學——以 SPSS for Windows 為例（第五版，新文京出版社，2015）

如何撰寫文獻探討：給社會暨行為科學學生指南（譯作，心理出版社，2014 二刷）

小學數學教學資源手冊——推理與解題導向（心理出版社，2009）

中學數學教學資源手冊——推理與解題導向（心理出版社，2009）

微積分、工科微積分、高科微積分

1993 年國民小學數學教科用書（全套）第一冊至第十二冊

會員 美國 NCTM 會員

美國 IEEE 會員

歐洲 WSEAS 會員

International Group for the Psychology of Mathematics Education 會員

台灣數學教育學會永久會員兼第一、二屆理事

台灣科學教育學會永久會員

台灣感性工學學會永久會員

馬秀蘭

現任　嶺東科技大學教授

曾任　高中教師

　　　國立台中教育大學、勤益科技大學兼任教授

學歷　美國北科羅拉多大學教育數學博士（Ph. D.）

　　　美國北科羅拉多大學理學碩士（M. S.）

　　　國立台灣師範大學理學學士（B. S.）

e-mail　hlma@hotmail.com.tw

著作　學術論文數百餘篇

　　　專書數十餘冊，包括：

　　　統計學——以 Microsoft Excel 為例（第八版，新文京出版社，2016）

　　　統計學——以 SPSS for Windows 為例（第五版，新文京出版社，2015）

　　　如何撰寫文獻探討：給社會暨行為科學學生指南（譯作，心理出版社，
　　　　2014 二刷）

　　　小學數學教學資源手冊——推理與解題導向（心理出版社，2009）

　　　中學數學教學資源手冊——推理與解題導向（心理出版社，2009）

　　　微積分、工科微積分、商科微積分

　　　二專數學（全）、五專數學（一二三四）、五專數學（全）

會員　International Group for the Psychology of Mathematics Education 會員

　　　台灣數學教育學會永久會員兼第一屆監事

　　　台灣知識創新學會永久會員

簡介

　　本書是本實用指南，以供學生在撰寫關於社會和行為科學方面文獻探討的複雜過程中使用。重點在探討刊登在學術期刊上的原創研究及相關的理論文獻。然而，本書的大多數指南也能被用於其他題材的探討。

給讀者的話

　　本書提供社會和行為科學相關領域學科的學生作為撰寫期中報告時的參考。通常，他們以前的訓練沒包括諸如：搜尋原創研究和有關理論文獻報告的資料庫，分析特殊樣式的文獻，及如何將蒐集到的眾多文獻，整合（synthesize）為一致且有凝聚性的陳述。相反的，過去的訓練只是教導我們如何使用二手資料來源（例如百科全書，刊登在大眾媒體上的報告，以及綜合他人報告的書籍）。此外，也不會教我們在撰寫社會行為科學方面報告的慣例及常規。本書為彌補這些缺陷，將以詳細的、一步一步的方式來指引學生，說明如何使用第一手資料來源來撰寫具綜論性的文獻探討。

　　研究時通常要準備關鍵性的分析數據，如果學生先前沒有接受過類似訓練，就開始著手做他們的碩士論文（thesis）和博士論文（dissertation），建議學生們先閱讀此書再著手進行，將更得心應手。撰寫一篇論文或長篇論文是件有壓力性的工作，本書應可作為學生在撰寫論文的文獻探討章節時，平靜心靈及邏輯思考上的參考之用。

　　總而言之，凡是為準備投稿於期刊出版物而撰寫文獻探討的個人，或是需要在申請研究計畫案提供文獻者，將會發現這本書的助益。

本書特點

相較於其他教科書，本書有以下特點：

- 本書著重於撰寫原創研究的批判性文獻（critical reviews）。
- 它透過有系統的、多步驟（multistep）的撰寫過程指引學生。
- 書中提及的步驟具有系統化，並挑選學術期刊做例子說明。
- 每一章節都可用來幫助學生撰寫出具體的成果，這成果將會是合乎標準的文獻探討。

對教師的建議

許多大專院校開出「論文寫作」（writing-across-the-curriculum）的課程，要求全部學生在整個課程中都要寫論文。這樣的課程目標令人欽佩，同時許多教師迫於時間壓力，僅教導他們課程上的傳統內容和利用少許的時間來教導寫作。本書在寫作過程中的明確步驟全部以範例說明，這使這些教師覺得實用，也讓學生得以獨立應用。除此之外，許多教授們「自然而然」（naturally）就能寫好論文，但是並未花很多心力或接受如何教導寫作的訓練。本書可作為補充教材，透過提供詳細的寫作過程指南，解決上述的兩難。

大多數人對於論文寫作，來自學者 Kamhi-Stein 在 1997 年所發表的「單獨寫作」（one-shot writing assignment）（p. 52）[1]。教師會在學期初規定要完成「關於指定題目寫作報告」（Write a paper about "specific topic"）的作業。即使學生可能在完成報告的過程中，經歷一些不連貫的階段，我們一

---

[1] Kamhi-Stein, L. D. (1997). Redesigning the writing assignment in general education courses. *College ESL, 7,* 49-61.

般還是會將這項作業視作個人的作業。實際上，在寫包含有文獻探討的報告時，這篇報告的品質大都依賴著我們能謹慎處理每個步驟。

本書在每章末的作業，是用來指導學生了解寫作過程的各種步驟和階段。教師可以修改這些作業活動，並做為另外一系列的作業，此一系列的作業可以併進寫論文訓練課程的教學大綱。因此，本書適宜兩種讀者：(a)想要將多步驟寫作方法融入課程大綱的教師；和(b)須獨立完成論文寫作中計畫和執行各項步驟的學生，例如在探討文獻章節時有所助益。

■ 有關第三版的內容

本版已更新多數的範例。另外增加兩章：第六章（質性研究的文獻分析）和第七章（製作表格來摘要文獻）。除此之外，本版比先前的版本收納更多文獻探討的範本。這些文獻探討的範本及第一、八、九、十章章末的作業活動，能作為課堂討論的題材。

■ 謝辭

在此感謝筆者的指導教授 Theodore J. Crovello 博士，允許筆者能延後完稿的預定時間，甚至在筆者擔任學務長時，鼓勵筆者繼續追求專業和學術的成長。

在此感激筆者的編輯 Fred Pyrczak 博士，為本書提供建議並協助第一章和第五章內容的研究設計。在此也感激加州大學洛杉磯分校的同仁，尤其是致力於多步驟寫作方法的 Marguerite Ann Snow 博士及 Lia D. Kamhi-Stein 博士。上述的三位博士提供無數有益的建議，多數已成為最後定稿的一部分。當然，疏誤之處是筆者該負的責任。

Writing Literature Reviews: A Guide for Students of the Social and Behavioral Sciences

▥ 回饋

　　倘蒙各界不吝指正，可促使本書的下一版更加完善。你可使用 e-mail 帳號 Info@Pyrczak.com 與我聯絡。

Jose L. Galvan
洛杉磯，加州

獻詞

獻給我的女兒 Melisa，一位具有創造力、獨立的作家。

 譯者序

　　學術論文的寫作不同於文藝作品的創作，兩者都是知識的製造者，但前者亟需科學的方法、過程與論證，故寫作時要有所本，即所謂的「站在巨人的肩膀上」。這就是為什麼要寫文獻探討的原因。

　　我們得以接觸本書第二版原文書，是 2004 年透過國立台中教育大學數學教育系所謝闓如博士所介紹，初閱後就覺得這是一本好書，值得推薦給全球華人。2006 年原文書出版了第三版，由心理出版社取得翻譯權，我們陸陸續續，寫寫停停，校校（校稿）停停，一下子六年過去了。六年間，馬博士先升教授了，吳博士想不開又去唸了一個博士學位，之後也升教授了，於此其間，吳之先父源祿（1933-2009）先生暨吳之先母李染（1934-2012）女士，相繼逝世，對本書之進度，不無影響。本書中文版雖然較慢出版，但對文獻探討的寫作，仍極具參考價值。

　　本書不但詳細而具體的舉例說明文獻探討的寫作過程暨要領，更提供了「最後定稿的綜合自編檢核表」，以利自我審核文獻探討的完整性，藉以提升文獻的品質。所以，凡是要寫作期末（中）報告、專題報告、博碩士論文、學術論文者，必當人手一冊。

　　本書的完成，要感謝聖約翰大學數位文藝系系主任吳順治博士，暨國立台北科技大學商業自動化與管理研究所教授林淑玲博士（前輔仁大學國際貿易與金融學系系主任）於百忙之中，提供了甚多意見。

　　末了，最感謝心理出版社董事長洪有義先生、總編輯林敬堯先生之熱心幫忙，編輯李晶小姐細心又費心的編輯，才使得本書能如此順利的出版。

　　本書成書費時良久，雖力求完美無缺，但疏漏之處在所難免，尚祈讀者先進，不吝賜予指正，毋任感荷！

吳德邦、馬秀蘭　謹識

2012 年 4 月

如何撰寫文獻探討
給社會暨行為科學學生指南

Writing Literature Reviews: A Guide for Students of the Social and Behavioral Sciences

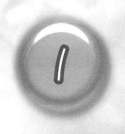

寫作學術文獻的探討：概述

本書將引導社會行為科學的研究，提供其論文探討的一般性需求，在本書中，你將可學習如何使用原始資源來進行社會行為科學研究之文獻寫作，顯然，最一般的原始資源是期刊中實徵性的研究報告，且依循期刊中的四種素材描述：(1)理論性的文章；(2)文獻回顧文章；(3)軼事性報告；(4)專業操作與標準報告。這些乃是依據我們寫作時，寫作過程的回顧，這樣的回顧包含本書所做的其他摘要。

回顧原始資源之介紹

為什麼聚焦於實徵性的研究報告？

本書著重在學術期刊中研究的原創（original）報告。因其是研究的第一手資料，因為這樣，這些報告是資料的原始資源（primary sources），其提供了研究方法的詳細報告，並對研究發現進行詳細的描述和討論；相反的，書本、雜誌、報章，及電視廣播所呈現的研究摘要報告，則往往是二手資源（secondary sources），僅提供大致性的結果描述，對於所使用的研究方法未能詳細呈現。身為學者，我們應該要重視基本性、原始性的資料，而事實上，我們的指導老師也會要求我們在文獻回顧探討的資料中引用原

始資源。

　　社會行為科學的研究期刊，也有豐富的**實徵性研究**之原始報告，這些有關觀察的**實徵性研究**會提及**系統性的觀察**，當研究者事先計畫觀察對象、觀察的特徵、如何觀察，及其他等等，則稱該研究是具有系統性的研究，而對任何科學而言，實徵性研究是其基礎，因而研究所獲得的結果應要相當謹慎小心，例如，應列出實徵研究最重要的三個主要議題，以及研究探討可能的問題（如下所示）。

● **議題一：取樣**（sampling）。大多數的研究僅對個別樣本進行取樣，並將其結果推論到一些較大的群體（常稱作母群體）上。再者，大多數的研究使用一些有偏差且不具代表性的樣本，例如，假設一教授在進行一項研究，僅使用其所指導的班級作為樣本，或一研究者寄出一些問卷並僅回收了40%的問卷回來，很明顯的，這些樣本必然無法作為母群體的代表。

　　問題：評論者在解釋研究結果時，須考慮到取樣方式造成的誤差。研究結果的可信度，常取決於樣本的取樣瑕疵的多寡。

● **議題二：測量**（measurement）。大多數的實徵性研究所使用的測量工具應假設其有某些瑕疵，例如，假設研究者使用自陳式問卷，進行校園中吸食大麻的相關研究，雖然對受試者保證他們的回應是會被保密且匿名的，但有些受試者可能並不想透露出其非法的行為。相反的，有些受試者可能想自誇做出了一些犯法的行為，但實際上他們卻很少或未曾如此，因此，應如何從中擇一呢？一種是進行個人的訪問，但這樣的測量方式亦是要求受訪者揭露其非法的活動，而另一種取代方式則採用隱藏式的觀察，但這樣的方法卻是欠缺道德的。然而，若觀察並非隱藏式的進行，參與者可能會改變他們的行為，因為他們知道自己是被觀察的。如你所見，並無完美的解決辦法。

問題：評論者須能考慮測量誤差的可能性，反問自己測量的方法是否公正，研究者是否使用了一種以上的測量方式？若是，不同的方法是否產生了一致的結果？

- **議題三：辨認問題**（problem identification）。研究者往往僅測驗了問題的一部分——大都是非常小的一部分，這裡有一範例：假設一位研究者想要研究回饋在班級中的使用情形及其對創造力的影響。首先，會以為這個研究問題似乎是很易於安排、管理的，直到考慮到回饋有許多種類——許多不同程度的表揚、可能給予許多不同形式的獎勵物品，以及其他因素等等。另一問題是創造力有許多不同的認定方式、表達方式，例如，創造力可以許多不同形式的藝術呈現出來，如：舞蹈、音樂。更多的創造力形式可以呈現在心理科學、口語表達、寫作溝通，以及其他等等。沒有研究者能擁有這樣的資源來檢驗全部的項目。取代的方式是研究者可能選擇其中一種或兩種讚美方式，以及一種或兩種創造力的表現形式，並以有限的班級數來進行檢驗。

問題：評論者需要對不同的研究報告在其給定的領域中進行問題的整體定義，逐個報告中尋找其一致性與描述，與此同時並謹記每位研究者對他自己研究的問題的定義，或多或少會不同於其他人。因為實徵性的研究僅提供大約程度的真實情形，而在研究問題中，研究的範圍必須要有所限制，創造綜合的整體就像拼圖遊戲，大多數的拼塊是不見的，而許多可得的拼塊並非以完整的樣貌呈現。

考慮以上所呈現的三個議題，你必須試著總結「回顧實徵研究的原始報告是困難的」之事實，無庸置疑的是，有時確實如此。然而，若你選取了一個自認為有趣的主題，並全面閱讀該主題的研究，將很快的沉浸在具有吸引力的主題上。在社會行為科學的大量主題中，對於這些可得資料的解釋至少有一些是持相反意見的，因此，你可能很快發現自己應像個評審

委員，審慎思考研究者應具有的凝聚力及邏輯論點，以期有最強的實證等等，這會是個具吸引力的活動。

你也可能做出錯誤的結論，認為僅有強烈學習研究方法及統計的學生，可理解原始的研究報告，當然這樣的研究背景是相當有幫助的，然而本書是希望給所有聰明、仔細的讀者，若讀者們能小心且仔細地回顧所給定的主題，必可從中了解實徵性研究的整體。原始研究報告之作者並非僅呈現孤立性的統計資料，取而代之的是，他們常提供有關其研究主題之先前研究的討論、基本概念的定義、相關理論的描述、他們用這個方式做研究的理由，以及藉由修飾研究法之限制所獲得研究結果之詮釋。因此，一個有技巧的作者，報告原始實徵研究時，將引導你透過素材來了解，甚至當你不了解該研究的術語及統計時，都能引導你讓你容易理解。

最後的一點考量：仔細閱讀自己在文獻探討中所引用的相關文章是必要的，僅閱讀研究文獻一開頭的摘要可能會誤導你，因為欠缺周詳地閱讀，會使你誤導你的文獻探討的讀者，因而，完整的閱讀每一篇所引用的文獻，對自己而言是重要的職責。

另一種原始資源：理論性的文章

並非每一篇期刊文章皆是原始研究的報告，例如，有些文章的寫作目的是詳細地批評一個已存在的理論，或是為了提出一個新的理論。請記得，理論是一般性的解釋，用來說明變數湊在一起的原因、這些變數間的關係，以及特別的是變數間如何互相影響。作為一系列統一的架構，理論可幫忙解釋看似不相關的實徵性觀察如何緊密結合並產生意義，這裡有一簡單的範例：

我們來看看寂寞的相關理論[1]。在其他事情中，此理論可從情感寂

---

[1] 本例取材自 Stroebe, W., Stroebe, M., Abakoumkin, G., & Schut, H. (1996). The role of loneliness and social support in adjustment to loss: A test of attachment versus stress theory.

寞（由於欠缺依附他人的親密情感而來的寂寞）及社交寂寞（由
於欠缺親密的社交網絡而來的孤立與寂寞感覺）來區分，此理論
提供許多社會及行為研究的重要線索，例如，此理論預測喪失親
密情感依附的配偶者，其將會封閉情緒上的接觸，而經驗到無法
因社交支持而減緩其寂寞的感受。

　　注意有關所舉範例中的兩件事，第一，以理論為基礎的預測與一般認
為：「因為失去重要親友而感到寂寞的人，將會因家庭或朋友的社交支持
而減少其寂寞的感覺」相反。然而，理論提出一般認為的情形僅在最佳且
少數的真實情境中出現。特別的是，家人及朋友將能減緩社交寂寞，但對
減少更深入的感受及潛在而破壞性極大的情感寂寞卻是無效的。要注意的
是，理論的預測與一般的常識是相反的，並不是不尋常的事。事實上，就
是這樣的理論特徵而對了解人的情感及心理世界有相當大的貢獻。
　　第二，寂寞的相關理論可透過實徵性的研究來測驗，研究者研究失去
重要親友的人，問他們心裡寂寞的程度，以及他們接受社交支持的形式和
強度。為使其更具實用性，理論必須要經得起實徵方法的測試，以幫助科
學界判斷它的效度。
　　在回顧文獻的工作上，若能區別出用於主題的主要理論，則工作可以
變得更簡單，實徵研究報告的作者常要區別基礎的理論，並討論其結果是
否與理論一致。依據他們在理論性文章的參考文獻中所給你的指引，能提
供你一個思考的架構，以發現一些刊載在學術期刊上較為特別或狹小範圍
的研究主題。事實上，你可能會選擇採用一個或更多的理論來架構你的研
究，換句話說，一個文獻探討的主題可被用以重新審視相關理論的研究。

Journal of Personality and Social Psychology, 70, 1241-1249。此寂寞理論是以「依附理
論」為基礎且為「依附理論」的延申。詳細的討論，請參閱：Atkinson, L., & Goldberg,
S. (2004). *Attachment issues in psychopathology and intervention.* Mahwah, NJ: Erlbaum
Associates。

以下所說非常重要：能幫助我們更加了解一種或更多理論的文獻探討，它是有可能對作者的研究領域產生重要貢獻，因為理論常對很多關心人類事務的領域提供更寬闊的線索。

文獻探討的文章

期刊常包含有文獻探討的文章[2]，亦即是能審視一些特別主題的文獻的文章，大部分像是你在使用本書時會寫的文獻探討。大多數的期刊在徵稿時，論文審查會有較高的標準，不僅在分析的部分要寫得嚴謹，要能呈現給讀者該主題最新的資訊，而且也應該提供能增進知識的嶄新洞見，這些洞察可能有許多形式，像是：(1)解決以往研究的基礎衝突；(2)解釋一主題研究結果的新方法；(3)安排未來研究的方向或路徑，使該領域能有更進階研究的潛力。因此，透過準備文獻探討的過程，可知文章要刊載在期刊上不是一件簡單的事。事實上，當你開始以一主題進行回顧時，並不保證你將能達到洞察的境地，並能通過期刊編輯者的門檻。然而，若你依循本書所給予的指引，強調分析與整合文獻的重要性（亦即，要用批判的眼光看待文獻，將它抽離出來，有時候分成一小段和小片；而後，再用一種新的形式把它們重組在一起），你將能比一般的學術寫作者有較佳的機會，可以寫出更適合出版的文獻。

當學生發現其主題在學術期刊上已被眾人評論，他們可能覺得當初自己應選擇一個不同的主題，但這並非是一個必要而聰明的決定，也不需感到沮喪。相反地，這些學生應感到慶幸，有思考他人的作品及洞見的優勢。意即，有些人的研究可建立在其他人的研究之上，或者可提出贊同或反對的觀點作為研究題材。寫作是個人化的過程，因而，兩人對相同文獻主體

---

2 有些雜誌也刊載書評、測驗評論，以及其他產品和服務的評估。這些將不在本書的考慮範圍。所以，在本書中「評論文章」（review article）泛指「文獻探討」（literature review）的文章。

Writing Literature Reviews: A Guide for Students of the Social and Behavioral Sciences

的回顧，也很可能寫出完全不同但潛在性相同而具有價值的文獻[3]。

軼事報導

當你針對某個特殊的主題做文獻探討，你或許會找到某些文章是基於某人經驗的軼事報導的。一則軼事是某個恰好被注意到的經驗描述（對比於研究的描述，仔細思量過的研究是當發現到某人或是為了蒐集某獨特現象中最好的資訊下所規畫出來的）。有些期刊將目標鎖定在專業人員，例如臨床心理學家、社會工作者和老師，這些期刊中的軼事報導是常見的。例如，一位老師會寫一篇關於班上成績落後的學生，其成績進步的文章，其他老師可能會對此有興趣並認為值得去了解其潛在意涵。但是，如果是從科學角度來看，如此的軼事，是有嚴重缺陷的。在沒有控制變項與比較的情況下，我們無從得知老師使用什麼教學方法讓學生成績進步。或許學生的進步不是由於老師努力所促成的，反而是由於家中的某種機制或是服用醫生開立符合過動症的藥物，而非老師的知識。基於上述限制，軼事報導在文獻處理時應該要更為謹慎，當軼事報導被引述時，應該要清楚標示出此為軼事報導。

專業實務與規範的報告

有些期刊是讓專業人員發表實務與規範的文章，例如某一州在數學教育上採用新的課程標準，或是提議立法讓臨床心理學家能合法開立藥物。關於此主題的文章不斷被引述後，或許這類文章是值得做文獻探討的。

3　請記住，實徵知識是曾經體驗的過程──不是一堆事實。實徵研究不能證明什麼，而是用來達到各式各樣的信度的。所以，研究者的「詮釋」可能有所不同，即使是對同一個主題來探討相同的文獻。

寫作歷程

我們已經討論過你可能會去閱讀的一些文章類型（亦即實徵性的研究報告、理論性的文章、文獻探討的文章、軼事報導的文章，和專業實務與規範的報告），我們將再簡要地考量這本書中會用到的歷程。

整合文獻探討（換言之，找到文獻、閱讀文獻、用心分析文獻）與寫文獻探討的區別，是重要但常被忽略的概念。不用說，文獻在找到後，必須先閱讀與分析文獻，才能去寫這份文獻。更甚者，寫文獻探討有其進程。在構詞和修辭的領域，這些進程正確的泛指寫作的過程。它們包括：(1)計畫；(2)組織；(3)設計；(4)編寫；(5)重組改寫。特別的是，歷程包括訂一個主題或選擇文獻來探討（計畫）；分析、整合、評價讀過或組織過的文章（組織）；寫一個初始設計（編寫）；重寫再設計以求徹底、連結，和正確無誤（重組改寫）。這樣的寫作歷程就類似當你上大一新生的英文課，你被要求寫一篇分析小論文一樣。本書依此組織討論寫作歷程的步驟。

為特殊目的而寫作

寫文獻的第一要素就是思考寫作的理由。探討實徵性研究可以提供很多的目標。它們是組成一篇研究論文（長短或複雜度皆符合教授的標準）的要素。期刊的論文，文獻的探究往往簡短，重點放在此研究問題原理的闡述或者該研究的假設。相反的，碩士論文或是博士論文的文獻，通常是想建立作者周密的支配運用在該主題的探究上，典型的情況下這樣的文章也有比較長的篇幅。明顯的，這些不同的目的導致文獻探究有不同的長度與風格。第二章將描述這些文章的不同。

計畫寫作

計畫怎麼寫的部分有兩大任務，一是定義主題，另一是找到研究的相

關文獻。這些步驟相互關聯，因為你如何決定主題，將影響你的文獻定義，而文獻也將接著影響你設定的主題。有時，你的指導教授指定某個研究主題，有時則是完全由你決定。設定主題的歷程是第三章的第一步。

第三章接著要處理相關期刊研究的選擇。研究型圖書館並不是像一般的圖書館。搜尋圖書館書庫對你來說助益良多，然而它可能有時成功，有時不成功，因為一間圖書館的館藏很不同，得看它當時的資源、館藏，甚至是借閱資料者的惡意破壞。一個比較好的方法是尋找電腦資料庫和網路資源。請圖書館員教你如何著手，或者你可以參與某個電子資源的工作坊。透過本書，你會學到幾種尋找資料庫的方法。然而，請記住每種資料庫都有其特色。之後會仔細介紹其差異。

在你找到足夠多與你的主題有關的文章後，你需要閱讀和分析它們。這步驟稱為**分析**，包括閱讀與記筆記。也就是說，當你閱讀時，你切割作者的文章成幾部分或幾個要素。因為你將分析一定數量的文章，你需要有系統組織的筆記。分析歷程的一部分是篩選你筆記的要素，留住有關的部分，摒棄你不需要的部分。這部分在第四章會詳加討論。

當你閱讀與分析文獻時，有時需要一些更特殊的想法見解。舉例來說，如果你的文獻探究是你計畫中的一部分，你要注意到第五章和第六章所描述的。這些章節會幫助你有技巧的分析這些文獻。

組織你的注意力與思考力

確定以上的步驟後，你需要著手整合，就是將每個小部分組成完整的一篇新文章。想想看：你閱讀的每篇文章都是完整的，而在你的研究筆記中，你寫下了每篇文章的一部分，接著你再把它們重組成一個新的架構。在創造出新架構後，你再來評價內容。也就是說，對於這些文章的品質和重點，你必須有自己的評價。這些都包含在第八章中。這時候，你或許想建立一些表格來歸納總結原先研究的結果。第七章會教你怎麼做。

撰寫初稿、編輯，以及重寫稿件

　　接著，你必須寫初始設計。基於你觀眾的立場，你必須想好要用形式化還是非形式化的語言。一個有效能的作者，是會意識到讀者的期待。寫給對某領域學有專精的教授的學期報告，就不同於碩士論文，其讀者是好奇於此主題，但不一定要有足夠的知識。一篇碩士論文的文獻探究不同於公開出版的期刊或是課堂報告的文獻探究。你應該要區分主要的次主題和從你的筆記中決定模式，例如取向、相同之處、對立之處和一般性原則。這些步驟都包括在第九章中。

　　再來你要確定論述是清楚、有邏輯和有證據支持的，而且沒有錯誤。第十章會幫助你確定你的論述對你與你的讀者是有意義的。第十一章描述如何確認你文獻探討的第一步是正確無誤的。

　　本書最後兩章是寫作歷程的最後兩步：編輯和重寫。這些是重複的（也就是不斷反覆出現）。對於寫過兩三篇以上文章的專業作者是不陌生的。第十二章提供一些指引來幫助寫作歷程的進展。最後的十三章則是提供一些詳細的檢核細節來確定你文章的完整性。典型的學術創作需要你準備正確無誤的文章資料，而這份檢核清單將幫助你達成這個目標。

第 1 章的活動

1. 找到一篇你領域中的實徵性研究的原始報告，閱讀後，回答以下問題（如何找到一篇期刊文章會在稍後章節討論。這時候，簡單的找一篇即可。你的圖書館員或指導老師可以幫你在學校圖書館找到一本有特色的期刊，讀過有興趣的論文文章中的表格並且拷貝答案帶到課堂上）。提醒老師你要在這樣的活動中處理一篇特殊文章。

　　A.有無明顯抽樣問題？試解釋之（請不要只有閱讀次標題「抽樣」的章

Writing Literature Reviews: A Guide for Students of the Social and Behavioral Sciences

節，因為研究者有時會在整篇文章中提供額外的資訊，尤其是緒論中，會指出他們與別的研究者抽樣上的不同，或者是在文章最後面，也會討論研究結果推論上的限制）。

B. 有無明顯的測量問題？試解釋之。

C. 研究者有無解釋狹義上的問題？範圍太狹小嗎？試解釋之。

D. 你注意到哪些缺點嗎？試解釋之。

E. 整篇中，你有想過這篇研究對未來知識上的貢獻嗎？試解釋之。

2. 閱讀本書後面第一篇文獻探討範本（Review A）回答以下問題。注意你在學過更多關於文獻探究寫作歷程後要再讀一次。以下的問題是第一次問你。之後，你要能詳細的評論文章。

A. 你清楚的定義出文獻主題嗎？他們有指出限定的範圍嗎？（舉例來説，它只限定在某個時候嗎？它只處理某些方面？）

B. 評論者寫了一篇具結合性的論文並且幫助你對於子題逐次的了解嗎？試解釋之。

C. 評論家綜合和評論該文獻或者只是總結而已？

D. 從頭到尾，你有想過這篇研究對文獻探究有貢獻嗎？試解釋之。

如何撰寫文獻探討
給社會暨行為科學學生指南

Writing Literature Reviews: A Guide for Students of the Social and Behavioral Sciences

為特定目的寫作的考量

　　雖然本書所提供的指引適用於任何的文獻探討寫作，但你仍會期望能依據寫作目的來改變你的寫作技巧。本章包括三個最常見的文獻探討類型和每一類型的讀者：(1)文獻探討作為課堂的學期報告；(2)作為碩士論文或博士論文的一個章節；(3)當成期刊論文的一部分簡介。

文獻探討作為課堂的學期報告

　　文獻探討作為課堂的學期報告可能頗為困難，因為工作牽涉到：(1)選擇一個對你來說是新研究領域的主題；(2)在你或許不熟悉使用的資料庫中認出和找出適當的研究文章數目；(3)在三到四個月中書寫及編輯一個結構良好的碩士論文。結合上述情況，大部分的教授期望你在他們最少的指導下，在課堂外去準備評論的文章。當然，他們也期望你的文獻探討能有完整及充分的研究。而這本書將幫你完成此目標。

　　謹記這些困難的因素，你必須小心的去計畫你的學期報告主題。首先，在學期初你應該要確認你了解這個作業，及盡可能知道教授期望的東西。因此，在課堂上你應該不要猶豫去提出與作業有關的問題。記住那些你不了解不清楚的部分，其他學生也可能不了解，你提出的問題可能會幫

助到他們[1]。再來，你必須按部就班的進行寫作程序。確認你有足夠的時間去遵循這本書所提到的步驟，包含主題的選擇；閱讀及評量相關研究的文章；整合及組織你的筆記；寫作、更改、及改寫你的作業；並且修正編輯及堅持形式的要求[2]。它可以幫助你找出幾週的學期時間及安排出一個時間表。以下是為期十五週的學期時間建議表。

範 例 2.0.1

階段一　圖書館的初步查詢和選擇主題
　　　　在第三週結束之前完成

階段二　書單和初步報告概述
　　　　在第六週結束之前完成

階段三　擬訂報告初稿
　　　　在第十二週結束之前完成

階段四　修改過的最終草案
　　　　在第十五週結束之前完成

　　指導教授對於書面評論的長度和引用參考文獻數量的期望也許大不相同。為介紹概括論述而寫的學期報告，指導教授也許只需要簡短的評論，也許極短的幾行字，至少五到十篇參考文獻的打字篇幅。對於這樣的評論，你將需要嚴謹挑選引用有一致性的參考文獻，通常選擇那些最重要或者最

---

[1] 其他學生一般來說，應該不會有興趣在課外或辦公時間對教授提出特殊的問題。例如：你計畫上研究所並想寫比教授要求更為廣泛的文章，或你先前文獻探討的課所寫的文獻探討文章，你想擴充它而非重寫。

[2] 在社會和行為科學一門中，最重要的樣式指南是《美國心理學會出版手冊》（*Publication Manual of the American Psychological Association*）。它可從多數學院和大學書店購買，或上網購買（網址 www.apa.org）。

當前的。為上面部分的課程，指導教授也許要求多些參考文獻的長篇評論。最後，對學校的研究生班級而言，你的教師可能不會限制篇幅或參考文獻的數量，而是盼望你去評論許多研究報告，因為你必須針對你的主題寫出統整的文獻探討。

　　鑑於在有限的時間內寫文獻探討作為一篇期末報告，你的題目通常應該是狹窄的。首先，尋找一個明確定義的領域，特別是如果你對一個領域不熟悉。選擇主題的一個好方式，就是審查教科書各章節裡的子標題。例如，一本教育心理學教科書也許有一章創造力，其中包括創造力定義的細目，創造力的測量和在教室裡培養創造力。以此為例，假設你對在教室裡培養創造力特別有興趣，讀這個部分，你也許會發現書中作者提及競爭在促進創造力的作用此論述有一些爭論（即，老師可否藉由提供獎勵來培養創造力？）。這題目聽起來似乎是一個可作為你實驗研究的主題，因為當你尋找這個題目的期刊文章[3]，你可以找到的文章比你完成學期作業所需還多。如此，你能進一步的縮小題目範圍，將你的評論限制在處理：(1)小學樣本；和(2)藝術類。

　　如果你沒有題目選擇權並且由你的指導教授指派題目，盡快開始查詢你的文獻並且向他（她）報告你遇到的任何困難，譬如：發現與指派的題目相關研究太少（或許，題目可能擴大或你的指導教授能指示你文獻搜索的另外來源），或有太多研究（或許，題目可能太狹隘或你的教授能幫助你辨認其他細目，譬如：近期碩士論文的評論）。

　　有一個對短時間內準備文獻探討作為學期報告的結論是，對你早期草稿的回饋，機會是有限的，因此你自己要負起許多編輯的責任。當你安排時間表時，留些時間針對你的草稿去請教指導教授，甚至在會面時可以這麼做。最後，在你交上報告前，你應該使用本書末尾的自我編輯指南，幫助你解決一些常見的問題。

---

[3] 搜尋電子資料庫重點放在怎樣使查詢縮小範圍，在下個章節會詳細談論。

寫一章碩士論文或博士論文的文獻探討

在本書中，碩士論文或博士論文中「回顧該章」是文獻探討的類型中最複雜的，因為在你開始你的研究前，已預期你準備好文獻探討的開頭以做為研究提案的一部分。在檢閱你的研究問題的過程中，處理文獻探討是你要進行的步驟之一，因此你可能必須一再解釋題目或修正你的研究問題。

在寫文獻探討章節的學生經常問：「我必須引用多少研究文章？」另外，他們也會問：「我應該花多長的時間去做探討？」當他們沒有在批判研究的文章數量和在批判章節的長度二者中任何一方預設一個最小量時，有些學生會覺得挫敗。通常，這件事的變化標準將取決於題目的性質和文獻的數量。

你應該為你的文獻探討建立兩個主要目標。首先，試圖提供綜合的（comprehensive）和最新的（up-to-date）主題回顧。其次，試著去證明你對你研究的領域有徹底的了解。記住文獻探討將為你的研究提供基本原理，而你完成這些目標的範圍將有助於推測你的計畫被接受的程度。注意這些在你領域中有助於知識主體的目標，反映出你著手任務的嚴肅性。這幾年已形成的幾個傳統，反映學術界對碩士論文或博士論文寫作有多嚴格。其中包括研究提案的辯護，已完成的碩士論文或博士論文的答辯，還有被圖書館接受成為館藏前，需對資料最後做一次小心詳細的檢查。

有些學生會在寫碩士論文或博士論文的文獻探討這章時有所延誤。畢竟，他們常沒有設定時間表。因此，為自己設定一個時間表是很重要的。有些學生發現和指導教授擬定一個非正式的共同研討時間表是有用的，或許設定完成不同階段的期限涉及整體的過程。在這本書裡所描述的指南將提供這方面的幫助。你應該和口試委員採用一個規律的諮詢模式去確保你仍緊扣重點且符合要求。

最後，對一篇碩士論文或者博士論文計畫準確性的期望程度是相當高。

這將要求你所撰寫的文章的程度遠超過學期研究報告這種程度。不僅你的文字必須符合你的領域中所使用的特殊格式手冊，而且它也應該毫無細節上的錯誤。在第十一章的指南和第十三章中自編檢核表，將幫助你完成這些。在編輯你的文章之前的幾天，確定你有足夠的時間去著手你的草稿，並且期望在給你的指導教授一份文獻探討的草稿之前，用自我編寫的指南檢查幾次。

期刊論文的文獻探討

在期刊發表的學術碩士論文研究的文獻探討，是本書所提及的三種批判類型中最直接的，它通常比另外兩種類型簡短，且更容易引起注意。因為它主要的目的是提供較特殊和狹窄的研究報告的理論和背景。

另一方面，這些探討經過比碩士論文和博士論文更嚴苛的檢驗，相關期刊中的研究論文會定期的被在這研究領域中具有領導地位的學者評價，這表示這些文獻探討不僅僅反應研究主題的現狀且要完全無誤。再次強調，第十三章中有個自編檢核表須小心使用。

一般來說，在研究完成之後，研究者會相隔一年多才發表期刊論文，通常會發生學生在決定改寫其碩士論文或博士論文成比較短的期刊論文。如果這跟你情況一樣，去尋找在你的研究領域中最新發表的期刊議題，保證你的文獻探討基礎是來自於你領域中最新發表的作品。

雖然期刊內容不盡相同，但是期刊中的文獻探討經常被認為一定要跟緒論相結合，也就是說，研究的緒論是用來介紹給讀者了解研究主題和目的，這種探討著重在獨特的研究中要建立科學的方法，還有在這個領域中有什麼貢獻。它應該有助於證明原先研究報告中的理論（論證）。所以，它要比碩士論文或博士論文的文獻探討更專精。

第 2 章的活動

1. 你寫文獻探討的目的是什麼？

   A.當作班級報告。

   B.當作碩士論文或博士論文的其中一章。

   C.當作期刊論文的緒論。

   D.其他：_____

2. 如果你正在寫文獻探討當作報告的話，你的指導教授有沒有先告訴你特殊的主題？如果有，把主題寫下來，並寫下任何你想問的問題。

3. 如果你正在寫文獻探討當作報告的話，你的指導教授如果沒告訴你特定的議題，簡單的描述二到三個議題（如果你不清楚，多看書尋找議題）。

4. 如果你寫的是碩士論文或博士論文的文獻探討，把你的主題寫下來。

5. 如果你寫的是碩士論文或博士論文的文獻探討，你完成第一份草稿的時間是什麼時候？跟你的指導教授說明進度表並取得回饋。

6. 如果你寫的是要發表在期刊上的研究報告的文獻探討，寫下研究目的，為你的研究目的或假設命名，在你讀完關於你主題的文章後，修正你的目的或假設。如果需要修正的話，要根據文獻修正（記得研究目的或假設應該直接有條理的從文獻探討中得來）。

7. 如果你正在寫的是碩士論文或博士論文的文獻探討，你至少要讀三篇被口試委員認同過的碩士論文或博士論文的文獻探討文章，這些通常會被收藏在大學圖書館。找時間跟指導教授討論他對你文獻探討的期望。把指導教授對你文獻探討的期望記下來。

Writing Literature Reviews: A Guide for Students of the Social and Behavioral Sciences

題目選擇與文獻鑑定

「我應該從哪裡開始？」這可能是學生準備寫一篇文獻探討時最常提的問題。當沒有明確的答案時，這章是用來說明很多專家學者和研究人員開始的過程。記住寫是一個個別的過程，因此這裡描述的程序可視為路線圖而不是作為一項指示。透過這個章節，你將能發展出幫助你開始寫一篇有效的文獻探討的兩種重要概述：你的題目的書面說明和你的閱讀書目提供討論的初稿。

顯而易見，在任何種類學術論文裡的第一步是決定你將寫什麼，而此論文遵循的明確方法將取決於你所寫的文獻探討的目的。前面章節描述你在寫文獻探討時，最普通的三種原因。

在任何這類型的文獻探討內，你通常要縮小你題目的定義範圍。範例3.0.1 提供一個非常一般的題目。實際上，很多一流大學會教授研究課程並且描述文獻的廣大樣貌。

範 例 3.0.1

一般的主題：學童語言的習得

顯而易見，在範例 3.0.1 的主題能用來作為文獻探討基礎之前，必須考

慮縮小其範圍。隨後的步驟將指導你透過這個範例引導出更好的選擇過程。

>>>步驟 1：搜尋合適的資料庫

在你選擇資料庫並且搜尋它之前，你需要至少選擇一個一般的主題。假定你選擇在範例 3.0.1 的主題：學童語言的習得，因為這個主題非常一般，將產生超出你需要（如同你在下面所見）的參考文獻。雖然如此，從一般題目開始通常是合適的，看看有多少文獻，然後把題目縮小到更容易搜尋的範圍，而你將在這章裡學習到這個過程。

使用範例 3.0.1 的題目進行一般搜尋，將產生數以千計的資料。因此，你應該指定一套參數以集中結果。例如，你可以把搜尋限制在被推薦的期刊文章，或者你能指定出版日期的有限範圍，或許只追溯五到七年。範例 3.1.1 的結果，便是以範例 3.0.1 使用的一般題目「學童語言的習得」為樣本，在《教育資源情報中心》（*Educational Resource Information Center, ERIC*）資料庫搜尋而得，在這裡提出依序的步驟：

範例 3.1.1

步驟	記錄的筆數
用「語言習得」搜尋：	6,985
把搜尋限制在期刊文章和出版日期 　　　在 2002 年：	429
更多限制對搜尋「語言習得」和 　　　「學童語言」：	128

範例 3.1.1 是如何搜尋的：

1. 在 www.eric.ed.gov 查詢 *ERIC* 資料庫。

2. 點擊 "Advanced Search"。

3. 在 "Keywords (all fields)" 的第一個區域，輸入 language acquisition（語言習得）。

4. 在 "Publication Type" 中點擊 "All"，可進行勾選，接著點擊 "Journal Articles"。

5. 在 "Publication Date" 中在 "From" 區域輸入 "pre-1966"，在 "To" 區域輸入 "2004"。

6. 點擊 "Search"，可得 6,985 條期刊文章的記錄，如範例 3.1.1 所示。

7. 點擊 "Back to Search"。

8. 將 "Publication Date" 在 "From" 區域改成 "2002"。

9. 點擊 "Search"，可得 429 個期刊文章的記錄，如範例 3.1.1 所示。

10. 點擊 "Back to Search"。

11. 在第一個領域的 Keywords 留下 language acquisition，並且把 child language（學童語言）加進第二個領域的 Keywords。

12. 點擊 "Search"，可得 128 個期刊文章的記錄，如範例 3.1.1 所示。

（譯者注：各種文獻資料庫的網址，常因公司重整而有所變動，建議從各大專院校圖書館的網頁開始搜尋各個資料庫的連結。）

　　注意：每篇文章由資料庫鑑定，會提供你一個摘要（即概要）。附錄 A 包含了一百二十八個標題和摘要，即是用上述的那些過程獲得的。值得注意的是在這個範例裡使用 *ERIC* 資料庫，是因為它的收錄是綜合的並且重點圍繞在教育的幾門學科上。其他資料庫，例如 *PsycINFO* 和《社會學文摘》（*Sociological Abstracts*），將產生集中於其他領域的結果[1]。

>>> 步驟 2：如果你的參考文獻清單太多，請縮短它們

　　範例 3.2.1 提供五個根據 *ERIC* 搜尋的樣本而來的可校訂的題目。在這

---

[1] 與 *ERIC* 不同，*PsycINFO* 和《社會學文摘》資料庫只提供有訂購者使用。大多數學術圖書館都有訂購，允許學生和教職員工免費使用。

個範例裡，被校訂的題目說明了附錄A中重新分類的那些文章是根據研究的主要領域（這些領域是由對文章的標題和摘要進行回顧而來的）。取決於你的課程的具體本質和它所提供的學術學科，現在你能透過選擇範例3.2.1 中一個題目來縮小你的題目領域。這些類別僅是在說明過程。實際上，附錄A可以被重新分類成很多其他類別。此外，你將注意到一些文章會出現在一個以上的類別裡。例如，附錄 A 中的第13筆參考文獻已經被歸類到兩個類別裡：(1)父母在學童語言習得中的角色；(2)習得兩種語言。此外，注意到並非全部文章都需要被分類。例如，如果你的主要興趣在英語習得過程，你可以刪除非使用英語的學童的文章，以避免它們參與更進一步的分析。

範 例 3.2.1

可能的題目領域，由附錄A提供的參考文獻號碼：*ERIC*搜尋的樣本；粗體字號碼是有關自閉症。

有特別需要的學童語言習得

　　樣本參考文獻號碼：**5**, 12, 31, **42**, **43**, 46, 47, 48, **49**, 55, **57**, 83, 84, 91, **93**, 96, 97, 98, 99, **101**, **113**, 116, **120**

父母在學童語言習得中的角色

　　樣本參考文獻號碼：4, 13, 16, 23, 32, 67, 68, 90, 115

習得兩種語言（雙語）

　　樣本參考文獻號碼：13, 18, 19, 20, 21, 22, 27, 30, 52, 69

習得語法架構和種類

　　樣本參考文獻號碼：26, 88, 102, 105, 107, 112, 118, 121, 122, 128

幼兒的語言習得

　　樣本參考文獻號碼：1, 10, 40, 53, 64, 77, 79, 81, 125

在分類完期刊文章的檔案，如範例 3.2.1 中所示之後，仔細檢查那些可能作為你文獻探討的題目的子集。例如，在「有特別需要的學童語言習得」中有九篇文章是探討自閉症小孩。在上面的範例裡，這些號碼被加粗。如果九篇文章還不夠達成你的目的，就進行下面的步驟 3。

>>>步驟 3：擴充參考文獻內容

如果你的文獻探討沒有足夠的參考文獻，當然你可以進一步往 2002 年之前搜尋。尋找歷史文獻的討論在下面的步驟 14。

如果你使用 *ERIC*，透過點擊 *ERIC* 記錄中的 "Details"，你也可能連接到另外的參考資料，接著進到連結（即畫底線的字），會出現作者們的名字。例如，附錄 A 的第一篇 *ERIC* 記錄，點擊作者的名字後，提供了同一個作者另外十三筆的參考文獻，包括書、教師指南和期刊文章的文獻。因為學術界學者傾向於針對一個特定的題目，在一段期間內持續的研究與寫作，這些文獻常常和手邊的題目十分相關（像是「幼兒的語言習得」）。

此外，當檢查一個 *ERIC* 期刊文章記錄時，你點擊 "Details"，然後檢查該文章 "Descriptors" 的清單。附錄 A 第一篇文章的描述詞請見範例 3.3.1。這些是有關的題目，點擊其中一個，你將可進行搜尋與這些題目有關的文章，你可擴充你參考文獻的清單，經由鑑定另外的有關文章。

範 例 3.3.1

與附錄 A 首篇文章在記錄上相關的描述詞：

照料者角色；認知發展；嬰幼兒教育；早期的經歷；情緒智商；嬰兒；語言習得；動作發展；家長的角色；社會發展；思考技能；學步兒；視覺感知；詞彙。

藉由搜尋 *ERIC* 也是可能可以找到資料的，例如在會議提出的報告、

課程指南、碩士論文和博士論文，都可以用來補充已被鑑定的期刊文章。為了找到可以提供另外參考的來源，在 *ERIC* 開始搜尋處，跳離 "All" 檢索（看本書裡第 21 頁上的方塊文字），然後進行另一搜尋。值得注意的是一本期刊裡刊登一份報告，它通常必須經過專門領域的一名或多名編輯和社論顧問或者評論家的審查。這個例子顯然不是如此，無論如何，*ERIC* 數據庫內涵蓋許多類型的資料。此外，注意到 *ERIC* 並不會去判斷那些資料裡的訊息的審慎性或者品質。因此，一些非期刊資料的訊息比起期刊文章是不那麼有參考價值的。

>>> 步驟 4：考慮尋找未發表過的研究

搜索未發表過的研究將是另一種增加你的參考文獻清單的方法（參閱步驟 3）。另外，你可能想要尋找未在期刊發表、出版的研究，因為這些研究可能有潛在的重要性[2]。一項有潛在性重要的研究，期刊沒有出版它的理由可能如下：

1. 潛在的、重要的一些研究甚至從未被提交至期刊成為出版物。例如，博士論文和碩士論文因太長而不能在一本學術刊物裡出版，用於出版則必須大規模的重寫。博士論文和碩士論文的很多作者不想承擔下這個重寫的過程。另外，當他們的研究結果與他們的假設不一致時，一些研究人員可能覺得洩氣。與其照期刊的意思完成研究，還不如重新處理比較有成果的部分或改走別條方法。

2. 一些期刊編輯和專業評論家可能對研究者所發表的文章結果沒有顯著差異，或者不能確認研究假說的研究有偏見。

找到未發表過研究的一個方法，是聯繫出版研究的作者，問他們在你的題目上是否知道任何未發表過的研究結果[3]。例如，他們可能做過研究，

---

[2] 不在期刊出版的研究通常稱為未出版的研究，它們可能以列印形式在某些學術圖書館內提供使用。

[3] 聯繫訊息，例如實體地址或者電子信箱通常是提供在研究文章附註的第一頁上，或者接近文章結束時，就在參考清單的前後。

但決定不適合出版，或者他們可能知道學生已經在做相同的事。第二種方式是透過網際網路搜尋電子數據庫。範例 3.4.1 中說明了一個團隊的研究人員做了什麼。

範 例 3.4.1[4]

描述如何進行未出版研究的搜尋：

我們透過搜尋回顧和傳播中心（Centre for Reviews and Dissemination, 2001）以及科克倫非隨機學習方法組織（Cochrane Non-Randomised Studies Methods Group, 2004）所建議的資源，去試圖含括未出版的研究。

1. 我們尋找報告、討論論文，以及在：(1)格雷文獻的訊息系統（System for Information on Grey Literature）（http://arc.uk.ovid.com/webspirs/login.ws）；(2)美國技術情報服務處（National Technical Information Service）（http://www.ntis.gov/search/）；和(3)英國圖書館公共目錄（British Library Public Catalogue）（http://blpc.bl.uk/）當中的文章。

2. 我們尋找在：(1)護理和聯合保健的多重索引（Cumulative Index to Nursing and Allied Health）（http://www.cinahl.com/）；和(2) ProQuest 數位博士論文（ProQuest Digital Dissertations）（http://wwwlib.umi.com/dissertations/gateway）中的博士論文和碩士論文。

3. 我們搜尋記錄在國家研究名錄（National Research Register）（http://www.update-software.com/national/）內所有的同期作品，並檢查合格的研究。

4. 我們尋找在：(1) ISI 研討會論文集（ISI Proceedings）（http://portalt.wok.mimas.ac.uk/portal.cgi?DestApp=ISIP&Func=Frame）；和 (2)zetoc（http://zetoc.mimas.ac.uk/zetoc/）中的研討會論文集。

---

[4] Shenkin, S. D., Starr, J. M., & Deary, I. J. (2004). Birth weight and cognitive ability in childhood: A systematic review. *Psychological Bulletin, 130,* 989-1013.

>>> 步驟 5：根據你的題目陳述，寫出初步的草稿

當你已經確認適當的參考文獻，你便能再檢查你已有的文章清單，並且為你的文獻探討選擇一個更具體的題目[5]。你題目陳述的第一個草稿應該試圖命名你將調查的領域。思索這個陳述是一個描述性的詞語而不是一頁短文或者一章標題。在範例 3.5.1 中呈現兩個題目的陳述：一個在語言學，另一個在心理學領域的文獻探討。注意到這些初步草稿仍然非常普遍。

範 例 3.5.1

心理學：

自閉症孩童的語言習得

語言學：

習得語法架構和種類

在範例 3.5.1 的每個題目都可能由一個特定族群，例如：「幼兒」來更進一步的縮小範圍（例如：非常年幼的自閉症孩童的語言習得）。

>>> 步驟 6：熟悉線上資料庫

目前所有大學圖書館都提供電子資料庫，以往手工查詢資料的方式已被電腦化搜尋所取代。因此，熟悉你學校圖書館的電子資源是重要的。假如你是線上資料庫的新手，你必須參加一個研討會或課程去學習如何使用這些資源，以及仔細閱讀任何關於你的大學資料庫資源的手冊。如前所述，

---

5 在這時，要你決定最終的題目仍言之過早。你應該要做的是讀完你已經找到的一些文章。

Writing Literature Reviews: A Guide for Students of the Social and Behavioral Sciences

本書告訴你的只是一些資料庫的一般入門，而非所有有關它們的詳細內容。

>>> 步驟 7：確認自己本身研究領域的相關資料庫

　　每個學術領域已發展出屬於自己的資料庫給學生或學者使用。在你搜尋初期，你必須確認自己本身研究領域的專業資料庫。除了在圖書館得到的資訊以外，你必須請教你的指導教授，你的主要研究中列為優先的資料庫為何，然後，你能夠找出它們可從何處取得，以及資料是否能從你家或宿舍被取用。

　　表一是以加州大學洛杉磯分校的圖書館為例，列出可使用的資料庫資源。此表並不詳盡，事實上，較大規模的學術研究圖書館提供比此表更多的研究服務。如果你是一個小學校的學生，建議你調查你的學校圖書館是否在你的研究領域裡，有與較大規模的機構維持合作關係。

>>> 步驟 8：熟悉資料庫的組織架構

　　如表一所述，線上資料庫包含數種文件資料的概要，有期刊、書籍、研討會論文、專題報告及政府文件。就你從第一章所知，本書著重在學術期刊中有關探討的部分，因為在這些資料庫裡數千種期刊中的每一篇，都有單獨的記錄此篇文章的專門資訊。換句話說，你在一個資料庫中所搜尋到而被列出的每一筆資料，將被連結到另一個資料目錄，對此筆資料有較詳盡的說明。例如，每一則記錄會包含很多內容，有：文章標題、作者、期刊來源、出版日期、摘要及一連串的描述（如描述文章內容的專門用語、片語）。你能夠運用一個或數個條件來縮小你的搜尋範圍。出版日期、期刊來源及作者是常被用來作為縮小搜尋範圍的條件，不過最常被使用的方式，是指定一個或數個字詞來搜尋。

表一　圖書館資料庫一覽表

資料庫名稱	學科範圍	資料庫統計
Basic Biosis	生命科學（Life Science）	300,000 筆資料，來自 350 種期刊。 1994 年至今，每月更新
CINAHL	護理（Nursing）、 聯合保健（Allied Health）、 生物醫學（Biomedical） 及消費者保健（Consumer Health）	352,000 筆資料，來自 900 種期刊。 1982 年至今，每季更新
Dissertation Abstracts （博士論文摘要）	完整系列的學術主題	1,566,000 筆資料。 1861 年至今，每月更新
ERIC	教育及相關領域	956,000 筆資料，來自期刊、書籍、碩士論文及未出版的報告。 1966 年至今，每月更新
LLBA	語言學及語言行為摘要	250,000 筆資料，來自期刊、書籍、博士論文、書籍評論及其他媒體。 1973 年至今，每季更新
Medline	護理（Nursing）、 公共衛生（Public Health）、 藥劑學（Pharmacy）、 運動醫學（Sports Medicine）、 精神醫學（Psychiatry）、 牙醫術（Dentistry） 及獸醫學（Veterinary Medicine）	9,305,000 筆資料，其中包括 3,500 筆來自國際已出版的期刊。 1985 年至今，每月更新
MLA	文學（Literature）、語言（Language）、語言學（Linguistics）及民俗學（Folklore）	1,308,000 筆資料，來自 4,000 種美國及國際期刊。 1963 年至今，每月更新

（下頁續）

資料庫名稱	學科範圍	資料庫統計
NCJRS	懲戒（Corrections）、毒品與犯罪（Drugs and Crime）、未成年案例（Juvenile Justice）、法律強制（Law Enforcement）、統計學（Statistics）、受害者（Victims）	140,000 筆資料，包括期刊、政府資料及未出版的報告。1970 年至今，定期更新
PAIS International	社會科學，著重同期的社會、經濟和政治議題，以及公共政策	451,000 筆資料，來自期刊。1972 年至今，每月更新
PsycINFO	心理學及相關領域，全文使用Psy-cARTICLES	1,249,000 筆資料，來自 1,300 種期刊。1887 年至今，每月更新
Social Sciences Abstracts（社會科學摘要）	社會學（Sociology）、心理學（Psychology）、人類學（Anthropology）、地理學（Geography）、經濟學（Economics）、政治科學（Political Science）及法學（Law）	562,000 筆資料，來自 400 種期刊。1983 年至今，每月更新
Social Work Abstracts（社會工作摘要）	社會工作及相關領域	30,000 筆資料，來自期刊。1977 年至今，每季更新
Sociological Abstracts（社會學摘要）	社會學（Sociology）、社會工作（Social Work），及其他社會科學	519,000 筆資料，來自 3,000 種期刊。1963 年至今，雙月更新
Sport Discus（運動討論）	運動醫學（Sports Medicine）、體育（Physical Education）、練習（Exercise）、生理學（Physiology）、生物力學（Biomechanics）、心理學（Psychology）、訓練（Training）、教練教學（Coaching）、營養（Nutrition）	344,000 筆資料。1970 年至今，每季更新

>>>步驟9：先使用一般字詞搜尋，然後限制其輸出結果

除非你有一個預定的特別主題，否則你應該從資料庫的分類詞語中的一般字詞開始搜尋。如果分類詞語無法搜尋到，你可以用你正在研究的主題中有描述到的標記或片語來找。如果這個做法導致資料太多，你可以透過和（and）增加另外的字詞來限制。例如，假設你搜尋「社會」和「恐懼」，你將只得到有提到這兩個字詞的文章。舉例說明：搜尋心理學的主要資料庫——*PsycINFO*，如果使用「恐懼」搜尋 2000 年到現在的資料，總共有七百七十三筆（主要來自期刊），但若用「社會」和「恐懼」找尋同時期的資料，則有四百八十四筆。最後，以「兒童」和「社會」和「恐懼」搜尋，則只有七十筆。

另一個從電子資料庫有效限制資料輸出量的方法，是限制字詞只從標題及／或摘要中搜尋，此限制在 *PsycINFO* 及其他一些資料庫中被容許。使用這些限制將幫助剔除那些字詞只在內容中出現的資料，因為一篇主要討論恐懼的文章，幾乎都會在這兩個重要地方的其中之一被提及（注意：在一未被限制的搜尋裡，所有資料的內容都會被搜尋）。在 *PsycINFO* 資料庫搜尋中，限制「恐懼」只從標題及摘要中搜尋，從 2000 年至今一共找到六百七十一筆資料，這比未限制條件找出的七百七十三筆少了一百筆多一點。若加上「恐懼」必須在標題及摘要同時出現的額外限制，找到的資料為二百五十一筆，比原來的七百七十三筆少了相當多。

>>>步驟10：細分主題

若你要為你所選的題目做說明並寫一篇簡介，那麼，合理的選擇一個範圍較窄的題目是必要的。範圍太廣的題目會費時費力，尤其你只是為了一學期的課寫一篇簡介。題目的簡介太廣易使主題不明確，讀者無法了解你已經完全掌握了資料。因此，你應該更細分的訂定你的主題範圍。

範例 3.10.1 就是一個主題範圍太廣的例子。雖然作者定義了四歲小孩

的英文會話能力，但是仍太廣。顯然的，作者欲從聲音及文法系統來進行研究。若是如此，此篇完成的簡介，不是有一兩本書的長度的手稿，就是在此太廣題目上只呈現出表面處理的資料的手稿。

範 例 3.10.1

一個有太廣目的的主題：

本文針對學童語言習得進行研究。本人將簡述學童在自然環境下學習說話所得之資料，從最早的聲音開始到完整的句子。研究對象為出生到四歲說英語的小孩。

範例 3.10.2 是修改範例 3.10.1 的版本。要注意的是，作者將簡介著重在語言的具體方面，而且更清楚的說明有兩個主要目標：(1)已被研究的口語特徵；(2)描述已知的範圍內學童遵循的發展路線。即使這個題目很可能已有了很詳盡的研究，這個主題仍能為作者將來的文獻探討提供一個合適的陳述。

範 例 3.10.2

修改自範例 3.10.1 的更具體的版本：

本文描述已知的有關學童如何描述時間和以時間做參考的能力，包括動詞的使用和其他包含在動詞詞組的特色。第一，我將試圖描述學習動詞詞組特色的範圍，其次，描述學童們發展更龐大的時間語言能力的過程。

>>> 步驟 11：以當前的研究開始並逆推回去

　　最有效開始某領域研究的方法是從最當前的期刊文章開始。如果你判斷一篇最近被發表的文章與你的題目有關，文章的參考目錄或參考書目將對於你的研究提供有用的線索。以附錄 A 而言，一個好策略能讓你獲得與你的研究題目有關的文章，影印每一本最後的參考目錄，針對附錄 A 內容來比較，並決定你的參考書單。要發展你的書單要記住兩個重要的標準：書單應該(1)呈現主題的相關知識內容；(2)如果你將文獻探討作為進行研究的前言部分，先要提供適當的上下文。

>>> 步驟 12：搜尋和主題相關的理論性的文章

　　如同在第一章學到的，與題目直接相關的理論性的文章應該包含在文獻探討中。但是如果在社會和行為科學中進行典型的文獻搜尋，大多產生實徵性的研究的原始報告，因為這些類型的文件掌控了學術期刊。假如尋找和你題目有關的理論性的文章有困難，那可以把「理論」當成你的描述詞語。使用關鍵字「社會」和「恐懼」和「理論」在 *PsycINFO* 資料庫中查詢，找到了五十份文件，包括範例 3.12.1 在內，這些文件顯然會對計畫撰寫關於社會恐懼理論的人有所幫助。

範例 3.12.1

使用關鍵字「理論」推行搜尋，所獲得的文章：

Chen, Y. P., Ehlers, A., Clark, D. M., & Mansell, W. (2002). Patients with generalized social phobia direct their attention away from faces. *Behaviour Research & Therapy, 40,* 677-687. 摘要：這個實驗測試患有社會恐懼的患者在情緒的表達上是否與對面孔的注意力有關。一個修改過的點探測變

化表測量〔受試者〕是否更注意面部表情或家用品。二十個患社會恐
懼的〔受試者〕（平均年齡 35.2 歲）在家用品的部分，能較快辨識出
他們的恐懼感，不管臉部表情是正面的、中立或負面的。相反的，二
十個控制組（平均年齡 36.1 歲）沒有情緒的起伏。結果和社會恐懼的
理論一致，此理論強調，外在社會暗示對保持社會焦慮，扮演遞減的
角色。

　　重要的是，我們應該注意到有經驗的研究報告的作者，經常且必然的
將和他們的研究相關的理論文獻提供在文獻參考中。你應該藉由查找參考
文獻來搜尋它們。

>>> 步驟 13：尋找「評論性」文章

　　在前一個步驟中是使用「評論性」此字詞，當作尋找探討文獻時的關
鍵字。早先出版的評論性文章在計畫新文獻探討時非常有用，因為它們對
辨認文獻在研究領域上的廣度和範圍有很大的幫助。與典型的研究文章相
比，它們通常包含更加全面完整的參考目錄。

　　值得注意的是：一些期刊只出版文獻探討的文章，一些則出版強調實
徵性研究的原始報告，然而當其他期刊有禁止出版文獻的編輯政策時，偶
爾由此領域領導研究者出版文獻探討的文章。如果你知道在你的領域出版
文獻的期刊名稱，你也能輸入重要的關鍵字在資料庫搜尋[6]。這應該與你的
主要搜尋分開，另外搜尋，因為它會將你的搜尋限制在那些期刊之中。

　　在 *PsycINFO* 資料庫使用 "substance abuse" 和 "treatment" 作為一個關鍵
字（描述詞語），在任何領域進行查詢，和以 "review" 為標題做搜尋，只

6　在心理學方面，例如，《心理公報》（*Psychological Bulletin*）是一本致力於文獻探
　　討的重要期刊。《教育研究回顧》（*Review of Educational Research*）則是教育研究
　　批判的期刊。

分辨了包含吸毒者治療文獻的四十九篇潛在有用的文章。範例 3.13.1 示範了兩個例子。

範例 3.13.1

兩篇藉由搜索 "review" 所得到的文章：

Hopfer, C. J., Khuri, E., Crowley, T. J., & Hooks, S. (2002). Adolescent heroin use: A review of the descriptive and treatment literature. *Journal of Substance Abuse Treatment, 23,* 231-237.

Leri, F., Bruneau, J., & Stewart, J. (2003). Understanding polydrug use: Review of heroin and cocaine co-use. *Addiction, 98,* 7-22.

>>> 步驟 14：確認重大或經典研究和理論學家

最後，最重要的是，你得確認你所研究的主題中的重大研究或理論學家（換言之，這即是對一個主題或問題在歷史重要性上發展的理解）。令人遺憾的是，一些研究者認為這是枝微末節。不過，若缺乏重要經典研究的知識，你將無法了解你所研究之主題的來龍去脈。如果你正在寫一篇期待成為被深入探討的碩士論文或者博士論文，沒有引用重要經典研究，可能被認為是一處嚴重的瑕疵。

在文獻上檢索的初期，鑑定歷史上重要研究往往是不容易的。然而，某些期刊論文的作者明確地注意到這些，如範例 3.14.1 所示。

範 例　3.14.1[7]

選錄自鑑定經典理論學家和有關的研究的一篇研究文章：

Rogers 的傑出貢獻是，他是最先試圖透過開放會談（session），公開他的觀察，使心理療法的性質去神祕化。在 1940 年代，他出版了有效療程的書面副本。超過五十年來，許多研究者如 Porter（1943）、Snyder（1945），甚至最近的 Brodley（1994）都曾使用這些副本，已經實際測量出治療師如何影響個案的表現。關於這個問題，Gill（個人通信，1991 年 8 月 28 日）也寫道：「我也認為Rogers為提出書面會談的第一人，為他贏得許多讚揚，從他開始，許多人已經提升了如此做的勇氣，但是他是第一位。」（p. 311）

　　當閱讀你所選擇的文章時，你會經常注意到某些作者的名字反覆被提及。例如，如果你廣泛的閱讀關於社會因素對學習的影響，你將發現許多作者引用 Albert Bandura 社會學習論的研究文章。關於這一點，基於下列兩個理由，將使你用 Bandura 的姓名作為關鍵字來進行資料庫查詢：(1)去找尋他理論上所寫的要點（注意你必須使用第一手資料，而非使用經過他人釋義的二手資料）；(2)為了尋找引導他產生此理論或者最初提出證實理論的早期研究。記住提出理論的人們經常引領研究並且出版以支持他們的理論。幫助他們建立理論的早期研究最可能被視為是「重大的」或「經典的」。注意當你以這樣的目的進行資料庫搜尋時，你的搜尋不應該限制在近年出版的文章。在論文作者欄中以 "Albert Bandura" 為關鍵字，在論文題目欄中以 "social" 為關鍵字，並且在其他的關聯檔案欄中以 "learning"

7　Kahn, E., & Rachman, A. W. (2000). Carl Rogers and Heinz Kohut: A historical perspective. *Psychoanalytic Psychology, 17,* 294-312.

為關鍵字，在 *PsycINFO* 資料庫中進行所有年份的資料搜索，包含較早的資料搜尋，如範例 3.14.2 所示。

 範 例 3.14.2

一項領導研究者和理論家的早期研究：

Bandura, A. (1969). Social learning of moral judgments. *Journal of Personality and Social Psychology, 11,* 275-279.

最後，參考相關的學術教科書。教科書作者經常追尋重要主題的歷史，且可能提及他們所認為的最經典研究。

第 3 章的活動

1. 首先，熟悉你所屬領域的電子資料庫（參閱本章之表一，可得到資料庫的部分目錄）。你可藉由參加你就讀的大學圖書館所舉辦的專題討論會或者自行閱讀及操作相關資料，以熟悉你所屬領域的電子資料庫。注意現在有很多圖書館查詢系統允許你從你家中搜尋他們的線上資料庫，但是你或許將需要使用一個大學電腦帳號才能如此做。一旦你熟悉資料庫，請選擇一資料庫完成其餘的練習。

2. 如果你的指導教授已經分派給你一個有關特定主題的學期研究報告，請你使用與你主題相關的一個簡單描述片語來進行資料庫搜尋。如果你是進行獨立研究，選擇你所感興趣的一個領域，並且使用與之相關的一個簡單描述片語來進行資料庫搜尋。這搜尋將會顯示出多少引用文獻呢？

3. 由你的搜尋中檢索兩個或三個記錄並且找到符合的清單。比較這三個清單

並且注意它們的共通性及差異性。

- 寫下與你的計畫題目相關的三個精確的描述詞語。所選擇的描述詞語能反映出你個人對主題的興趣所在。
- 當你開始時,選擇一個簡單片語,你認為這些描述詞語是更具體還是更一般呢?為什麼?

4. 現在使用你剛剛修改的描述詞語來進行搜尋。

- 首先,利用修改搜尋來選擇更多的記錄。
- 然後,利用修改搜尋選擇更少的記錄。
- 如果你使用連接器 AND,它導致更多或是更少的來源?你認為為什麼會產生這樣的結果呢?
- 如果你使用連接器 OR,它導致更多或是更少的來源?你認為為什麼會產生這樣的結果呢?

5. 如有必要,更進一步的縮小搜尋,使你只剩下五十到一百五十筆文獻資料,並且列印搜尋結果。

- 仔細瀏覽列印清單以確認幾個可能的子類。
- 把新的種類與你原先的主題做比較。
- 更精確的定義你的主題,並且確認與你新主題相關的文章。準備一張這些文章的參考清單。

分析文獻的一般指南

現在你已將整組文獻做了初步的分類，你應該在撰寫文獻探討前，開始分析它們的過程。這章被設計來幫助你完成這個過程。其中兩個重要結果是：(1)參考清單的工作草稿；和(2)一套可包含關於各篇文章具體、詳細的資訊的筆記卡片。這是在你開始寫文獻探討之前，需要準備的兩種東西。

>>>指南 1：瀏覽文章並摘錄概要

當你選擇這些文章，你一定讀過文章的標題，而且應該也已讀了文章的摘要（像是總結），這些摘要常被多數期刊放在各篇文章的開頭。其次，你應該閱讀各篇文章開頭的前幾段，作者通常會對他們的問題範圍提供一些介紹。這將會給你有關於作者的寫作風格以及他們對研究問題的看法的一種感受，然後在「研究方法」之前，跳到最後一段，那些通常是研究文章文本的第一主要標題。傳統上，研究人員會在這段陳述他們的具體假說、研究問題或研究目的。接著瀏覽文章的其他部分，標記所有的標題和副標題，瀏覽各個分部的文本，但不要讓自己陷入困難或混亂的枝微末節。此時你的目的僅是在得到概要。

藉由遵循這指南，你就是在預習（pre-reading），這指南是一個由閱讀專家廣泛推薦，作為閱讀報告技術的第一步之技術。由於預習給你報告的

目的和內容的概要，能幫助你，讓你後續的工作能不至於專注在細節上，而是將注意力能保留在醒目的重點上。如同下個指南所建議的，藉由預習，你將能得到資訊幫助你依類別來編組文章。

範例 4.1.1 以期刊裡的短篇報告中典型的主標題為例。

範 例 4.1.1

標題（接在研究者的姓名及研究機構之後）

摘要（整個報告的總結）

〔在摘要之後接著寫相關文獻的探討簡介；典型地，標題不可以稱作「簡介」（Introduction）。〕

研究方法

　參加者（或主題）

　步驟（或測量、觀察或工具）

結果

討論（或結論、含義）

較長的文章常有另外的標題，例如假定、定義、實驗性治療、限制等等。瀏覽這些部分將能幫助你在詳讀這些文章時，從開始到結束能夠更為順暢。

研究文章的最後標題通常稱為「討論」或「討論與結論」，研究者常在這個標題下的前幾段重申或總結他們的研究目的、研究方法和主要研究結果。如果此研究包含了許多統計資料，可能對你造成困難，而詳讀這部分可幫助你了解該研究。

>>>指南 2：根據你的概要（參見指南 1），按類別編組文章

對於你要描述的文章做分類，你大概已經累積許多研究的類別的文章了。你也可能選擇以任一個方式來組織它們，但普遍做法是先依題目和副主題，然後再按年代順序在各個副主題之內組織它們。範例 4.2.1 顯示一篇壓力與人類免疫系統的參數之間關聯性的文獻探討，可能將文章依類別和次類別編組的範例。

範 例 4.2.1[1]

I. 壓力的概念化（定義）

　　A. 敏銳的時間限制引起的壓力源

　　B. 簡要的自然主義引起的壓力源

　　C. 壓力事件的序列

　　D. 慢性壓力源

II. 免疫系統的概要

　　A. 免疫系統的分類

　　B. 免疫分析

III. 壓力和免疫系統之間的關聯性

IV. 壓力、免疫系統和健康之間的模型

　V. 誰對於減輕壓力的免疫變動是脆弱的

---

[1] 引自 Segerstrom, S. C., & Miller, G. E. (2004). Psychological stress and the human immune system: A meta-analytic study of 30 years of inquiry. *Psychological Bulletin, 130,* 601-630.

範例 4.2.2 顯示在中國和移民中國的家庭中，父母的管教方式和學童的表現結果之間的關係所做的研究，將文章依類別和次類別分類，以作為文獻探討的可能編組方式。

範 例 4.2.2[2]

I. 父母管教方式的概念
   A. 西部人口的研究
   B. 交叉文化研究
II. 中國家庭的父母管教方式和學童的表現結果
   A. 父母親的控制
   B. 父母親的溫暖
III. 儒家思想以及它對中國家庭的衝擊

如果你同時依各類別或次類別閱讀所有該類別文章，將文章依類別來組織，將可促進你的分析能力。如果我們從最後一篇開始讀和這個題目有關的所有文章，會更容易綜合父母親的溫暖作用（參見範例 4.2.2 第 II-B 點）的相關文獻。

>>>指南 3：在讀文章之前組織自己

在詳細閱讀文章之前組織自己是很重要的。你將需要一部電腦、一疊筆記卡片來寫你的評論，並準備幾疊有自黏性的標籤紙，用來辨認值得注意的評論。你可以使用不同顏色的標籤紙標記不同的副主題、不同的研究方法、評論文章或標竿性研究，或其他需要註明的，或可能幫助你組織你

---

2 引自 Lim, S.-L., & Lim, B. K. (2003). Parenting style and child outcomes in Chinese and immigrant Chinese families: Current findings and cross-cultural considerations in conceptualization and research. *Marriage & Family Review, 35,* 21-43.

的回顧的。如果你使用一台電腦，你能使用差異較大的不同顏色（可利用文書處理程式），代替筆記卡片中不同顏色的標籤紙。

>>> 指南 4：在你的筆記中使用一致的格式

在你組織了文章之後，你應該開始閱讀這些文章。當你閱讀、總結重點，並且將它們記在筆記卡片內時，你可以設計一個格式來記錄你閱讀文章的筆記，且全部使用同樣格式。在這個階段的過程中如果你以一貫性的方式，編輯你的筆記，之後當你開始寫文獻探討時，會很有幫助。因為文章內容已被註記了，之後你遇到可觀的變異橫跨研究，你的筆記應該是一致和足夠詳細，以使你能描述其差異性和相似性。範例 4.4.1 推薦一個格式來記錄你的筆記。當你逐字複製作者的內容時，要記得標註頁數；直接引文應該伴隨頁數，如果你能註記頁數，以後將會節省你許多的時間。為了準確性，你要再確認你的文章。

 4.4.1

作者的姓、名

文章標題

出版年份

學報名、冊數、頁數

註記（回答以下問題）：

1. 這篇文章的要點是什麼？

2. 描述所使用的方法學（包括參加者人數、控制、治療等等）。

3. 描述研究結果。

4. 這篇文章有何著名的部分？（它是否是標竿性研究？它是否有缺點？它是否是一項實驗性研究？它是否是定性或定量的？等等。）

5. 特別注意與你的探討主題相關的具體細節（有需要就做）。

範例 4.4.1 中的重點可作為引導你通過這個過程的範例。實際上，你可以選擇刪掉一個或更多，或者你可以決定其他更加適當的方式。你可能需要為每個來源創造幾張筆記卡片。像你也許有一張卡片用來記錄每篇文章的要點，另外一張則記錄使用的研究方法等等。

使用分開的卡片於記錄問題或關注一篇特殊文章，或者是你所專注於能夠達到研究效度的文章，都是有用的。這些筆記以後可能被合併到你的文章裡，可能是在你的討論或結論中，而使用分開的卡片可以節省你寶貴的時間。如果你決定製作表格以摘要在你的文獻探討中的研究分組，則這些卡片將是相當有用的。製作表格指導在第七章有介紹。

就每篇文章而言，一張卡片應該包含完整的書目細節。這篇文章的其他卡片應該編碼一部分的書目信息：例如第一位作者的姓、文章標題中一個關鍵詞和出版年代。

>>> 指南 5：在文獻尋找關鍵術語的明確定義

無需訝異，不同的研究者有時用不同的方式定義關鍵術語。如果看法和你所書寫的有主要差異，你就得在定義上做標記。實際上，如果有幾個不同的定義，準備分開的卡片來記錄定義是很有用的。

如果要了解定義術語的重要性，不妨看看在範例 4.5.1 中「正義節目」和「基於娛樂的正義節目」的定義。它排除的節目是超過一個小時之久且根據真實案例的研究事件。另一位研究者不用這些排除的定義，也許會得到不同的結果。作為評論者，你將會注意到定義上的區別，因為它們也許從不同的研究幫助解釋差異的結果。

範 例　4.5.1[3]

考慮了特殊「風格」，或電視娛樂的一般類別（Gitlin, 1979），「正義」節目（有時稱警察影集、罪行影集、法律秀或者律師秀）被定義為將焦點放在刑法系統的某部分，例如執法、刑事訴訟、法院或懲戒的半小時或一小時電視節目。此外，基於娛樂的正義節目被定義為虛構；即角色和事件是虛構的，它們不刻畫真實角色或實際事件。採用這些定義，研究者發現了十三個基於娛樂的正義節目正在播映⋯⋯包括：《NYPD 藍色》⋯⋯（p. 18）。

　　特別記錄下來你能引述或摘要的值得信賴的定義（即定義由專家提供），例如，範例 4.5.2 的作者在文獻探討中援引的定義是來自專業協會。

範 例　4.5.2[4]

美國按摩療法協會（American Massage Therapy Association, 2003）定義了按摩療法為一整套柔軟的手工操作（manual soft tissue manipulation），包括抓握，引導運動，並且／或者施加壓力於身體。

　　對相關術語的定義要分開註記。例如，範例 4.5.3 分別定義廣義名詞「嫉妒」與狹義名詞「愛情嫉妒」，並與羨慕的定義做區別。注意，範例 4.5.3 出現的文獻探討在 2005 年出版了，裡頭提供較舊的定義。如果它們仍是有效用的，則引用較舊的定義本質上也沒什麼錯誤。

---

[3]　Soulliere, D. M. (2003). Prime-time murder: Presentations of murder on popular television justice programs. *Journal of Criminal Justice and Popular Culture, 10,* 12-38.

[4]　Dryden, T., Baskwill, A., & Preyde, M. (2004). Massage therapy for the orthopaedic patient: A review. *Orthopaedic Nursing, 23,* 327-332.

範例 4.5.3[5]

嫉妒（jealousy）被定義為「一種想法、情感和行動的複合體，它可以引發失落感或威脅到自尊和／或存在感或愛情關係的品質」（White, 1980, p. 222）。愛情嫉妒是從競爭者那裡接收到對愛情關係的威脅，而引發的一套想法、情感和反應（Guerrero & Andersen, 1998b; Teismann & Mosher, 1978）。嫉妒發生在人們渴望盡可能保有與某人的一段關係，這段關係是已擁有的，與羨慕（evny）相較，羨慕是有關渴望現在並未擁有的某事或某人（Guerrero & Andersen, 1998b）。

注意，在文獻探討的開頭提出關鍵術語的定義，通常是一個好想法。

>>>指南６：尋找關鍵的統計資料，以用在你文獻探討的起始處

使用一組分開的卡片，註記你可能會想要在你的文獻探討起始處引用的關鍵統計資料。範例 4.6.1 列舉出有關移民和難民經濟適應議題的文獻探討的第一句話。你可以注意到，與一個一般陳述，例如「許多在美國的人是在外國出生的」這句話相比較，若能引用具體的百分比數據來說明，會是一個較佳的選擇。

---

5 Fleischmann, A. A., Spitzberg, B. H., Andersen, P. A., & Roesch, S. C. (2005). Tickling the monster: Jealousy induction in relationships. *Journal of Social and Personal Relationships, 22,* 49-73.

範例 4.6.1[6]

美國人口中大約 10% 是在外國出生，預計將來還會依比例持續成長（Doyle, 1999; U.S. Bureau of the Census, 2001）。那些問題之一……

　　在文獻探討的起始處引用統計數據是具彈性的，因為一些標題的本身較其他部分更常使用這種方式表現。不過，從你開始計畫以數量來說明時（例如，一些青少年……；經常，投票者寧願……），若數量具有意義，則人們會想要知道。我們可在 www.census.gov 中找到社會和行為科學的相關統計資料。

>>> 指南 7：與你主題相關的文獻須更用心探討

　　如果你發現和你所探討的主題相同或相關的文獻文章（像是文章僅是由文獻探討所組成，並非一篇研究的原始簡介），請仔細閱讀並做下記錄，將有助於你統整你的文獻探討。範例 4.7.1 的作者們簡短地綜合近期他們所探討的文獻。

範例 4.7.1[7]

一份有關五個國立大學學生飲酒情形的調查探討（O'Malley & Johnston, 2002），概述了過去二十來所累積的主要發現：超過三分之二的大

6　Potocky-Tripodi, M. (2004). The role of social capital in immigrant and refugee economic adaptation. *Journal of Social Service Research, 31,* 59-91.

7　O'Hare, T., & Sherrer, M. V. (2005). Assessment of youthful problem drinkers: Validating the drinking context scale (DCS-9) with freshmen first offenders. *Research on Social Work Practice, 15,* 110-117.

學生喝酒，而且40%的人是酒精狂熱者（舉例來說，在兩個星期內喝了五次，甚至更多），實際上，自 1950 年代以來，酒精使用的比率並未改變。

>>>指南 8：為相關重要文獻準備小卡記錄

在文獻探討裡很少使用直接引證，因為過多的引證會影響敘述的流暢度。因此，研究者常比原來的作者歸納和解釋更多重點，雖然原作者能提供較詳盡的研究細節。然而，若有實例作為舉證，則更適用在文獻討探中。例如：以範例 4.8.1 來說，作者探討的是家庭中的領導地位，而在探討的起始處，作者用一個經濟組織的領導階層做類比。引證主要在簡潔的概述原作者的重要論述。請留意這也是他們在其文獻探討中唯一引用的引證。

範例 4.8.1[8]

根據 Bennis 和 Nanus（1985）所描述，「一個經濟匱乏的首都可以借貸，一個貧困的地方可以遷移，但是若缺乏領導階層，生存機會是渺小的。」（p. 20）

另一個合適的引證是以法律事件舉證，而且確切的措辭是很重要的，此時措辭有小小的改變也會影響它的合法性。範例 4.8.2 包含了此類的引證，它出現在這份探討的第一句話。

---

[8] Galbraith, K. A., & Schvaneveldt, J. D. (2005). Family leadership styles and family well-being. *Family and Consumer Sciences Research Journal, 33,* 220-239.

Writing Literature Reviews: A Guide for Students of the Social and Behavioral Sciences

範例 4.8.2[9]

在 2003 年 11 月 18 日，麻州最高法院法庭（SJC）宣布，找不到「任何本質充足的理由來否認同性伴侶的婚姻」，並且開始命令州政府把結婚許可證發給同性夫妻。

請注意在範例4.8.1和4.8.2的引證是相當簡短的。在一份文獻探討中，過於冗長的引證是不適當的（舉例來說，多於幾個字句的範圍）。畢竟，探討應該是一篇原創的綜合結論，不是再將一篇已出版的素材重新發表。

>>>指南 9：尋找有力的方法學

我們不可能找到一篇單一的研究文章，它的定義結果是符合人類環境下每個觀點的。不可避免地，有些研究比其他研究扎實，而你必須在你的探討中將這些有力論證記錄下來。詢問你自己這些證據有多有力，並牢記於心：你所扮演的角色，就是個評論者，你有權利和責任做這些主觀的評估。

研究文章的強度可能取決於研究方法學的使用。一份研究的方法會超越早期的資料蒐集技術嗎？研究的強度是取決於文章的多少或它的普遍性嗎？以多樣性的方法是否就可論證研究將導向相同的結論？這些或其他類似的問題將導引你決定特定研究的強度。定義方法學的強度將在第五、第六章探討其細節。

>>>指南 10：反思方法學上的缺點

當你在察看研究文獻時，你應該會注意到你所遭遇的問題。當發現問

---

[9] Lannutti, P. J. (2005). For better or worse: Exploring the meanings of same-sex marriage within the lesbian, gay, bisexual, and transgendered community. *Journal of Social and Personal Relationships, 22,* 5-18.

題時，你必須使用過去辨認優點的步驟來處理。例如，你必須判斷作者的研究方法是否在主題裡被賦予新的解釋。明確的說，如果使用一個創新方法學，它是適當的嗎？抑或是它引出可替性、可供選擇解釋的可能性？是否使用了恰當的研究樣本？研究上的發現是否跟類似的研究一致？不管研究者的推論是否有根據，一個明智的人必須判斷其在文章中所呈現的證據是否足夠？

在這裡，最好能一起批判一堆研究，特別是這些研究有相似的缺失。一般而言，當你探討文獻時，並不適合（inappropriate）去註記每一個研究的每一個缺失。而是註記個別研究群的大部分缺失，並關注跨研究群間缺失的型態。舉例來說，如果你探討的研究報告之子題（subtopic）中，都是以非常小的樣本為基礎，你可以在分開的卡片上註記這一件事，這些卡片是註記與此相關聯的文章。

研究論文的作者經常討論他們自己研究論文上的缺點。當然在文章裡任一處都可以討論這些缺失，不過在研究報告結尾處的「討論」（discussion）章節來探討這些缺失，會是比較一般、常見的做法。這些通常被視為是研究論文上的「限制」。範例 4.10.1 顯示如此的狀況。針對這些自我揭露方法學上的缺點的觀點去做筆記是重要的。

範 例 4.10.1[10]

對社會工作實務而言，（當代研究的）結果與建議是建立在一個非機率性的小規模樣本上，而此樣本來自於一個單一供應者組織。此外，他們疾病的嚴重性不被考慮……因此，社會工作實務結果和含義，應該要將這些限制考慮在內。

---

[10] Lee, J. S. (2004). A profile of diabetic African American elderly receiving home health care: Implications for social work practice. *Journal of Social Work in Long-Term Care, 3,* 13-30.

>>> 指南 11：辨別主張與證據

　　文獻探討裡常犯的一般錯誤是描述出一位作者的主張（asseration），其主張彷彿是研究所發現的結果。為了避免這種錯誤，確定你已經了解作者的證據及他的解釋。一個發現的取得來自實徵證據的呈現；而主張是作者的意見。

　　在範例 4.11.1 中，讀者可以很容易分辨段落中的主文主張，以及最後以實證為基礎陳述的句子。楷體字是重點所在。

範例 4.11.1[11]

導致暴飲暴食的危險因素中，最讓人關注的是節食（Lowe, 1994）。節食被認為是增加個人過量飲食以對抗卡路里被剝奪的效應的風險。節食也可能造成暴飲暴食，因為違反了嚴格的飲食規定可能造成毫無節制的飲食（禁止—違反機轉）。此外，節食伴隨著一種機轉：由依賴心理信號轉變到由認知控制過度飲食行為，這個認知過程被打斷時，便引發了個別難以防守的毫無節制的大吃大喝。支持這些的主張中，節食導致暴飲暴食發生於青少女身上（Stice & Agras, 1998; Stice, Killen, Hayward, & Taylor, 1998），並在成熟的女性中，其嚴重的熱量損失導致大吃大喝的機率提高（Agras & Telch, 1998; Telch & Agras, 1996）。（p. 132）

>>> 指南 12：在之前的研究結果裡辨別主要趨勢或樣式

　　當你撰寫文獻探討時，你有責任在你回顧研究文章的結果裡，指出主

---

[11] Stice, E., Presnell, K., & Spangler, D. (2002). Risk factors for binge eating onset in adolescent girls: A 2-year prospective investigation. *Health Psychology, 21,* 131-138.

要的趨勢或者樣式。這可以形成一般化，據此，你可以一般化各種各樣的文章。在範例 4.12.1 中，最初是出現在某一文獻探討的最後一段。注意支持範例內的一般性參考文獻在那篇選錄前的部分就已經說明過了。

範例 4.12.1[12]

回顧這九個研究，「關節炎的自助課程」已經能享有一個建立完善的研究體，這個研究體以支持其功效和高效益的成本。（p. 60）

當然，你或許不能像寫範例 4.12.1 的評論者一樣幸運。從一篇文章到另外一篇文章在結果方面或許會不一致。當這種情況發生時，你應該試著讓讀者理解。例如，你可以說明歸納的結果，它可能是整理許多文章的成果或是一個具有最權威研究方法的文章的歸納。不論意見是否被接受，只要你明確地講解你歸納的準則。再一次提醒你在分析階段仔細記錄將對你有所幫助。

>>>指南 13：辨認文獻的分歧

在文獻中發現一個重大的分歧是每個研究生的夢想，特別是它可能形成學生的碩博士論文寫作的重要關卡。實際上分歧是經常存在的，因為其對於研究者在這些領域研究上呈現出可觀的障礙。這些分歧應該在文獻探討時被提及，同時討論它們為什麼會存在。如果你覺得你辨認的歧異應該要被提出來，你應該在計畫寫文獻探討時提及它、記錄它並將它考慮進去。

---

12 Brady, T. J., Kruger, J., Helmick, C. G., Callahan, L. F., & Boutaugh, M. L. (2003). Intervention programs for arthritis and other rheumatic diseases. *Health Education & Behavior, 30,* 44-63.

>>>指南 14：辨認各研究間的關係

　　當你閱讀清單外的文章時，要記錄那些可能存在於研究中的所有關係。例如：指標性的研究文章可能會造成一個新的後續探索，由其他新的方法進行，或者兩篇文章也許探索同樣或相似的問題，但是用不同的年齡組或語言組。在你的文獻中指出這些關係是很重要的。在你寫作時，你有可能會想要談論那些相關的研究內容。

>>>指南 15：為每篇和你的研究題目緊密相關的文章做筆記

　　試著將你文獻的重點維持在你選擇的研究主題上。在你的文獻探討中涵蓋一些與你研究不相干的內容是不適當的。所以，你的筆記應該包含與你主題相關的具體方面研究的明確文獻。

　　如果你確定沒有其他文獻對你的研究主題有直接影響，那麼你可以回顧周邊的研究，但這應該要慎重進行。Pyrczak 和 Bruce（2005）引用在洛杉磯被實施作為課程創新的全年學校日程表的範例，如範例4.15.1。

> **範 例** 4.15.1[13]
>
> 例如：當洛杉磯首先開始實施全年學校日程表時，並沒有和這個主題相關的研究出版。然而，是有研究關於：在學童輪流上課的傳統學年計畫、學年長度，是否影響學生的學習成就和暑期輔導的效率如何等方面。學生在寫關於洛杉磯課程計畫的碩博士論文時，必須引用這些周邊的文獻，以呈現他們管理文獻的能力，並能完成一個全面性且有組織的文獻探討。

---

[13] Pyrczak, F., & Bruce, R. R. (2005). *Writing empirical research reports: A basic guide for students of the social and behavioral sciences* (5th ed.). Los Angeles, CA: Pyrczak Publishing.

這樣的範例是少見的，在你得到結論但又沒有研究能具體支持你的研究主題前，建議你要去請教你的指導教授。

>>>指南 16：評估你參考清單的流通性和涵蓋性

當你讀完蒐集的文章，你應該再次評估你的參考目錄，去確保它的完整性和時效性。文獻探討應顯示出它代表在這個主題範圍內最新完成的工作。根據經驗，用從目前算起的五年間距作為一個涵蓋範圍的嘗試性界限，記住只要涵蓋範圍是保證有效的，你將可以進一步擴展到更過去。以你的探討想要呈現主題的歷史概要為例，你必須達到超過五年的間距。然而切記關於文獻探討，讀者期待你報告當前最流行且可利用之研究。因此你應該清楚交代你的理由：為什麼文獻探討包含不是潮流的文章（例如，這文章是否為經典文章？是否在一特定的主題上展示了唯一的證據？它是否幫你了解研究技術的演變？）。

要包括多少文獻探討才夠？是一個很難回答的問題。一般來說，你最優先考慮的事，應該是確定你是否讀了當前最可利用的研究。然而你應設法在你需要的範圍內完整詮釋你的題目，而不是盡可能在完整的範圍內這麼做。你的指導教授或教職員顧問可以幫你確定多少文獻才是夠的。

 ## 第 4 章的活動

說明：參考第三章末尾進行的活動 5 當作文獻資料來源的列印清單。

1. 從這個清單取得兩篇文章，並瀏覽每一篇的內容。
   - 作者是否在文章一開始時，對文獻探討的內容做了總結？如果是那樣，標記這個總結作為未來的參考。
   - 作者是否用了小標題？
   - 直接先掃視以「方法」為標題的短評，作者是否對他們的假說、研究問

題或研究目的做了描述？

- 在沒有讀任何其他文章內容之前，寫一則簡要的敘述來描述每一篇文章是關於哪一方面的內容。

2. 以你清單上所有列出的文章的概要為基礎，對你文獻探討的範疇和子範疇做適當的預報。再次閱讀文獻來源的列印清單，並試著以大範疇和子範疇來將它們做分類。再用這些範疇和子範疇來創造出描述你研究主題領域的一個草案。

3. 仔細回顧你的草案並選擇你首先要閱讀的文章。在每一個範疇裡，從最初的研究開始進行到目前的研究。如此你便有了初步的閱讀清單了。

量化研究的文獻分析

在前面的章節裡，已建議你在寫文獻探討之前，註記你所閱讀的研究論文中重要方法的優缺點。本章節將在一些你想要註記的點上為你提供訊息，特別是量化研究的研究方法。那些已經選修了研究方法課程的人，就該知道本章節只是非常簡短的概述一些重要問題。

>>>指南 1：注意那些研究是量化還是質性

因為量化研究中，研究者會把訊息簡化為統計值，例如平均數、百分比等等，他們的研究文章很容易看出結果。如果一篇論文中，有一個主要部分是以統計資料的結果呈現，可以大膽的說那就是量化研究。從 20 世紀到 21 世紀，社會科學和行為科學大都是量化研究，因此與質性研究相比較，你很可能找到更多的論文是屬於量化研究。

量化研究中所強調的部分包括：

1. 開始於一個或更多的明確申明的假說，這假說在整個研究期間保持不變[1]。這些假說的效度只在那些數據被分析之後被評量（即，當數據被蒐集時，假說不受變化的影響）。

---

[1] 量化研究人員有時從具體的研究問題或者目的開始而不是一個假說。像假說一樣，研究問題或者目的在整個研究期間保持不變。

2. 從特定的母群中選擇一個非特定的樣本（像是透過從一頂帽子中抽出名字而取得的一個簡單隨機樣本）。

3. 使用相對大樣本的參與者（通常，就一個實驗來說至少三十名，而有時為了國家調查會多達一千五百名）。

4. 用可以被客觀記錄的工具進行測量，例如多項選擇成就測試和強制選擇問卷，由參與者標記選擇的態度量表或者人格量表。

5. 使用統計值呈現結果並且經常對樣本來源的母群進行推論（即，推斷那些研究人員透過研究一個樣本所獲得的發現，類似於他們研究整個樣本來源的母群所得到的發現）。

質性研究被應用於社會科學和行為科學方面也有很長一段時間，但是應用於其他領域，則是近幾十年的事。要分辨「質性研究」有時是容易的，因為在文章的標題中，經常包含「質性」這個語詞。而做質性研究的研究者通常也會在他們的論文或其他報告中，提出他們的研究是屬於質性研究[2]。你也可以根據研究中的摘要或研究的主題來鑑定研究是否屬於質性研究。

質性研究中所強調的部分包括：

1. 研究通常從一般的問題開始，沒有強調嚴格、特定的目的和假說來進行研究。因為某些問題而必須蒐集數據，假說可能就此出現，但是當數據被蒐集時，假說可能會因此在研究過程中受到影響。

2. 選擇樣本時是採用立意樣本，而不是隨機樣本。例如，一個質性研究者可能接觸到參加一個特別門診的海洛因成癮者，對於戒除成癮者的問題，門診部的這些病人或許可以提供有用的回應。換句話說，質性研究者在選擇一個樣本過程中，使用他們的判斷，而不是機械化、客觀的過程，例如隨機從一頂帽子中抽出名字。

3. 使用一個相對小樣本，有時小到像是例如已經得到師鐸獎的一名數

---

[2] 注意：量化研究人員很少明確地說明他們的研究是量化的。

學教師（這是一個立意樣本──篩選一個被認為是具有重要資訊潛在資源的人）。

4. 以相對非結構性工具進行測量，如半結構式開放問卷面訪（即參與者沒有「機會」選擇），在自然脈絡下非結構性的行為觀察等等。

5. 密集測量（例如，與那些參與者共處較長的時期，以獲得對所關心的現象更深入的了解）。

6. 結果的呈現主要或專門只用文字，並強調對特定立意樣本研究的理解，且通常不強調或者忽視類推到較大的母群。

如你所見，透過比較上面所列的兩大項目，當你要評估研究的優缺點時，量化和質性研究間的分別，就變得很重要。本章提出評估量化研究的主要指導方針。當你為了準備一篇文獻探討而評估與綜合研究報告時，你應該考慮這些指導方針。而評估質性研究的指導方針將在下一章提出。

>>> 指南 2：注意這個研究是實驗還是非實驗性

實驗研究是為了研究目的而給參與者一些實驗處置，再評估其影響。例如，在一個實驗過程中，給一些過動的學生服用利他能（Ritalin），而其他過動學生則給予行為治療（例如回饋系統的有系統應用），以評估兩種處理方法對減少教室紀律問題的有關效力（注意幾乎所有實驗都是量化的）。這目的很明顯的是要了解每個處置的效果如何，以及哪個處置是較有效用的。更常見的目的是鑑定因果關係。

非實驗研究，是測量參與者的特性，但並不試圖改變他們。例如，過動學生可能透過晤談以理解他們自己破壞性的教室行為，但研究人員不會嘗試治療那些學生。這樣的一項研究可以是量化（研究人員使用高結構性的面談問卷供學生選擇，再統計結果做出結論）或者是質性（研究人員使用半結構性或非結構性的面談問卷[3]，並用文字來總結主題、模式或理論的結果）[4]。

---

[3] 此外，一個質性研究人員很可能進行相當長的晤談和也許不止一次的晤談。

[4] 顯而易見，實驗研究幾乎都是量化的，非實驗研究則可能是量化或質性的。

這裡有個重要的告誡：不要養成將全部研究稱為實驗研究的習慣。例如，如果你正評論非實驗研究，應稱它們為「研究」，而非「實驗」。「實驗」一詞只能用在為了觀察處理方法的影響，而實際施行在參與者身上的處理方法。

>>> 指南 3：實驗時，注意哪些參與者是以隨機方法分發

參與者被隨機分發到處理方法的實驗，稱為**真實實驗**。隨機分配是保證處理方法沒有分配偏見（即，由於是隨機分配，所以不會具偏見有系統的分發較具破壞性學生給予行為治療處遇，而其他學生分發到服用利他能的治療）。如果其他情形都一樣，則真實實驗比起使用其他分配方法的實驗要來得重要，例如在一所學校使用那些學生作為實驗組，而在另一所學校的一些學生作為對照組。注意學生並沒有正式隨機分配到學校。因此，兩所學校的那些學生之間可能早已存在重大的差別，而推翻了這個實驗結果的解釋（例如，社會經濟地位、語言背景或自由選擇，像發生在藝術、科學等等的磁石學校）。

>>> 指南 4：注意在非實驗研究中檢驗因果議題

這種調查因果問題的實驗法（對處理條件進行隨機分配），被廣泛地認為是最好的量化方法。不過，它有時不能實行或者不可能用某些模式對待參與者。例如，如果一個研究人員為了探索父母離婚和孩子被中學退學之間是否相關，而要求一些父母為了此實驗結婚或離婚，顯而易見，這是不可行的。對於這個研究問題來說，最好是找一些被退學的和沒被退學的孩子，研究他們有無重要的相似部分（例如社會經濟地位、他們就讀學校的品質等等）。然後檢視他們父母的離婚率與假設的方向是否相同[5]。與父

---

[5] 如果研究人員有相當多的資源和長的時間，一預測研究的進行可從孩子們入學到畢業，去留意退學和沒退學的以及父母離婚的。這縱貫性方法（longitudinal method）

母未離婚的孩子相比較，離婚父母的孩子有稍微高的被退學比率。這意味著離婚引起更高的退學比率嗎？不一定。研究者可能得根據其他原因再下結論。這僅僅是其中一個原因：或許因為離婚的父母不容易與人相處，且較不易與他們的孩子相處。這可能是在與孩子的溝通狀況上出現問題（並非離婚），那也會使孩子被退學[6]。

我們正考慮的研究是原因－比較（或者採取措施後信以為真）的例子研究。當使用它時，一個研究者觀察一種目前的條件或結果（例如退學），並且搜尋過去可能的原因變項（例如離婚）。因為就檢驗因果律來說，原因—比較研究，比真實實驗更容易有錯誤，所以當一個結論是基於這種原因—比較法而來時，你應該要特別加以留意。另外，你應該考慮是否有研究者可能忽略的其他似是而非的原因的解釋。

>>> 指南 5：考慮施測工具操作的重測信度

量化研究者將他們使用的測量（例如測驗和問卷）稱為工具。因此，工具操作（instrumentation）指的是他們測量主要變項的過程。

信度指結果的一致性。舉個例子：假定我們實施一週的大學入學考試，然後下週給相同的受試者重新施測。假如在第一週得高分的受試者在第二週也傾向於得到高分，那麼這個考試會被認為是具有信度的[7]。透過計算一個相關係數，一次試驗的信度可以被計量。相關係數的範圍從 0.00 到 1.00，而 1.00 表示完美的可靠性。量化研究者一般認為 0.75 或者更高的係數表明

也不如這種實驗法適合，因為可能使鑑定因果關係的變項變混亂（即，許多變項比離婚更可能導致退學行為，而研究人員可能無法控制所有變項）。

[6] 如果這限制仍然不清楚，更進一步看看這個例子。基於研究的問題，假設一獨裁政府為了降低退學率，規定父母離婚不合法。如果退學的真正原因是父母缺乏人際互動技巧，防止離婚將沒有預期的效用，因為它被誤認為是真正的原因。相反的，政府本應規畫幫助父母改進他們人際互動的技巧，特別是與他們的孩子相處。

[7] 同樣的，第一週得分低的受試者在第二週也得低分就是信度高。

足夠的信度。我們稱這類型的信度為**重測信度**[8]。

當你分析一項量化研究時，檢查關於工具操作的部分，看看那些研究者是否提供關於他們在研究過程中使用的工具的信度訊息。通常，這訊息非常簡短，就像範例 5.5.1。

範例 5.5.1

在研究過程中有關重測信度的一個簡短陳述：

兩次施測間隔為兩週的工具操作，其重測信度為 0.81，這表明有足夠的信度（Doe, 2005）。

儘管範例 5.5.1 的陳述非常簡短，但它向你保證你分析的研究，其研究者已經考慮過信度的重要問題。另外，它提供你一個可以查閱有關如何確定信度的參考（即，Doe, 2005）。

>>> 指南 6：考慮施測工具操作的內部一致性信度

重測信度關注的是超過一段時間的結果的一致性（詳見指南 5），而內部一致性信度則是指在某一時刻當下的結果的一致性。要理解這概念，可試著想想只有二題代數題目卻有多項選擇的測驗。假定受試者答對一題，另一題答錯。這表明缺乏內部一致性，因為我們了解考生的代數知識有所改變（這一題和下一題有所不同）〔即，在這個測試項目，考生獲得一分，而在其他測試項目，考生獲得零分（這是在單個項目上最低的評分）〕。把這個概念擴大到一次測驗許多項目和受試者，如果那些受試者答對任何一個考試項目，則他們傾向於答對其他考試項目（反之亦然），那這個測

---

[8] 決定信度的其他方法超越了本書的範疇。

驗被稱為有好的內部一致性信度。更廣泛地說，內部一致性指的是，藉由其受試反應是類似於在其他項目中的受試反應，以了解一個考生的能力[9]。

　　缺乏內部一致性表示有些項目無法如陳述般加以運作，這有很多原因造成這個狀況。一個明顯的原因是有些項目可能是含糊的，使得有很多知識的受試者選了錯誤的答案。當然，這不是我們所願的。

　　內部一致性信度最常透過計算 Cronbach α 係數來檢查，如同相關係數，α的範圍一樣是從 0.00 到 1.00，數值超過 0.75 通常便表明了此研究有足夠的內部一致性信度[10]。範例 5.6.1 顯示在一份研究報告裡如何提出α。

範例 5.6.1[11]

在研究報告中的簡短陳述裡有關兩種信度的類型：

這項研究所關心的結果是一個自陳報告的暴力行為……常模的範圍從 0 到 70；得分愈高表示行為愈暴力。在一次小規模試驗中，Cronbach α 係數是 0.75，和重測信度……相關是 0.76（Birnbaum et al., 2002）。

　　儘管範例 5.6.1 的陳述非常簡短，但它向你保證研究者已經考慮重測信度和內部一致性信度。另外，它也提供你關於信度和內部一致性怎樣被確定的更多參考訊息（即，Birnbaum et al., 2002）。

---

[9] 換句話說，一個內部一致性相當高的研究工具，可以看成是一組同質性項目的組合（即：所有項目傾向於相似的技巧，態度等等）。

[10] 如果你學過統計，你知道相關係數也會有負值。然而實際上，當估計信度和內部一致性時，它們總是正值。

[11] Blitstein, J. L., Murray, D. M., Lytle, L. A., Birnbaum, A. S., & Perry, C. L. (2005). Predictors of violent behavior in an early adolescent cohort: Similarities and differences across genders. *Health Education & Behavior, 32,* 175-194.

>>>指南 7：考慮工具操作的效度

一項工具（像是大學入學考試）在它測量所想測量的程度上據說是有效的。例如，由大學入學考試去正確推測誰未來在大學裡能成功，這考試被稱為是有效的。實際上，並沒有工具是絕對有效的。例如，大學入學考試充其量只適度有效。

在效標關聯效度的研究，受試者在一個工具（像大學入學考試那樣）的得分與其他測驗工具（像是大學裡新鮮人的 GPAs 一樣）的得分有關，效標關聯效度的有效範圍是透過計算一個相關係數以描述其關係而確定。當完成時，所導致的相關係數被稱為效度係數[12]。一般來說，超過 0.30 的係數表明研究目的足夠有效。範例 5.7.1 顯示關於大學入學考試的預測效標關聯效度的一個簡短陳述。稱預測是因為入學考試在某一時刻當下實施，而結果（GPAs）在過後才被測量，其目的是確定預測 GPAs 有多高分。

範例 5.7.1

在研究報告中的簡短陳述裡有關預測的效標關聯效度的情況：

使用考取一所小型文學院的二百四十位受試者的樣本，Doe（2005）與 XYZ 大學新生入學考試的成績相較。發現測驗有足夠的效標關聯效度（$r = 0.49$）。

範例 5.7.2 顯示一個關於同時效標效度的簡單陳述。形容詞「同時」是指兩個測驗在幾乎同時實施。

---

[12] 效度係數是符號為 r 的相關係數。

範 例　5.7.2

在研究報告中的簡短陳述裡有關同時效標效度（預測）的情況：

在一項以前的研究，Doe（2005）採用由有訓練和有經驗的採訪者蒐集而成的戒煙資料在戒煙問卷上得到相關分數。問卷在同一天給予那些有參加訪談的參與者。訪談資料是用來判斷問卷調查標準的有效性，發現問卷有良好的效標效度（$r = 0.68$）。因此，用戒煙問卷測量戒煙行為是一種合理有效的方法，並可取代更昂貴的訪談過程。

　　另一種主要的效度是**建構效度**。這名詞是指任何類型的基本資料研究都能藉由一項工具的效度弄清楚。建構效度研究可採用很多形式，大部分超出本書的範圍。不過，要說明這樣的一項研究可能如何進行，可參考範例 5.7.3。

範 例　5.7.3

在研究報告中的簡短陳述裡有關建構效度的情況：

在新的 ABC 焦慮量表（ABC Anxiety Scale）與既有的貝克憂鬱量表（Beck Depression Inventory）上得分有相關，且相關性為 0.45。這個結果與主要的理論和以前的研究一致（例如，Doe, 2004），那表明焦慮不安的人有一種適度的傾向是沮喪的。因此，這個相關性對於新憂慮量尺的效度提供間接證據。

效度的最後主要類型是**內容效度**。內容效度透過讓一位或更多位專家評估一項工具的內容來確定。成就測驗的內容效度是特別重要的，例如，藉由設計用來測量是否達到教學目標的成就測驗，我們可要求專家比較教學目標與材料，確定其配合的程度。內容效度也能由其他類型的工具確定，就像範例 5.7.4 說明的。

範例 5.7.4

在研究報告中的簡短陳述裡有關內容效度的情況：

在這個實驗過程中使用嬰兒發展檢核表作為測量結果。在一項以前的研究中，Doe（2004）報告它由三位發展心理學的教授判斷有足夠的內容效度。

>>>指南 8：考慮工具對特別研究目的的效度

一項在以前的研究過程中合理有效的工具，用在其他研究上未必特別有效。例如，一個顯示供青少年使用是有效的態度量尺，可能在另一項研究內，供更幼小的孩子使用，會有一些未知數的效度。因此，如果研究的目的是研究更幼小孩子的態度，工具的效度可能是未知的。用更一般的術語來說，一項工具的效度與一項研究的目的有關。它可能在某個目的的研究過程中（例如，確定青少年的態度），比起另一項研究在一些不同的目的時更有效（例如，確定幼小孩子的態度）。

>>>指南 9：注意研究過程中被測變項的不同

當你檢查各種已出版的研究中，你感興趣的一種變項已經被測量，你會發現不同的研究者常使用不同的工具測量變項。例如，一位研究者可能

用一份強制選擇的問卷測量學校的態度（例如，參與者回應的選項由「非常同意」到「非常不同意」），而另一位研究者可能會使用一個觀察教室行為的檢核表，表明積極或消極的態度（例如，孩子在教室工作上合作的情形）。如果經過使用不同的工具研究結果發現是相似的，則支持結果。顯而易見的，研究中結果的差別可能可歸因於工具操作的差別。

　　值得注意的是測量過程的一部分是決定從哪些來源去蒐集數據。例如，研究暴力少年犯的行為，一個研究者可以從參與者的同儕尋找資料，另一個研究者基本上可以使用相同的問題，從參與者本身找尋資料[13]。不同的對象使用工具的差別，也可能使結果不同。

　　根據上述，你應該可以透過歸因於工具操作的研究尋找模式。例如，是所有支持同樣結論的研究，都使用一種方法或工具類型，還是支持不同結論的那些研究，都使用不同的方法呢？如果你的筆記顯示這種情況，你可能考慮做一個陳述，像範例 5.9.1 裡的那樣。

範 例 5.9.1

一個文獻探討的說明指出測量方法上的差異（令人滿意的）：

兩個使用問卷調查法的研究支持青少年間吸入劑的使用是非常罕見的（低於 1% 的一半），而三個使用面對面訪問的研究則提出發生率多於 5%。

　　注意範例 5.9.1 的資訊遠多於範例 5.9.2。

---

[13] 例如，受試者被問到：「你在上禮拜和人吵架了嗎？」而他的同學也許被問到：「你的朋友小翰有告訴你他在上禮拜和人吵架了嗎？」

範例 5.9.2

一個文獻探討的說明未指出測量方法上的差異（令人不滿意的）：

「青少年吸入劑使用的發生率」這個研究得出繁雜的結果，兩個研究報告指出發生率是非常罕見的，而其他三個研究指出發生率多於 5%。

>>> 指南 10：注意受試者取樣的方式

大多數的量化研究者只研究單一被抽樣的樣本，從這個樣本來推論到母群體。你應該注意的是，這個被研究的樣本是否具有母群體的代表性而可能可以被推論。從一個量化研究者的觀點，隨機抽取一個樣本是最好的。

遺憾的是，大多數的研究者不能使用隨機樣本（至少沒有用他們純理論的做法）。這是由於以下兩個原因。第一，很多研究者使用有限的資金工作，而且和有限的合作企業接觸，而這些對取得隨機樣本而言是必需的。因為在社會和自然科學方面大部分研究者是教授，所以他們通常以他們授課的學院或大學的學生作為樣本。當然，大學生可能不能推論到其他群體。

第二，即使一個隨機樣本被抽樣出來，被挑選出來的成員總是有些會拒絕參與。在問卷調查中，特別困難的是回答比率經常是顯著的低。而這並不那麼令人驚訝，例如，一個隨機樣本是一個職業公會（例如：國中小教師公會）的成員，在一個全國性的問卷調查中，只得到 25% 的回函率。

研究若沒有隨機抽樣以及低回答率就要相當小心的解釋。這樣的研究通常被當作是試驗性的，因為它們沒有提供穩固的證據。

Writing Literature Reviews: A Guide for Students of the Social and Behavioral Sciences

>>>指南 11：注意受試者人口統計資料之備註

文獻中受試者人口統計資料[14]的備註也能夠幫助你確認樣本。例如研究者研究工作福利的轉變，使用居住在城市的樣本跟使用居住在農村的樣本，會得到不同的結果嗎？受試者城市—農村身分的差異（一種人口統計的特色）是否有助於解釋調查結果上的差異性？注意，你不能確實的回答這些問題，但你可以在你的文獻探討提出這個可能性。此外，人口統計的特性在研究報告中經常被提到的是性別、種族、年齡和社經地位。

研究報告中沒有詳細的人口統計資料，通常效用會比研究報告中有詳細的人口統計資料者來得少。

>>>指南 12：注意差異的程度，不只是達統計顯著

當一個研究者指出研究結果在統計上達顯著水準時，此份研究報告就意味著研究結果的差異性是由單一隨機因素所影響。但這不表示差異性必然很大。很多的統計書都會花很多章節來解釋此現象。然而，接下來的分析可以幫助你了解這個重點：假設參議院中 A、B 候選人勢均力敵，A 比 B 多十票，這真的是很微小的差距，但卻相當具有顯著性（換言之，在非常仔細精準的點數過票數之後，我們可以很明確的找到一個很微小的非隨機因素所造成的差異性）。

即使有些微小的差異性通常都能達到顯著水準，但還是要注意在文獻中所發現的差異性大小[15]。假設你讀了很多研究，這些研究都指出電腦教學對於英語作文的幫助不大，但是在增進學生學習成就上卻達到顯著水準。

---

[14]「人口統計資料」是受試者的出身背景特性。

[15] 愈來愈多的量化研究者提出一種統計量，這種統計量被稱為「實驗效果」（effect size），用來測量一組受試者中個別受試者之間的差異性大小。在本書後面討論統計量時，你用這個粗略的指南重新探討文獻會遇到這個統計量：實驗效果低於 0.25 意指微小的差異，實驗效果高於 0.50 意指大的差異。

那麼你就必須在報告中指出差異性的大小，就像範例 5.12.1 一樣。假如你在你所讀的文獻中找到一個適當的說明，你就要寫出如下的研究結果。

範例 5.12.1

有一個在美國不同大學所進行的真實實驗，實驗組接受英語作文的電腦輔助教學，實驗組得到一個很小但比對照組在數學成就上有顯著的差異性。一般來說，這樣的結論只在選擇題的測驗上達到大約 1%的顯著性。儘管它們達到顯著，但是這些微小的差距卻使得在使用電腦教學上增加很多花費，造成另一個基本問題。

>>>指南 13：量化研究有其缺陷

　　所有的量化研究都會有不同類型的錯誤，所以沒有任何一個研究可以被用來證實有絕對且正確精準的答案。事實上，這就是為什麼你在原文的研究論文報告中整理蒐集這些證據之後，你必須從這些不同的證據中去權衡所有證據的真實性，才能達到合理性的結論。從此處，我們得到一個重要的警示：討論實驗研究的結果時絕對不要用「證明」（prove）這個詞。實驗研究並不提供證據，只提供證據的程度，這個研究提出的證明比另一個研究有力。當分析研究文獻時，要注意在每一個文獻中的證據是如何被確認的。相同的，你也要在你的文獻中，再次強調這些研究結果提出的強而有力的證據。

　　這一則指南又引出另一個重要原則。很明顯的，你不能夠期望能分析或討論你所引用的每一篇文獻中的每一項缺失，因為研究中充滿了缺失。相反的，你應該注意主要的缺失，尤其是你計畫在結論中強調、重複提出的研究。此外，你應該盡可能的批判群體研究的方法論。例如，你可以指出所有你參考的群體研究都有相同的缺點。當你在閱讀這些文獻時，好好

Writing Literature Reviews: A Guide for Students of the Social and Behavioral Sciences

的做記錄，將幫助你找出這些共同性。

總結意見

　　這個章節只簡短的提出你在準備寫文獻探討的內容時，對於量化研究報告所應注意的一些主要的方法學上的議題。當你在讀你所選擇的文獻時，因為其他研究者也會在他的論文中批判別的研究者，所以你會發現更多額外的資訊。仔細的閱讀這些文獻，將有助於你更完整的理解你正在重新閱讀的這些研究文獻。

第 5 章的活動

說明：找到一份量化研究的原始報告，最好和你探討的主題有關，並回答下列問題。為了學習目標，你的指導老師可能會選擇分派一篇文章讓你們班上所有的學生去閱讀。

1. 在你找的報告中有什麼特色讓你相信它是一個量化研究的範例？

2. 這個研究是實驗性的研究還是非實驗性的研究？你是根據什麼下這個決定？

3. 假如這個研究是實驗性的，參與者是隨機被分派的嗎？假如不是，他們是如何被分派的？

4. 假如這個研究是非實驗性的，研究者是否企圖去檢驗因果問題？假如是，研究者是用原因－比較方法嗎？請解釋之。

5. 使用什麼種類的測量方法（工具）？研究者是否提供足夠的資訊允許你去判斷他們研究的適當性？假如是，按照他們提供的資訊，你認為他們的研究是適當的嗎？假如不是，有關測量方法還有什麼額外的訊息應該被提出來？

6. 研究者如何取得受試者的樣本？是從母群中隨機抽樣嗎？如果這個研究是

一個問卷調查，回答的比率是多少？

7. 研究者是否詳細的描述受試者的人口統計資料？請解釋之。

8. 假如研究者指出研究結果在統計上達顯著水準時，在他的討論裡研究結果是否有很大的差異性？根據你的看法，這樣的差異是否大到能夠實用的重要性？請解釋之。

9. 研究者是否經由研究限制的因素來評論自己的研究？請解釋之。

10. 根據你在問題 1 到問題 9 的回答，簡單的敘述研究時你不能避免的主要缺失。

質性研究的文獻分析

質性和量化研究之間的主要差別在之前第五章的指南 1 已描述了。本章撰寫時假定你已經根據那指南工具仔細考慮過。第五章強調在寫文獻探討之前量化研究的分析，而本章則探索分析質性研究的標準。

>>> 指南 1：注意研究是由研究團隊或個人來進行

已出版的量化和質性研究經常是由研究團隊來進行，與量化研究過程相比，使用團隊在質性研究過程中更重要。例如，一名量化研究者給予一客觀態度量表計分，並且使用一個統計套裝軟體分析數據，任何人只要小心使用這些計分，並鍵入這些數據，則其獲得的結果與原先研究者的結果相同是很合理的。但是，質性研究者採用的是開放式、半結構式晤談，所得的原始數據通常是由那些參與者在晤談時說的多頁副本所組成，不同的研究者可以有不同分析並且解釋這樣的數據，提出分析數據的有效性問題。但是，如果一個研究團隊分析一套質性數據並且達成共識，則會比由個人處理的研究結果讓讀者更能信服。

由團隊來進行研究不是必要的。實際上，可能沒有時間讓其他合格的研究者與一個研究者合作，或是一篇論文或一篇長篇論文是研究者要作為個人研究報告的。當遇到這種情況時，特別重要的是，讀者要檢查看看這些人在進行質性研究時，是否至少使用了指南 3 和 4 所描述的技巧之一。

>>>指南 2：當有研究團隊時，注意最初是藉由個別處理的數據分析

研究者在分析一組質性資料時，會先獨立分析（即，沒有諮詢彼此），這是為了防止一個或更多研究者，在解釋資料時受到其他人影響。最初分析之後，研究者接著解決任何歧見，通常藉由討論達成共識。在範例 6.2.1 中描述了這個過程。

範例 6.2.1[1]

獨立分析後達成共識的描述：

由研究團隊分析質性數據……我們首先獨立細察原始數據，使參與者所有回應趨於相似。其次，我們結合內容相似的結果，最後，我們將所有數據做成項目清單，並且取得共識。

其他事情是等同的，由一群研究者首先獨立的分析資料，然後共同討論他們的分析以達成共識的質性研究，是勝過沒有如此做的研究。

>>>指南 3：注意是否曾請教外部專家

向一位或更多外部專家求教，可以增加讀者對此一質性研究結果的信任。如果是個人（而非團隊）進行研究，則求教更形重要（見指南 1）。

質性研究者通常從外部專家處，取得足夠的資料分析結果作為參考，此稱為同儕審查過程。那些專家評論整個研究處理的過程，一如回顧數據分析的結果，專家通常被稱為審稿委員，如範例 6.3.1 裡所做的那樣。

---

[1] Schuck, K., & Liddle, B. J. (2004). The female manager's experience: A concept map and assessment tool. *Consulting Psychology Journal: Practice,* 75-87.

範例 6.3.1[2]

獨立分析後達成共識的描述：

審稿委員是一位非裔美籍女性博士生，她的專長在諮商輔導非洲移民和國際大學生。審核過程需要檢查保證原始數據被恰當分派到各領域，並且做出準確和完整的核心摘要。審稿委員提出幾個更改後的書面建議，而最初架構出領域和核心想法的那些研究者，則評估審稿委員的建議，並依一致的判斷做出更改。

>>> 指南 4：解釋資料時需顧及參與者

關於怎樣處理質性研究的文獻，重點是在，處理研究時所得的結果須能反映出那些參與者察覺的真實性。換句話說，質性研究的目標是理解參與者怎樣察覺他們自己的現實，而不是建立一個所謂的客觀現實。因此，質性研究者應該詳細記敘一份結果的試驗性報告，並且要求參與者（或者代表他們的樣本）檢閱報告，提出他們的看法。質性研究者將此過程稱為*成員檢查*。此方式最初的想法是，在質性研究過程中，那些參與者實際上是研究團隊的成員，所以他們有權檢查結果。範例 6.4.1 說明研究報告中如何描述此種情況。

2　修改自 Friedman, M. L., Friedlander, M. L., & Blustein, D. L. (2005). Toward an understanding of Jewish identity: A phenomenological study. *Journal of Counseling Psychology, 52*, 77-83.

範例 6.4.1[3]

使用成員檢查的描述：

經過最初分析後，要求三位參與者（一名男性和兩名女性）評論結果暫定的草稿，並且考慮它的準確度。總之，那些參與者同意草稿，能準確反映出全部參與者在焦點團體會談上的想法。不過，基於這篇文獻探討，有一核心概念的標籤詞語被修改。

然而質性研究本身若被判斷已經具足，則成員檢查便不需要了，這對單獨處理研究的個人特別有幫助（與研究團隊相反，他們彼此能反映出結果的準確度）。

>>> 指南 5：注意研究人員使用的是立意樣本還是方便樣本

你從第五章指南 1 的內容可知，質性研究者努力使用立意樣本。這些個人樣本，是研究者針對特別的研究主題，判斷什麼類型的個人可以是好的資料來源，再依此目的選擇而來。例如，一個質性研究者正在評估一個臨床計畫，他可能選擇幾個剛開始參與此計畫的人，或幾個已經參與一段長時間的人做晤談。選擇的標準可能也包括性別（例如，選擇一些男性和一些女性）、年齡，以及出席情況（例如，只選擇那些能正常參加的）。

相反的，方便樣本是指那些參與者只因為他們容易利用而被找來（即，合作方便）。例如，一名研究者找來幾個朋友參加此臨床計畫，並且參與者僅有他們幾個，因為他們很好用又很配合。注意質性和量化研究者都認

3　修改自 Friedman, M. L., Friedlander, M. L., & Blustein, D. L. (2005). Toward an understanding of Jewish identity: A phenomenological study. *Journal of Counseling Psychology, 52,* 77-83.

為方便樣本不可靠。雖然有時因為研究者有限的接觸和資源，只找得到唯一的類型作為樣本。然而，使用方便樣本產生的研究結果須謹慎解釋。

>>> 指南 6：注意參與者描述的人口統計資料

　　從第五章指南 11 可知，在你的文獻探討中準備分析研究時，不妨將參與者的人口統計資料也包含在內，針對研究題目提供相關的人口統計資料，研究的讀者可以「看到」那些參與者，並依此判斷樣本的準確度。例如，在範例 6.6.1 所描述的人口統計資料，是研究者研究家庭暴力如何影響婦女就業。如你所見，他們報告的人口統計資料和他們的研究題目相關。

範例 6.6.1[4]

在一項質性研究裡人口統計資料的描述：

　　參與者的平均年齡是三十八歲，範圍介於二十二和五十四歲之間。22%的婦女有接受一些中學教育，37.5%完成中學學業或有同等學力證書（General Equivalency Degree, GED），6%有一副學士學位，34%擁有大學或更高學位。69%的參與者是白人，22%是黑人，3%是美國原住民，6%是其他種族。71%回答者擁有未滿十八歲小孩，年齡從一到十八歲都有。

　　所有參與者在過去兩年都曾上班；87.5%是去年至今有工作，12.5%在過去二十四個月內曾有工作。回答者工作的部門有生產服務（93.5%）以及貿易企業（12.5%）。詳細條例，婦女受雇的職位包括食品雜貨店出納員、女侍者、汽車旅館人員、護士助手、工廠工人、機器操作者、摘煙草工人、錄影店經理、餐廳經理、接待員、油漆工人、健身俱樂

4　Swanberg, J. E., & Logan, T. K. (2005). Domestic violence and employment: A qualitative study. *Journal of Occupational Health Psychology, 10,* 3-17.

部經理，以及計程車司機。美國婦女的平均工資每小時在 5.15 美元（美國的最低工資）至 10 美元之間。

所有婦女都表示在她們的生活過程中經歷心理虐待，並且 78%報告在過去的一年，曾經歷一位親密伴侶的心理虐待。心理或感情暴力經常和肢體暴力、性暴力一起發生，包括言詞攻擊（例如嘲笑、言詞威嚇和辱罵）、隔離，以及文字威脅傷害（Dutton et al., 1997; Follingstad, Rutledge, Berg, Hause, & Polek, 1990）。所有婦女都表示她們的一生皆曾被踐踏，67.7%報告在過去一年曾被親密伴侶踐踏。所有婦女在她們人生中都經歷過肢體暴力（被推、被撞、踢或咬），75%報告在過去的一年曾遭肢體暴力。大約 88%的婦女表示曾遭受親密伴侶的嚴重暴力（被痛打、用武器攻擊，或真的被武器擊傷），59.4%表示過去的一年曾遭受親密伴侶的嚴重暴力。75%表示在她們的一生中曾遭親密伴侶性騷擾，而在過去的一年有三分之一的婦女曾遭到性騷擾。

>>> 指南 7：考慮是否能詳細描述質性分析方法的細節

既然說是「研究」，那麼分析數據的方法就要詳細的計畫，且要有系統。相對的，如果它是由完全主觀的討論所做出的原因觀察，則不夠資格稱為研究。

為了幫助讀者確定一份質性報告是否夠格稱為「質性研究」，質性研究者應該詳細描述他們是怎樣分析數據的。注意研究者光是宣稱「採用了紮根理論（grounded theory）」或是「分析是基於現象學研究（phenomenological approach）」，都是不夠的。範例 6.7.1，研究者是以「共識質性研究」（consensual qualitative research, CQR）作為分析方法，並提供參考資料，以便讀者可取得更多訊息。接著他們總結了分析中所採用的 CQR 的步驟。

Writing Literature Reviews: A Guide for Students of the Social and Behavioral Sciences

範 例 6.7.1[5]

使用共識質性研究方法學的描述：

　　使用共識質性研究（CQR）方法學（Bogdan & Biklen, 1992; Henwood & Pidgeon, 1992; Hill, Thompson, & Williams, 1997; Stiles, 1993）做出分析。CQR 是一種分析質性數據非常可靠和節省成本的方法，利用多個研究者達成一致的過程，並有系統的交叉檢查案例，得出具代表性的結果。當記錄開放式問卷的回答時，CQR 包括了三個步驟：發展和編碼範圍，建構核心想法，進而發展細目以描述跨案例的共通點（交叉分析）。

發展和編碼範圍

　　兩位獨立的研究心理學家根據討論的內容和焦點團體問題，將其中主題相似的資訊組合起來，發展出一份範圍或主題領域的清單。每位評論家先獨立鑑定他們的範圍，接著兩位評論家比較他們各自條列的範圍清單直到達成共識。最後得出的七個範圍是⑴男人的性；⑵女人的性；⑶有小孩家庭的重要性；⑷性角色和社會預期；⑸性或者含帶藥物和酒精的「派對」；⑹教堂和宗教；和⑺ HIV 帶原者。每位評論家，跟循全部調查者，獨立讀完副本，並且把句子或段落劃歸某一範圍。詳細重審範圍以避免重複編碼。評論家比較他們的編碼，討論差異部分，並且達成共識。

---

[5] Williams, J. K., Wyatt, G. E., Resell, J., Peterson, J., & Asuan-O'Brien, A. (2004). Psychosocial issues among gay-and non-gay-identifying HIV-seropositive African American and Latino MSM. *Cultural Diversity and Ethnic Minority Psychology, 10,* 268-286.

建構核心想法

　　兩位獨立的評論家跟循那些調查者，重讀全部原始數據，並且將這些數據總結成核心想法。這個過程叫做濃縮或者摘要，總結那些內容並且用幾個字準確反映出參與者的陳述，避開推論字眼。一旦組員獨立發展出核心想法，那些評論家和調查者就要再開會討論他們的想法，直到達成共識。

交叉分析

　　當在 CQR 的第一和第二個步驟時，那些調查者檢查個人的陳述，交叉分析的目的，是為了確定這些樣本裡的案例是否有相似之處。在此步驟，團隊須概覽這些個案，以確定這些個案間的相似點。獨立評論家和調查者在審視完個案的每一部分後，鑑定出所有核心想法，並決定哪些核心想法適合放入類目中。個別組員在單一領域內評論核心想法，並且分配到相關的類目。團隊再次比較類目，並且確定參與者自陳報告中的哪幾項是重要的。獨立的評論家和那些調查者取得共識之後，團隊檢閱交叉分析，確保每一核心想法都適合，且類目標籤足夠描述列舉的核心想法。

>>> 指南 8：注意質性研究者討論量化情形時是否提出數量

　　儘管研究是質性方面，但並不意味著就沒有量化的部分。例如，在質性研究過程描述參與者的人口統計資料時，使用統計是很合適的，如同範例 6.6.1，在平均年齡上提出一大堆百分比數字。

　　當描述結果時，並不希望出現這樣的陳述，例如「少數的參與者提到這項議題……」或是「許多參與者接受這項議題……」。

　　一種近似量化質性結果的方法是質性研究者所稱的逐字列舉，這僅僅表明報告中參與者的每一個陳述的明確數目。但這樣一來，質性研究結果

的報告中將塞滿了一大堆數字;變通辦法是建立量化類目以取代含糊的字眼,像是「許多」,範例 6.8.1 中有說明。在結果部分的開頭採用這樣的陳述,有助於確定這些研究者是如何使用術語。

範 例 6.8.1[6]

數量中關於含糊術語上變通的定義:

在隨後的結果部分列舉了數據。明確來說,「許多」是指超過 50%的參與者給予特別類型的回應;「一些」則是指在 25% 和 50%之間;而「少數」是指少於 25%。

其他也可比照處理。質性報告若能提供量化指標,對讀者將更為有用。

總結意見

這章只簡單提了一些主要的方法學的問題,當你在做質性研究報告中的文獻探討時,可參酌使用。當你為了文獻探討而選擇閱讀一些文章時,注意那些研究人員在決定採用何種方法的議題和決定上,可能會影響研究結果的有效性。

---

6 此範例取自 Orcher, L. T. (2005). *Conducting research: Social and behavioral science methods*, p. 72. Glendale, CA: Pyrczak Publishing.

第 6 章的活動

說明：找到一份質性研究的原始報告，最好和你探討的主題有關，並回答下列問題。為了學習目標，你的指導老師可能會選擇分派一篇文章讓你們班上所有的學生去閱讀。

1. 在你找到的報告中有什麼特色讓你相信它是一個質性研究的範例？

2. 此研究是由個人或研究團隊進行？

3. 不止一個研究者獨立進行結果的最初分析嗎？

4. 有同行評議的外部專家嗎？為了審核嗎？如果有，這會增加你對結果有效性的信心嗎？

5. 那些參與者有參加成員檢查嗎？如果有，這會增加你對結果有效性的信心嗎？

6. 使用的是立意樣本還是方便樣本，很清楚嗎？請解釋之。

7. 研究者有詳細描述那些參與者的人口統計資料嗎？請解釋之。

8. 研究者有提出一種質性數據分析的精確方法（例如，共識質性研究）？它的描述夠詳細嗎？請解釋之。

9. 研究者在結果部分有提供足夠精確的質性訊息嗎？請解釋之。

10. 根據你在問題 1 到問題 9 的回答，簡單的敘述研究時你不能避免的主要缺失。

製作表格來摘要文獻

在早先章節的指南幫助你選擇一個主題、辨認文獻和進行初步分析。製作表格來摘要文獻是一個可以幫助你得到深思熟慮的文獻概要的有效方式。另外，你在你的文獻探討中，可能想要含括一個或多個你所製作的表格，這也將提供文獻探討的讀者一個概觀。

>>> 指南 1：考慮製作一個相關名詞定義的表格

你所考慮的每一個變項應該及早在先前的文獻探討中被定義。製作一個相關名詞定義的表格可在以下兩個範疇幫助你和讀者。首先，若有一堆緊密相關的變項的定義，例如在範例 7.1.1 中，為了辨認相似和不同，表格可使瀏覽定義變得容易。

範例 7.1.1[1]

表 7.1.1　心理賦權的定義與煙草控制主動性有關

領域	屬性	定義
內省	專門領域效力	對「一個人組織和執行計畫的能力需要引發與控制煙草有關的特定轉變」的信念。
	被察覺的社會和政治的控制	有關一個人在社會和政治系統中的能力和效力的信念。
	參加能力	覺察能力：透過會議上的對談、團隊運作等，來參與和對團隊和組織的運作有所貢獻。
相互作用	資源知識	了悟資源是否存在支持小組和如何獲取它們。
	斷言	當不違犯其他個人權利時，有能力直接地、公開和誠實地表達你的感覺、看法、信仰和需要。
	主張	對影響結果的追求，包括在直接地影響人的生活的政治、經濟和社會系統和機關之內的公眾政策和資源分配決定。

　　其次，如果一個特定變項有各式各樣的定義，定義的表格是有用的。考慮按年代順序安排，看看這些變項隨著時間遷移，如何被定義。範例 7.1.2 說明這種表格的組織架構。

---

[1]　Holden, D. J., Evans, W. D., Hinnant, L. W., & Messeri, P. (2005). Modeling psychological empowerment among youth involved in local tobacco control efforts. *Health Education & Behavior, 32,* 264-278. Reprinted with permission.

範例 7.1.2

表 7.1.2　在各年代中有關虐待兒童的定義（1945 至 2005）

作者	定義	注解
Doe (1945)	定義……	第一個發表的定義。不包括精神虐待。
Smith (1952)	定義……	
Jones (1966)	定義……	第一個提及性虐待。
Lock (1978)	定義……	
Black & Clark (1989)	定義……	
Solis (2000)	定義……	德州的法律定義。
Ty (2003)	定義……	在最近的文獻中，廣泛被引用的定義。
Bart (2005)	定義……	

>>> 指南 2：考慮製作一個研究方法的表格

　　由於不同的研究方法可能導致不同的研究結果，製作一個研究方法的摘要表來使用是有幫助的，例如範例 7.2.1 便是如此。除了在範例 7.2.1 描述的方法之外，為了試驗（參閱第五章的指南 2 和 3），會希望其中包含表明每項研究使用實驗設計的型態（例如隨機化的控制組設計）。

範 例 7.2.1[2]

表 7.2.1　主要研究特徵（方法）

	Pope (1994)	Preyde (2000)	Cherkin (2001)
樣本數	n = 164	n = 98	n = 267
參與者	參加的診所	大學電子郵件和報紙上的廣告	給 HMO 的信函
提出的情況	不明的下背痛	急性的下背痛	持續的下背痛
按摩的類型	按摩	全面按摩	治療按摩
研究期間	沒表明	1 年	6 個月
結果估測	視覺類比量表	羅蘭傷殘問卷	症狀困擾量表

>>>指南 3：將研究結果整理成摘要表格

藉由增加額外的列或欄，將研究結果摘要成表格（參考指南 2）。

除了像範例 7.2.1 將作者的名字放在欄的最頂端外，也可以像範例 7.3.1 將作者的名字放在列的最前面。在這個範例中，可以輕易的摘要出研究結果。

---

[2] Loosely based on Dryden, T., Baskwil, A., & Preyde, M. (2004). Massage therapy for the orthopaedic patient: A review. *Orthopaedic Nursing, 23,* 327-332.

範 例　7.3.1[3]

表 7.3.1　宗教信仰與青少年性行為的長期研究

出版日期，作者	研究地點，年份，社經地位，樣本數	年齡或年級，性別，種族	宗教信仰檢測	性行為檢測	宗教信仰對性行為的影響
(1975) Jessor & Jessor	在落磯山區小鎮，1969-1971，中產階級，樣本數為 424 人	高中生，男女生，白人	有宗教信仰，會去教堂做禮拜	在 Time 1 曾經有過性行為	在 Time 1-Time 2 開始有性行為的高中女生，信仰較不虔誠且較少上教堂。
(1983) Jessor, Costa, Jessor, & Donovan	在落磯山區小鎮，1969-1972、1979，樣本數為 346 人，無性行為經驗者	1969 年時的 7、8、9 年級，男女生，白人	有宗教信仰，會去教堂做禮拜[a]	第一次性行為的年齡	有宗教信仰與上教堂頻率高者，其第一次性行為的年齡較晚。
(1991) Beck, Cole, & Hammond[b]	美國，1979、1983，樣本數為 2,072 人	14 至 17 歲，男女生，1979 年無性經驗的白人	青少年與父母信仰相同的宗教（天主教、受洗者、新教徒、基本教義派、習俗教派）	第一次性行為的經驗（有或無）	在 1979-1983 年研究中，信仰一般習俗教派（猶太五旬節教派、摩門教、耶和華見證教派）的白種青少年比起新教徒（聖公會、路德教派、衛理公會）發生第一次性行為時間較晚。受洗過的女性與基本教義派的男生比新教徒晚發生第一次性行為。

（下頁續）

---

[3] Rostosky, S. S., Wilcox, B. L., Wright, M. L. C., & Randall, B. A. (2004). The impact of religiosity on adolescent sexual behavior: A review of the evidence. *Journal of Adolescent Research, 19,* 677-697. Reprinted with permission.

出版日期，作者	研究地點，年份，社經地位，樣本數	年齡或年級，性別，種族	宗教信仰檢測	性行為檢測	宗教信仰對性行為的影響
(1996) Crockett, Bingham, Chopack, & Vicary	美國東部一間鄉村學校，1985，低社經地位，樣本數為 289 人	7 到 9 年級，男女生，白人	有去教堂做禮拜	第一次性行為的年齡	比較常去教堂的女生，其第一次發生性行為的時間較晚（超過 17 歲）。
(1996) Mott, Fondell, Hu, Kowaleski-Jones, & Menaghan[c]	美國，1988、1990、1992，樣本數為 451 人	1992 年，14 歲以上，男女生，白人（黑人與西班牙人婚生子女除外）	有去教堂做禮拜，和朋友上同一個教堂	早期（14歲）第一次性行為	比較常上教堂的人，且有同儕一起陪同到相同的教堂的人，其較少在 14 歲時就開始有性行為。
(1996) Pleck, Sonenstein, Ku, & Burbridge[d]	美國 (1)1988，樣本數為 1,880 人 (2)1990-1991，樣本數為 1,676 人	1988 年，15 至 19 歲，男生，37%黑人、21% 西班牙人，3% 其他	宗教的重要性，上教堂的頻率	在過去十二個月沒有使用保險套的性行為次數	比較常上教堂的青少男，其沒有使用保險套的性行為頻率較低。
(1997) Miller, Norton, Curtis, Hill, Schvaneveldt, & Young[e]	美國，1976、1981、1987，樣本數為 759 人	1976年，7 至 11 歲，男女生，白人、黑人	有去教堂做禮拜，對上教堂的態度	第一次性行為年紀（在第三波回顧報導）	對進行宗教活動持有正面態度的家庭較可能延後發生第一次性行為。
(1999) Bearman & Bruckner[f]	美國，1994-1996，樣本數為 5,070 人	7 至 12 年級，女生，白人、黑人、西班牙人、亞洲人	參加宗教活動（有信教）	第一次性行為(有或無)，第一次的年紀，懷孕的風險（有或無）	若不論年紀對第一次性行為的影響，則保守的新教徒和天主教徒比主流新教徒較少在 Time 1 和 Time 2 發生第一次性行為。
(1999) Whitbek, Yoder, Hoyt, & Conger	中西部州，1989-1993，樣本數為 457 人	8 至 10 年級，男女生，白人	有去教堂做禮拜，重要性（母親及青少年）	性行為（有或無）	媽媽對宗教的信仰與否將影響9 至 10 年級生發生第一次性經驗的可能性。有宗教信仰的青少年對第一次性行為有強烈的負面態度。

（下頁續）

出版日期，作者	研究地點，年份，社經地位，樣本數	年齡或年級，性別，種族	宗教信仰檢測	性行為檢測	宗教信仰對性行為的影響
(2001) Bearman & Bruckner[g]	美國 (1) 1994-1995 (2) 1996，樣本數為 14787 人	7 至 12 年級，男女生，白人、黑人、西班牙人、亞洲人	有去教堂做禮拜，重要性，祈禱的頻率	第一次性行為的年紀，有無避孕，處女的誓言（有或無）	不論是白人、亞洲人、西班牙人的青少年，宗教信仰高的人較會減少第一次性行為的風險。就黑人的青少年而言，宗教信仰與第一次性行為的風險是沒有關係的。相較於早期，宗教對中期和晚期青少年發生第一次性行為的影響比較大。在第一次發生性行為有無避孕與宗教沒有關係。

a. 宗教信仰檢測並沒有描述在該文中。

b. Data are from the National Longitudinal Survey of Youth (NLSY).

c. Data are from the National Longitudinal Survey of Youth (NLSY).

d. Data are from the National Survey of Adolescent Males (NSAM).

e. Data are from all three waves of the National Survey of Children (NSC).

f. Data are from Waves I and II of the National Longitudinal Study of Adolescent Health (Add Health).

g. Data are from Waves I and II of the National Longitudinal Study of Adolescent Health (Add Health).

　　注意在範例 7.3.1 不同研究結果的摘要，最好的方法通常以文字描述（非統計）來展現；通常這是展現結果的摘要最好的方法，若被統計的研究是直接且可以比較的，則呈現統計數據是可以被接受的。舉例來說，假如有五個研究要對高中學生盛行使用鼻吸劑的人數做估計，它們都是使用百分比來呈現結果的摘要，另一方面而言，假如主題的統計報告在研究之間顯示出差異性，則通常不會想要將它們呈現出來，因為它們是不能在不同研究間做直接比較的（例如：一個研究呈現的是百分比，另一個研究呈現的是平均數和中位數，另一個研究呈現次數分配，如此等等）。這是事實，因為讀者能檢視欄或列以注意到研究間的不同，而

檢視和比較欄位中混合的統計數據，很容易被搞混掉。

>>> 指南 4：當一個主題有很多文獻時，建立一種準則來決定哪些摘要須放在一個表格裡

一個插入文獻探討的摘要表是不需要包括所有研究主題的文獻。但是，如果只有一些文獻包含在其中，則你需要說明包含的準則，如範例 7.4.1 和 7.4.2 所顯示的範例說明，告知讀者，這種準則為何。

範例 7.4.1

列表準則（即，僅真實實驗）的描述：

表一概述了參與者的特點、應用的工具和結果的評估。本表只包括真實實驗（即，實驗中，參與者被隨機分配到實驗組及控制組）。

範例 7.4.2

列表準則（即，僅最近的調查）的描述：

表二摘要列出五個最新調查的題目的研究方法和成果。因為文獻的呈現取自不同時間的意見，最近一次調查提供了現行的公共輿論對這一問題的最佳顯示。

>>> 指南 5：當一個主題有很多文獻時，考慮製作兩個或更多表格來做摘要

即使有了列入研究表格的標準（見指南 4），在單一的表中，仍然可

能有太多的研究。在這種情況下,可考慮如何將文獻分組,這樣可為每個研究的小組製作不同的表格。舉例來說,一個表可能是將相關的議題總結而得的理論,另一個表則可能總結了量化的研究課題,而第三個表可能總結了質性的研究。

>>> 指南 6:文獻探討中的表格只針對複雜的資料

在整合文獻的早期階段,並沒有限制你可以自行創建多少表格以幫助文獻探討。不過,你應該在文獻探討的表列中,處理複雜的、可能很難讓讀者理解(即,難以說明的文獻探討)的問題。

一個文獻探討不應是一個表格的蒐集。相反的,它應是一個說明(用來總結、綜合和解釋文獻的主題),用少量插入的表格協助讀者以理解複雜的資料。

>>> 指南 7:討論在文獻探討中的每一個表格

文獻探討的敘述中應該要介紹或討論文獻探討內的所有表格。範例 7.7.1 說明了如何介紹或探討。

範 例 7.7.1

探討表格:

表一摘要了五個研究,研究中使用了貝克憂鬱量表審查這些認知行為療法的效果,作為測量結果。大致上,這些樣本數相當小,範圍由四個到十六個。儘管有此侷限,這結果驗證了使用認知行為療法的效果,因為所有實驗組與控制組相較之下,在統計上顯示憂鬱顯著消退。

當你討論每一個表格時,你不需要去討論其中的每一個元素。例如:範例 7.7.1 討論了一個表格,這個表格摘要了五項研究,然而這些樣本大

小，只使用了在原始文獻中所提起的兩項研究（樣本數為四和樣本數為十六）。

>>>指南 8：為每個表格做編號及下標題

所有表格應該都有編號（例如表一、表二……等），標題也一樣（即說明）。注意本章的所有表格都有編號及標題。

>>>指南 9：善用文書軟體製作表格

現代文書處理程式的特色，在於利用欄和列來協助製作表格。例如在 Microsoft Word 中，用滑鼠點選靠近螢幕上方的「表格」鍵（Table）[4]，你會得到選項來「插入」表格。點選「插入」鍵後，再點選「表格」鍵中的下拉式選單。就會產生一個對話框，讓你指定所需之欄與列的數量。最後會產生一個如下所示具有五欄四列的表格：

整理修飾表格時，你需要使用「表格與框線」工具列。在整理表格時，點選「檢視」鍵，然後從下拉式選單裡點選「工具列」，再點選「表格與框線」，此工具列便會顯示在你的螢幕上。移動游標到這個工具列（在上面的每個選項稍作停留），便會產生浮動工具箱來指示每個選項的功能。

---

4 一個底線字，比如 a 在 Table 這個字中表示是一個快速鍵，讓打字的人不使用滑鼠時，可以更有效率。例如，按住鍵盤上的 "Alt" 鍵再按一下 "a" 將產生下拉式清單，可不必使用滑鼠製作一個表格。

Writing Literature Reviews: A Guide for Students of the Social and Behavioral Sciences

例如：你會發現其中一個是「合併儲存格」。使用它能讓你合併這個表格的第一列，以填寫表格編號及標題。具體做法是拖曳滑鼠橫跨反白表格的第一列（第一列會變黑），然後，點選「合併儲存格」的選項，這個表格將會如下所示：

表格的編號放置在這裡。不能用斜體字（如「表一」）。表的標題放置在這裡（斜體的標題，每個字的第一個字母都要大寫，沒有句號）5。				

　　怎樣使用如 Word 程式當文書軟體來製作表格，已超出本書的範圍，只有少數實驗注意到在「表格與框線」工具列裡的浮動工具箱，它能讓人更方便的學習如何修飾表格。

>>> 指南 10：當表格因跨頁而分開時插入「接續本頁」字樣

　　表格並不會總是能順利的放在獨立的一頁裡，當一個表格因跨頁而分開時，在表格的底部標上「接續本頁」字樣，讓讀者知道翻頁來閱讀表格。在下一頁表格的第二部分頂端須重複標上表格的編號，跟著標上「接續上一頁」字樣。

---

5 這一個表格的格式和《美國心理學會出版手冊》內的指南一致。

第 7 章的活動

說明：假設你已閱讀過，經你評估而能置於你文獻探討中的文章。你即可以
閱讀的文章為基礎，來回答下列問題。

1. 你能計畫去製作一個定義的表格嗎？請解釋之。

2. 你能計畫去製作一個研究方法的表格嗎？它將包含哪些總結了研究結果的
行或列？

3. 你會應用準則來選擇包含在表格裡的研究嗎？請解釋之。

4. 你會預先插入一個以上的表格在你的文獻探討裡嗎？請解釋之。

5. 你是否考慮過如何討論你計畫要摘要一個或更多表格的文獻？

6. 你是否有使用你的文書軟體，來研究如何製作表格？它容易使用嗎？是否
感到任何使用上的困難？如果有，是否請教其他人（例如其他學生）來解
決你的困難呢？請解釋之。

撰寫文獻探討前的資料統整

　　此時，你應該已經閱讀並分析了一些期刊雜誌或是博碩士論文，有可能包含了如第七章提到的摘要表。現在應該將這些要點和表格資料統整在一起，這將會成為你的文獻分析的資料。換句話說，你現在可以開始撰寫論文的文獻探討了。這一章將幫助你去發展一個重要的初胚：詳盡的文獻大綱。

>>>指南 1：在開始撰寫之前考慮目的和聲明

　　首先問自己你寫文獻的目的為何；你是否試圖說服你的教授：在這一門課，你已付出足夠的努力來編寫學期論文？在一篇碩士論文或博士論文裡，你想要展現自己實地研究的知識嗎？還是，你建立研究脈絡的目的只是希望在一本雜誌裡出版研究而已？不同的情形會導致不同類型的最終產物，部分原因是作者的目的不同，部分原因是讀者的期望不同。文獻探討的三種類型可見第二章。

　　在確立你的目的並考慮你的讀者後，要為你的草稿發表適當的意見（或文體）。作者在編寫文獻探討時的態度應該是很嚴謹的，因為這是學術領域的要求。在傳統的科學寫作領域，作者不再強調自己，以便讀者集中注意力於內容。在範例 8.1.1，作者的**自我意見**明顯太多，它會在陳述聲明的內容上分散讀者的注意力。範例 8.1.2 較佳的原因則是將焦點放在內容上。

範例 8.1.1[1]

學術論文中不恰當的「聲音」：

在這篇文獻探討裡，我將顯示關於治療少年兇手的文獻是稀少的，這與少年殺人（Benedek, Cornell, & Staresina, 1989; Myers, 1992）以及暴力少年犯（Tate, Reppucci, & Mulvery, 1995）的文獻一樣，面臨同樣的問題。令人遺憾的是，我發現大多數治療的結果都是以少數的臨床個案報告為基礎，這些個案僅參考作者的評估與／或治療（例如，請參閱 Agee, 1979...）。

範例 8.1.2[2]

學術論文中合適的「聲音」：

在治療少年兇手方面的文獻是稀少的，這與少年殺人（Benedek, Cornell, & Staresina, 1989; Myers, 1992）以及暴力少年犯（Tate, Reppucci, & Mulvery, 1995）的文獻一樣，面臨同樣的問題。大多數治療的結果都是以少數的臨床個案報告為基礎，這些個案僅參考作者的評估與／或治療（例如，請參閱 Agee, 1979...）。

---

[1] 這是一個以範例 8.1.2 為基礎的假設範例。

[2] Heide, K. M., & Solomon, E. P. (2003). Treating today's juvenile homicide offenders. *Youth Violence and Juvenile Justice, 1,* 5-31.

值得注意的是：學術作者傾向於避免使用第一人稱。相反地，他們讓材料，包括統計資料和理論，替自己發言。這不是說第一人稱絕對不能使用。不過，傳統上非常少用。

>>> 指南 2：考慮如何重新整理你的筆記

既然你已經為你寫的論文建立目的、確定好讀者群，並且建立聲明，你應該重新評估你的筆記內容，確定你已經知道如何重新整理。在開始時，你應該認知到一篇論文若只提出研究一系列的註釋，經常成為無法讓人接受的研究報告。那麼在本質上，在敘述一棵樹之前，你應該先敘述一座森林。就一篇論文而言，你該使用你所閱讀過的文獻中的「樹木」，來建立你要的「森林」。為了建造一個全新的作品，當你在準備主題大綱時，應該要考慮這題目要概括彼此之間的關係，這在下一個指南會更詳細描述。

>>> 指南 3：建立一個追蹤你的論點之主題大綱

像其他類的論文一樣，首先，應該將你所遵循的論證脈絡呈現給讀者（這就是作文課中所謂的論文）。由此斷言，這可以說明一個論點或者一項建議的形式；然後，你應該發展值得且經驗證是正確的證明論證的路徑。這意味著你應該藉由分析和整合你目前探討的文獻，對主題形成判斷。

該主題大綱應設計為論證的路線圖，這在範例 8.3.1 中說明。請注意，它從一個主張開始（捐贈器官有嚴重的短缺，這被統計資料佐證，並且界定這個評論到「決定捐贈的心理要素」）。在這序論之後，是有系統的檢討相關領域的研究文獻（在主題大綱裡的第 II 和 III 點），隨後進行相關研究中方法學議題的討論（第 IV 點），最後以摘要、影響以及對未來研究的建議的討論和關於序論（在主題大綱第 I 點）的結論作為結束。

請注意，範例 8.3.1 選擇在一個單獨的章節討論研究方法的缺點（在主題大綱第 IV 點），當所有或許多的研究有同樣的缺點時，使用單獨一節來討論是特別適合。如果不同的研究有不同的缺點，最好在引用時能指出缺

點（而不是在文獻探討的單獨章節討論它們）。

由於下列綱要將在本章其餘部分被提及，請花一些時間仔細研究。請在本頁標示或註記以便之後提到它時，你便於參考。

 範例 8.3.1[3]

主題大綱示例：

主題：器官捐贈的心理層面：個人和至親的捐贈決定

I. 序論

　A. 建立主題的重要性（引用器官短缺的統計數字）。

　B. 定義「決定的心理要素」文獻。

　C. 描述報告的組織，這表示在大綱中剩下的主題將會被討論。

II. 個人死後的器官捐贈決定因素

　A. 捐贈器官的信念。

　B. 對捐贈的態度。

　C. 明確表示願意捐贈。

　D. 有關「個人決定」研究的摘要。

III. 至親的同意決定

　A. 捐贈他人器官的信念。

　B. 對至親捐贈的態度。

　C. 有關「至親同意決定」研究的摘要。

IV. 方法學問題和今後的研究方向

　A. 態度測量的改進和測量策略。

---

3 本大綱是取材自 Radicki, C. M., & Jaccard, J. (1997). Psychological aspects of organ donation: A critical review and synthesis of individual and next-of-kin donation decisions. *Health Psychology, 16,* 183-195.

　　B. 按類別劃分捐贈的大差異。

　　C. 更強的理論重點。

　　D. 跨學科議題。

V. 結論、影響和討論

　　A. 總結第 I 點到第 IV 點。

　　B. 需要完善的態度和決策的理論模型。

　　C. 目前的調查資料侷限在其範圍和應用上，在未來需要更複雜的研究。

　　D. 需要利用更多先進的數據分析技術。

　　E. 結論：心理學可以借鑑各分支學科以便對捐贈決定有所理解，如此才能界定介入策略。迫切需要增加現有捐贈器官的供應。

>>>指南 4：根據你的論證路徑重新組織你的筆記

　　在之前的指南裡描述的主題大綱是作者的論證路徑。下一步是根據大綱重新組織筆記。首先，將筆記編碼，依據它們在大綱中適當的位置。例如，實際筆記卡寫 "I" 註記引用捐贈器官短缺的統計數字，"II" 註記個人對器官捐贈的決定，"III" 註記至親未來的決定，和 "IV" 註記涉及到方法學的問題。然後，返回主題大綱並且具體的表明提到的特別研究。例如，如果 Doe 和 Smith（2005）引用捐贈器官短缺的統計數字，在主題大綱第 I 點的右邊寫上他們的名字。

>>>指南 5：在每個主題的標題間，標記研究之間的差異

　　下一個步驟是要在主題大綱上標記研究內容上的區別。基於任何差異，你必須思考是否把可以歸成一類的章節放在同一個子題裡。例如：關於捐贈器官的信念（在範例 8.3.1 第 II-A 點），在範例 8.5.1 中，文獻可以被歸納成五個子題。

範例 8.5.1

附加在範例 8.3.1 第 II-A 點的子題：

1. 宗教信仰
2. 文化信念
3. 知識（即，根據人們匯集各方的「事實」為基礎的信念）
4. 利他主義的信念
5. 標準信念（即，根據在特定的社團中可被接受的觀念為基礎的信念）

　　這些都將成為在第 II-A 點主題大綱內的附加子題。換句話說，當你界定附加的子題時，你的大綱也將變得更加詳細。

　　你將從不同研究結果的一致性中去思考其他種類的差異。例如，在範例 8.3.1 中，評論者即根據三篇論文中所提到在文化上的障礙，降低了西班牙裔美國人的器官捐贈數量，而另一篇論文則提到在這個族群中自願捐贈和關於移植問題的高層次體認。當討論這些差異時，必須透過提供研究的相關訊息來協助你的讀者，去注意到界定差異的可能解釋。是否前三篇的論文已過時，而後者才是趨勢？前三篇論文是否為蒐集數據使用了不同的方法學（即有負面結果的論文是檢測了醫院記錄，而有正向結果的論文是使用自陳式問卷）。當你寫文獻探討時，特別留意這些可以提供問題討論的差別。

>>> 指南 6：在每個主題的標題中，尋找明顯的差距或需要更進一步研究的領域

　　根據範例 8.3.1 中的主題大綱充分顯示，評論者注意到有許多對非洲裔美國人、亞裔美國人和西班牙裔美國人進行的跨文化研究，僅少數研究將焦點放在美國本地人。因此，任何結論可能不適用於後者。另外，這點可

能適合推薦作為將來計畫研究的領域。

>>>指南 7：規畫如何為相關的理論作介紹

理論性文獻的重要性在第一章已提過。你應該計畫簡單地描述每種理論。範例 8.7.1 是社會比較理論的一個簡要說明。注意作者開始於原始理論的摘要，然後繼續談論怎麼隨著時間的推移修改理論。這個架構幫助讀者更加充分地了解理論。

範 例 8.7.1[4]

一個相關理論的簡要定義：

Festinger（1954）的社會比較理論斷言：⑴個體有評估他們看法和能力的本能；⑵在缺乏客觀、非社會性的標準下，個體進行社會比較（即，他們將自己的看法和能力與其他個體做比較）；和⑶若情況許可，社會比較是人們常常和自己相似的人做比較。

相較於它原始的想法模式，社會比較理論已經經歷許多修正。首先，現在承認未追求的比較也許發生，並且用於比較過程的相關論點也許與個體並不那麼相似（Martin & Kennedy, 1993）。其次，社會比較也有可能發生於外在相貌的方面……

>>>指南 8：計畫討論並提出與個人研究相關的理論

你應該考慮如何進行個人的研究（通常範圍較小），以幫助定義、說

4　Morrison, T. G., Kalin, R., & Morrison, M. A. (2004). Body-image evaluation and body-image investment among adolescents: A test of sociocultural and social comparison theories. *Adolescence, 39,* 571-592.

明或推進理論概念。通常，研究者會指出他們的研究與理論的關聯性，將幫助你思考這個問題。從你文獻探討內相關的主題大綱中指定一個或更多理論進行討論，如範例 8.3.1 中的第 V-B 點所做的，表明評論者將談論對明確定義之理論模型的需要。

如果在你的研究範圍有其他論點的理論，應討論那些支持己方理論的文獻，記住，在研究結果和理論預測之間的不一致，也許起因於理論模型的盲點或者是研究方法上有缺失。

>>> 指南 9 ：計畫去做定期性的摘要，在文獻探討接近結尾時再做一次

摘要你從各階段文獻探討裡所得的推論、分類和／或結論是有幫助的。舉例來說，在範例 8.3.1 的大綱中，需要在文獻探討的兩點之間做出摘要（即：II-D 和 III-C 兩點）。在文獻探討裡，冗長又複雜的主題通常必須要有它們自己單獨的摘要。這些摘要可以幫助讀者了解作者所採取的方向，而且讓讀者可以稍停然後思考，把困難的材料內化。

你或許已經注意到範例 8.3.1 的最後一個主題（主題 V）需要之前出現過的所有材料的摘要。用一篇已包含重點的摘要來當做篇幅較長的文獻探討的最後一部分，通常是比較恰當的。這可以告訴讀者，什麼是作者最主要的論點，然後鋪陳對於作者的結論和他（她）所提出的影響的討論。在一篇較短的文獻探討中，可能不需要摘要。

>>> 指南 10 ：計畫提出結論和影響

注意結論就是一個對於主題了解狀況的陳述。範例 8.10.1 說明一個結論。注意它沒有顯示有「證據」。評論家應該侷限於現有證據並且討論證據的可信度（例如，「似乎可以這麼結論……」，「結論可能是…」，「有利的證據顯示……」，或者「證據壓倒性的支持結論……」）。

範例 8.10.1

根據不同文化對於器官捐贈態度的研究，似乎可以做出安全的結論（加重語氣）：不同文化族群對於器官捐贈的態度非常不同，而且一些有效的干預策略必須考慮到這些文化的差異處。明確的說……

　　假如在一個主題中證據分量沒有明顯支持某一結論（壓倒性勝出其他結論），就要這麼說。範例 8.10.2 說明這種技巧。

範例 8.10.2

雖然大部分的研究都顯示方法 A 是比較優良的，但是也有一些研究指出方法 B 的優點。在缺少其他證據下，很難結論出（加重語氣）……

　　一個影響通常就是對個人或組織對於現有的研究應該做什麼的陳述。換句話說，一個評論家通常應該做出一些建議，這些建議就是根據研究探討所做出似乎可以保證的行動。因此，靠近一個主題大綱的結尾處，通常可以預期包含「影響」這個標題。範例 8.10.3 就是一個影響，因為它建議一個用於特定族群的干預或許是有效的。

範例 8.10.3

在這篇文章裡探討的證據主體部分表明，當研究亞裔美國人時，干預 A 好像最能保證增加這個族群的器官捐贈數量。

　　起初，一些新手作家相信他們應該只要描述得自已出版的研究報告中的「事實」，而不要冒險提供他們自己的結論和有關的影響。記住，對一個主題做完全仔細地文獻探討的人，實際上，已經成為這方面的專家了。對於知識基礎（結論）我們應該向誰尋求建議，以及我們應該做什麼使自己變得比那些在研究主題上有最新知識的專家更有效率（影響）呢？因此，去表達你對於主題知識了解的結論及跟隨而來的影響是恰當的。

>>> 指南 11 ：在文獻探討結尾處，計畫對未來的研究建議具體的方向

　　注意範例 8.3.1 大綱中，在第 V-C 這一點裡評論家計畫去討論未來的研究。當你計畫要說什麼的時候，記住若只是簡單的建議「未來需要有更多的研究」是不夠的。相反地，提出具體的建議，例如，如果全部（或幾乎全部）研究者都使用自陳式問卷，你或許會要求未來的研究使用一些其他蒐集資料的方法，比如直接觀察行為舉止和檢測那些有協調器官捐贈機構的記錄。假如有像美國原住民那樣的對照組，你可能會要求要更多有關他們的研究。假如幾乎所有的研究都是量化的研究，你或許會要求要額外的質性研究。可能性幾乎是無限的。你的工作就是建議在你文獻探討的領域裡可以使知識更進一步發展的方法。

>>> 指南 12 ：根據你的分析及細節充實你的大綱

　　在你開始寫第一個草稿之前，最後的步驟就是檢視主題大綱，並從文獻之中蒐集特殊的細節去充實這個大綱內容。在擴充大綱時，盡可能包含足夠的細節使你的研究計畫更為清楚詳盡。你須標註研究的優缺點，例如與文獻有關的差異、關係、主要的趨勢或型態等。最後，你的大綱應該有幾頁的篇幅了，並且你已準備好要寫你的第一份草稿。

　　範例 8.12.1 說明如果我們要為範例 8.3.1 小部分的主題大綱（特別是範例 8.12.1 中的第 II-A-l 點）補充額外的細節，我們看看它是否更加充實。

範 例 8.12.1

一個擴充過的大綱：

II.個人死後的器官捐贈決定因素

　A.捐贈器官的信念（將研究分類成五個主要的群組）

　　1.宗教信仰

　　　a.定義「宗教信仰」

　　　b.認同器官捐贈的宗教

　　　　(1)佛教、印度教（Ulshafer, 1988; Woo, 2002）

　　　　(2)天主教（Ulshafer, 1988）

　　　　(3)猶太教（Bulka, 1990; Cohen, 1988; Pearl, 1990; Weiss, 1988）

　　　　(4)新教（Walters, 1988）

　　　　(5)伊 斯 蘭 教（Gatrad, 1994; Rispler-Chaim, 1989; Sachedina, 2003）

　　　c.不支持它的宗教

　　　　(1)耶和華見證教派（Corlett, 2003; Pearl, 2004）

　　　　(2)正統的猶太教（Corlett, 2003; Pearl, 2004）

　　　d.其他來源：認為宗教是器官捐贈的障礙（Basu et al., 1989; Gallup Organization, 1993; Moore et al., 2004）

　　請注意到，範例 8.12.1 中的參考資料不只出現在一個地方。例如，Corlett 2003 年的報告在耶和華見證教派和正統的猶太教的討論下都有被提到。文獻書寫時，不適合只在一個地方引用。相反的，應該在多個適合的地方做引述。

第 8 章的活動

說明：針對你指導老師指派的每個文獻探討範本，回答下列問題。這些探討
的範本列於本書末。

1. 作者使用了適當的學術聲明嗎？作者使用第一人稱書寫嗎？請解釋之。

2. 每個主題間，作者的辯論合乎邏輯嗎？請解釋之。

3. 作者有指出更多的需求嗎？請解釋之。

4. 作者對於內容有提出定義、說明，或提出理論嗎？請解釋之。

5. 如果文獻過長，它有包含一篇或更多摘要？請解釋之。

6. 作者有清楚的結論和推論嗎？

7. 作者對未來研究有提出具體的建議方向嗎？

⑨ 撰寫初稿的指南

　　到目前為止，你應該已經在你的文獻探討主題中搜尋了一些文章，在文獻的特定細節上，做了詳盡的筆記，並且分析這些細節以便於定義所要研究的樣本、在各研究間的關聯、文獻主體的差距，以及特定研究的優缺點。在第八章，你已經重新整理筆記，並且發展出撰寫大綱時的細節步驟，就好比想像成你已開始在撰寫文獻探討一般。

　　換句話說，你已經完成了在撰寫過程中最困難的步驟了：文獻的綜合及分析、繪製你的論點路線圖表。這些初步步驟構成準備文獻的過程。剩下的步驟──擬稿、編輯、再擬稿，將需要你將你所找到的轉換成有價值的敘述報告。

　　接下來在此章所探討的指南將幫助你產生文獻探討的初稿。第十章的指南將幫助你發展出脈絡連貫的論述以及如何避免產生一連串的注解。第十一章會陳述有關格式、制式化和語言使用的額外指南。

>>> 指南 1：定義問題的範圍，但是避免陷入範圍太大的廣泛描述

　　通常，文獻探討的介紹應該從廣泛的問題範圍的定義開始，首要的規則是「從一般到特殊的問題」，在一開始所謂的一般是有限制的。看看範例 9.1.1，在文獻探討一開始便提出要探討高等教育，範圍太廣，所以在定

義任何特殊範疇或主題上是失敗的，你的文獻探討在一開始時，應避免廣闊的敘述探討。

範例 9.1.1

太廣泛的教育文獻探討的起始處：

高等教育對於美國和世界其他國家的經濟都是重要的。倘若沒有高等教育，學生將沒有辦法去應付及迎接千禧年所帶來的進步變化。

相對於範例 9.1.1，範例 9.1.2，同是在教育上的主題，但卻明確的是有關一個即將要評論的具體主題：減少大學生對酒精的消耗。

範例 9.1.2[1]

足夠具體的教育文獻探討的起始處：

與酒精有關的高犯罪率、交通事故和大學校園內的其他問題行為，已經使學校行政人員去執行用來降低大學生喝酒的行動（Abbey, 1991; Scott, Schafer, & Greenfield, 1999...）。

---

[1] Novak, K. B., & Crawford, L. A. (2001). Perceived drinking norms, attention to social comparison, information, and alcohol use among college students. *Journal of Alcohol and Drug Education, 46,* 18-32.

>>> 指南 2：在文獻探討批判之初，迅速指出被評論的主題是重要的

早在文獻探討的第一個段落時，即應表明主題的重要性。範例 9.2.1 的作者已經透過標題指出他們的研究涉及一個生或死的議題。

範例 9.2.1²

在文獻探討一開始處即表明探討主題的重要性：

在美國，從 1993 到 2002 年，就有超過 48,762 人在等候器官移植時已經死亡，但目前卻不能減低對器官捐贈的需求（Department of Health and Human Services, [DHHS]...2004）。更甚者，雖然個人在器官等候名單上的數量在 1993 年是 33,014 人，但等待器官移植的男人、婦女和孩童的數量，在 2003 年一開始的時候即高達 80,000 人（DHHS et al., 2004）。

當然，並非全部問題都具有和在範例 9.2.1 裡的那個普遍的重要性一樣。雖然如此，探討的主題應該對一些組織具有重要性且這點也應該被指出，如同範例 9.2.2，建立起對教育者在閱讀困難影響學生的態度上的理解的重要性。

---

² Siegel, J. T., Alvaro, E. M., & Jones, S. P. (2005). Organ donor registration preferences among Hispanic populations: Which modes of registration have the greatest promise? *Health Education & Behavior, 32,* 242-252.

範例 9.2.2[3]

文獻探討的第二段開始指出主題的重要性、學生有閱讀困難：

在學習障礙的學生，例如閱讀困難（閱讀障礙）的報告中，教育工作者的態度深深地影響他們察覺自己和在學校和生命中成功的模式（Helendoorn & Ruijssenaars, 2000...）。

>>> 指南 3：區分研究發現與其他訊息來源

如果你描述的觀點是著重在軼文趣事或者個人觀點而非基於研究發現，須明確指出資料來源。舉例來說，在範例 9.3.1 中的三種表達方式包含了關鍵字（例如：推測），這指出了材料是建立在個人觀點之上，並非研究結果。

範例 9.3.1

表達方式的一開始指出材料是建立在個人觀點之上（而非研究）：

「Doe（2004）推測……」

「它已經被建議……（Smith, 2004）」

「Black（2004）敘述個人經驗，指出……」

對照範例 9.3.1 和範例 9.3.2 的表達方式，範例 9.3.2 是介紹在文獻探討中以研究為基礎的發現。

---

3 Wadlington, E. M., & Wadlington, P. L. (2005). What educators really believe about dyslexia. *Reading Improvement, 42,* 16-33.

範例 9.3.2

表達方式的一開始指出材料是建立在研究之上：

「在一個全州的調查，Jones（2004）發現……」

「Hill（2004）對市區班級的研究建議……」

「最近的發現指出……（Barnes, 2003; Hanks, 2004）」

如果在一個論題上只有少部分的研究，你會發現首先先探討只描述了意見（缺乏研究作為基礎）的文獻的必要性。遇到這種情況時，在你的文獻探討中討論你個人的意見之前，請先以一般的陳述說明這樣的情況。這種技巧在範例 9.3.3 中有提到。

範例 9.3.3 [4]

說明指出研究的缺失：

……ERIC 資料庫包含……超過五百項 ERIC 的文件、期刊論文、專題論文，是有關「時段編課方式」這個主題。然而其中只有十件作品著重在學校傳媒中心脈絡的時段編課方式中，而沒有任何一份報告發現是建立在構思研究論文之上……。

這些現存的報告在本質上，大部分是屬於軼事的。Lincoln（1999）、Ready（1999）和 Richmond（1999）都提出了關於他們圖書傳媒中心時段編課方式對其影響的個人經驗，每一個討論……

---

[4] Huffman, S., Thurman, G., & Thomas, L. K. (2005). An investigation of block scheduling and school library media centers. *Reading Improvement, 42,* 3-15.

>>> 指南 4：指出為何有些研究報告是重要的

如果你相信一個特定的研究報告是重要的，請清楚的說明為何它重要。舉例來說，範例 9.4.1 的作者定義一個研究報告像是「在這個領域裡最大規模研究報告之一」，因此指出它的重要性。

範例 9.4.1[5]

說明為何一份報告是重要的（在這個實例中，是最大規模研究報告之一）：

在美國，「大哥哥／大姐姐」或許是最為人知的志工指導計畫。在這領域裡最大規模的研究報告之一（Tierney & Grossman, 1995），是九百九十五位年輕人在 1992 至 1993 年間在「大哥哥／大姐姐」配對中，被隨機分配到兩個群組中的一組：指導組或控制組（後者的年輕人被放入十八個月的等候清單中）。兩個群組都接受面談……

一份重要報告，會重複表達研究的某一部分發展的中樞觀點，如同一份指出一位重要研究者地位的逆轉或提出一項新方法論的研究論文。一份報告的這些特點和其他特點能強調它的地位如同一份重要的報告一樣。當一份報告格外重要時，記得你的文獻探討要明確的說明它的重要性。

>>> 指南 5：如果你正在評論一個當代的議題，請明確的描述時間架構

在開始你的評論時，標題上避免用不具體的參考文獻，像是「最近幾

---

5 Keating, L. M., Tomishima, M. A., Foster, S., & Alessandri, M. (2002). The effects of mentoring program on at-risk youth. *Adolescence, 37,* 717-734.

年，有愈來愈多關注在……」，這種開頭將留給讀者很多未解的問題，例如：哪一個時代開始涉及的？作者如何決定這「關注」是持續增加？誰變得更關注，是作者或者其他領域的人？當其他人對這主題無興趣時，作者最近是否有可能對主題更有興趣？

　　同樣的，問題的增加或關注的母體大小的增加，應該用明確的數字觀點或百分比和指出明確的年份。舉例來說，它不是很正式的去聲明只有「西班牙裔的人數在未來將增加」。範例 9.5.1 的作者避免了這個問題，他明確地引用的百分比和時間架構（楷體字增強了重點部分）。

範 例　9.5.1[6]

提出明確的時間底線：

根據美國人口調查局（2001）估計，有 3,280 萬名西班牙裔的人住在美國。這個估計指出，人數比例將從 1990 年的 10%提升到 2020 年的 14% 或 15%，屆時該族群將成為這國家四大種族之一（Garcia & Marotta, 1997）。Baruth 和 Manning（1999）寫道，墨西哥裔美國人佔西班牙裔人口總數的 61%。約有一半的……

>>> 指南 6：如果援引經典或里程碑式的研究，請確定它本身是如此

　　在文獻探討前，請確認你所鑑定的是經典的還是具有里程碑意義的研究。這些研究往往是已出版文獻的歷史發展中的關鍵點。此外，它們往往

6　Sharma, P., & Kerl, S. B. (2002). Suggestions for psychologists working with Mexican American individuals and families in health care settings. *Rehabilitation Psychology, 47,* 230-239.

負責制定一個特定問題或研究的傳統，它們也可能是將來文獻原始來源的關鍵概念或術語。不管它們的貢獻如何，你應確定它們的地位是經典或是文獻中的里程碑。看看範例 9.6.1，便是引用一個里程碑（此類型中的首例）的研究。

範例 9.6.1[7]

確定了里程碑式的研究：

雜誌廣告上的性別偏見的第一項內容分析（強調）是由 Courtney 和 Lockeretz（1971）所出版。這些作者發現，雜誌廣告一般反映了四個刻板觀念：(1)「一個女人，頂多是在家裡」；(2)「婦女不能做出重要決定或做重要的事」；(3)「婦女依賴和需要男人的保護」；和 (4)「男子主要將婦女作為性對象，他們對婦女的許多事不感興趣」。

>>> 指南 7：複製一個具有里程碑意義的研究，需提出並說明複製的結果

正如先前的指南所言，具有里程碑意義的研究通常將刺激更多的研究。事實上，藉由使用不同的參與者群體或調整其他研究的設計變項，大部分的里程碑式研究被複製了很多次。如果你是引述里程碑式的研究並已經複製它，你應該提到這一事實，並說明是否複製成功。範例 9.7.1 即是根據範例 9.6.1 而來的詳盡闡述。

---

7 Neptune, D., & Plous, S. (1997). Racial and gender biases in magazine advertising. *Psychology of Women Quarterly, 21,* 627-644.

範 例 9.7.1

重點複製：

在這研究的這段期間，許多其他的內容分析都複製這些結果（強調）
（Belkaoui & Belkaoui, 1976; Busby & Leichty, 1993; Culley& Bennett,
1976; England, Kuhn, & Gardner, 1983; Lysonski, 1983; Sexton & Haber-
man, 1974; Venkatesan & Losco, 1975; Wagner & Banos, 1973）。在過去
四十年裡，只有一個由 Courtney 和 Lockeretz（1971）所發現的刻板印
象顯示了改進的證據：婦女受制於家庭的形象。由於婦女進入職場的
人數愈來愈多，廣告也愈來愈多地呈現出她們在家庭之外的工作環境
（Busby & Leichty, 1993; Sullivan & O'Conner, 1988）。

>>> 指南 8：針對你的主題討論其他文獻探討

　　如果你發現有關你探討主題的一個早期已出版的文獻探討，對你而言
在你的文獻探討中討論這份出版品，是很重要的。在如此做之前，考慮下
列問題：

如何審查其他評論跟你的不同之處？

　　你是否超越了現狀甚多？

　　你是否用不同的方式劃定了題目？

　　你進行更全面的審查？

　　更加早期的評論者是否得出了跟你同樣的主要結論？

　　一如先前的評論者，你做出同樣的主要結論？

其他的探討是多麼值得你的讀者回顧？

　　如果有的話，他們可以藉由閱讀得到什麼？

他們能透過各種不同且有幫助的角度來看待這個問題嗎？

什麼是它的主要優點和缺點？

>>>指南 9：向讀者提到其他你將不會討論細節的議題

如果你認為有必要提及的相關議題不能涵蓋在你的深入探討回顧中，須適當的向讀者提到其他文獻探討，如範例 9.9.1。不用說，你的探討應完全涵蓋你選擇的特定主題。在你的主題中若只描述部分文獻（如你定義它時），然後就向讀者提到其餘部分的另一來源，那是不行的。然而，範例 9.9.1 的制式描述，對於指出文獻中讀者感興趣的部分，是有幫助的，但不會詳細探討你正在寫的文獻（粗楷體字為重點）。

範例 9.9.1[8]

向讀者提出其他可參照來源的詳細資料：

整個 20 世紀，在戰爭期間和之後，對心理創傷的影響的興趣已經達到了頂峰，與戰鬥有關的心理後遺症（當時稱為心理神經症）的第一次重大研究，於 1941 年由 A. Kardiner 出版（見 Kolb，1993，有更多細節描述）。處理二戰戰俘營倖存者帶來了一些見解……

>>>指南 10：證明論點，視同「沒有研究發現過這些論點」

如果你在文獻探討中發現值得提出的文獻缺失，請解釋你是如何獲得現有文獻缺失的結論，至少，要解釋你是如何建立你的文獻探討，及它裡

8 Ozer, E. J., Best, S. R., Lipsey, T. L., & Weiss, D. S. (2003). Predictors of posttraumatic stress disorder and symptoms in adults: A meta-analysis. *Psychological Bulletin, 129,* 52-73.

面包含的資料、年代及你使用的變數。你並不需要非常明確的指出,但讀者會期待你對於這個缺失提出論點。

為了避免誤導讀者,最好在你的文獻探討的前面寫出如同範例 9.10.1 的說明。假使你所指出的缺失並不存在,這個步驟會讓你避免遭受批評。換句話說,你告訴了讀者你是使用一項特定的搜尋策略,而指出缺失的。

範例 9.10.1[9]

描述文獻搜尋的策略:

我們使用了五種方法來找出相關的研究,第一,我們從過去出版有關於自我概念發展的文章(Demo, 1992; Harter, 1982, 1998; Wylie, 1979)和兩份最近有關性別不同在自尊方面的統合分析(Kling, Hyde, Showers, & Buswell, 1999; Major, Barr, Zubek, & Babey, 1999),探討參考文獻的清單;第二,我們在 *PsycINFO* 和 *ERIC* 資料庫,搜尋 1887 年(最早進入 *PsycINFO* 資料庫的資料)到 2002 年 6 月之間出版的文章,使用關鍵字為「自尊」及搭配以下文字:年齡差異、改變、一致性、連結性、發展、文獻探討、縱向的、統合分析和穩定;第三,我們將「自尊」這個關鍵字與每個含有先前定義文章的期刊標題配對(從關鍵字搜尋);第四,我們用一般自尊量表的名稱為關鍵字在 *PsycINFO* 資料庫裡搜尋(如:羅森伯格自尊量表、自尊問卷、Piers-Harris 自我概念量表),這些關鍵字搜尋中找到了 9,410 筆資料(其中 7,150 筆出自學術同儕評鑑的期刊雜誌);第五,我們藉由從 *PsycINFO* 和 *ERIC* 資料庫定義中,找到包含標準的參考文獻探討清單來搜尋相關的文章。

---

9 Trzesniewski, K. H., Donnellan, M. B., & Robins, R. W. (2003). Stability of self-esteem across the life span. *Journal of Personality and Social Psychology, 84,* 205-220.

>>> 指南 11：避免針對非特定參考文獻的一長串清單

在學術寫作方面，參考文獻被用於書面文件的正文，至少有兩個目的，第一，它們的作用在於讓作者的想法或直接引用、特定用字有適當的可信度，否則，會造成剽竊。第二，參考文獻是用來說明原稿所研究的範圍廣度，因此，在前言的段落中，舉例來說，最好提及關鍵的參考文獻，甚至有幾篇是在文獻探討中，會討論細節的重要研究文章。然而，不建議使用冗長且不是特別關於所要表達重點的清單。舉例來說，範例 9.11.1 在第一句中，羅列繁雜且非特定參考文獻的清單可能不適當，這些都是以經驗為依據的研究嗎？是否記錄這些作者對於問題的推測呢？某些參考文獻是否比其他的更重要呢？對於作者來說，讓讀者去參考一些重要研究案例是更好的，因為它們本身在特定領域中，包含了額外研究實例的參考文獻，如同範例 9.11.2 所闡示。

範 例 9.11.1

文獻探討的第一句話（太多非特定的參考文獻）：

許多作者指出：單親家庭的小孩比雙親家庭的小孩在學業成就表現上，承受較大的挑戰（Adams, 1999; Block, 2002; Doe, 2004; Edgar, 2000; Hampton, 1995; Jones, 2003; Klinger, 1991; Long, 1992; Livingston, 1993; Macy, 1985; Norton, 1988; Pearl, 1994; Smith, 1996; Travers, 1997; Vincent, 1994; West, 1992; Westerly, 1995; Yardley, 2004）。

範 例 9.11.2

範例 9.11.1 的改良版：

許多作者指出：單親家庭的小孩比雙親家庭的小孩在學業成就表現上，承受較大的挑戰（例如，參見 Adams, 1999; Block, 2002），有三個近期的研究，以觀察為依據為這個論點提供強烈的支持（Doe, 2004; Edgar, 2000; Jones, 2003），在這些研究中，以 Jones 的研究是支持性最強的，因其採用了在嚴謹控制下的全國性樣本來……

注意「例如」與「參見」的使用，這些用法表明了只有某些可能的參考文獻被引用，作為支持作者意圖表達的重點，你也可以使用拉丁文縮寫 *"cf."*〔意思是「比較」（compare）〕。

>>>指南 12：假如先前的研究結果是前後矛盾或截然不同的，則分別引用它們

對於研究來說，在同一個主題下產生前後矛盾或截然不同的結論是不常見的，遇到這種情況，則分別引用這些研究，讓讀者正確的詮釋你的文獻探討是重要的。範例 9.12.1 是讓人誤解的例子，因為它沒有註記之前的研究是根據被分為兩個極端的百分比範圍的群組，而範例 9.12.2 展示出引用兩個前後矛盾結果的較佳方法。

範 例 9.12.1

引用一個結果為前後矛盾的研究（不受歡迎的）：

在先前的研究（Doe, 2004; Jones, 2005），父母親支持公立學校學生穿制服的程度是相當不同的，從 19%到 52%都有。

範例 9.12.2

範例 9.12.1 的改良版：

在先前的研究中，家長對於是否要求學生穿校服的支持度，發生了很
大的改變。農村與郊區的學生家長所持的支持度各有不同，在農村學
生家長的部分，支持學生穿校服的，從原本只有 19%至後來的 28%
（Doe, 2004），而郊區學生家長則從原本的 35%至後來的 52%（Jones,
2005）。

>>> 指南 13：在碩士論文、博士論文與期刊論文中的章節，引用所有相關的文獻

當撰寫文獻探討先於原始研究報告之前的碩士論文、博士論文與期刊
論文時，通常應該先引用所有相關參考文獻資料，並且避免在文獻的後面
章節（如結果或討論的部分）引入新的參考文獻資料。請確認你已檢查過
整份資料，以確保文獻中的一節或一章是全面的。在第一次審查你的碩士
論文、博士論文與期刊論文的時候，可以翻閱以前的研究討論，將焦點放
在討論有關文章的結論部分。

>>> 指南 14：在文獻探討的章或節，強調你研究的需要

當撰寫文獻探討先於原始研究報告之前的碩士論文、博士論文與期刊
論文時，應該使用回顧探討，以證明自己的研究。另外也可以使用多種方
式，如指出你的研究是：(1)縮短文獻中的差距，(2)測試當前理論的一個重
要面向，(3)複製一個重要的研究，(4)使用新的或改進的方法學程序，再測
試一次理論，(5)旨在解決理論中的衝突等等。

範例 9.14.1 被列在一份研究報告的文獻探討部分，這個報告旨在探討使用大麻的自陳式報告和毒品檢測與治療方案意見間的關係，而在審查的文獻中，作者指出在先前研究文獻中的不足處，並說明他們的研究如何填補不足處。這對研究而言是一個強而有力的證明。

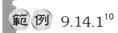 **9.14.1**[10]

一項研究證明：

本研究填補這三個不足處。首先，本研究側重於毒品治療的反應方案。具體的說，我們考慮的問題，如職業安全的敏感性、毒品的使用、和治療方案的類型。第二，我們特別集中於關係……

 ## 第 9 章的活動

說明：針對你指導老師指派的每個文獻探討範本，回答下列問題。這些探討的範本列於本書末。

1. 當要避免廣泛的陳述時，作者是否由定義一個廣泛問題範圍開始？請解釋之。

2. 作者是否指出：目前正在審查的主題，為何是重要的？請解釋之。

3. 作者有透過使用適當的措辭來區分研究成果和其他訊息的來源嗎？請解釋之。

---

[10] Paronto, M. E., Truxillo, D. M., Talya, N. B., & Leo, M. C. (2002). Drug testing, drug treatment, and marijuana use: A fairness perspective. *Journal of Applied Psychology, 87,* 1159-1166.

4. 作者是否撰文指出為什麼某些研究是重要的？請解釋之。

5. 如果作者評論的是主題的及時性，他（她）是否描述具體的時間架構？請解釋之。

6. 所引用的文獻資料是在一個具有里程碑意義的研究中提到的嗎？如果是，如何確定這個文獻資料具有里程碑的意義？有任何跡象顯示，這個文獻資料是複製的嗎？

7. 審查其他文獻，是否有關於同一主題的討論而未引用到？

8. 重新檢查自己的文獻，是否有其他評論引用有關的問題，而本身未詳細討論？

9. 在主題的某些方面，如果撰文說：「沒有任何研究上的發現」，這種說法是合理的嗎（正如本章）？

10. 作者有提交非特定參考交獻的一長串清單嗎？

11. 如果研究結果和先前結果不一致或截然不同，是否有分別引用它們呢？

發展具連貫性論文的指南

本章旨在引導你發展一篇連貫的文章,幫助你潤飾初稿。請記住,文獻探討不應針對你所閱讀的文獻寫成一系列連接的摘要(或注解)。相反的,文獻探討應該有一個明確的論述,並應以下述方式來發展:其中所有的元素,共同傳達一個理由充分的論述。

>>> 指南 1:如果你的文獻探討很長,在文獻探討開始時提供一個概述

當在寫一篇很長的文獻探討時,給讀者提供一個作者論述的明確藍圖是很重要的。這通常是在文獻探討前言部分就完成了,其中應包括文件剩餘涵蓋部分的概述。範例 10.1.1 說明了這一點。

範例 10.1.1[1]

在文獻探討之初的一個有效「藍圖」：

因著延遲或無法行動，他們將自己置身於不良的結果中，為什麼人類如此頻繁參與逃避決策？這裡我認為多樣性的選擇行為，可以作為個人潛在逃避決策的反思，個人所尋求的行為模式，是藉由延遲或選擇他們覺得無需做決定的選項，來逃避做決定的責任。這項文獻探討顯示，在所有這類情況下，是混合了對逃避而言，是些許好的、合理的藉口，和由情緒（如：懊悔和恐懼）所扮演的更複雜、值得質疑的角色這二者。這些問題形成本文的基礎：(1)在劃定邊界條件時，該根據人們的猶豫、遲疑或選擇對部分或沒有變化的選項不採取行動，而維持現狀，以及(2)解釋這種行為。

>>> 指南 2：文獻探討之初，明白陳述哪些會或不會被涵蓋在內

有些主題是如此廣泛，你的文獻探討無法完全涵蓋所有的研究。尤其你正在寫一篇學期研究報告，且你的指導老師有提出頁數的限制，或是發表一篇文章，其中文獻探討部分傳統上相對較短。在這種情況下，你在文獻探討開始時，應該精確陳述哪些會或不會被涵蓋在內（即你的文獻探討的界定）。範例 10.2.1 的摘錄說明這方針的應用。注意到文獻探討者首先提供一個定義，且指出他們的文獻探討包含了欺騙與撒謊（兩者可互換的）。然後，他們陳述這篇文獻探討會侷限於兩個標準。

---

[1] Anderson, C. J. (2003). The psychology of doing nothing: Forms of decision avoidance result from reason and emotion. *Psychological Bulletin, 129,* 139-167.

範 例 10.2.1[2]

文獻探討界定的論述：

我們定義中的欺騙是企圖誤導他人。那些誤解的人或自欺的人所接受的謊言不是謊言，但是文字所傳遞的主旨產生誤導的就是謊言。雖然一些學者區分了欺騙和撒謊（如 Bok, 1978），我們還是將兩者交替使用。如同 Zuckerman 等（1981）在他們的文獻探討中所做的一樣，我們限制了對行為者的分析，無需任何特殊設備的援助，這些行為者的行為就可以被人類的知覺所察覺，我們也限制了我們對於成人研究的文獻探討，且欺騙的動機可能與兒童的有顯著的不同（例如，Feldman, Devin-Sheehan, & Allen, 1978; Lewis, Stanger, & Sullivan, 1989; Shennum & Bugental, 1982）。

>>> 指南 3：在文獻探討初期明確說明你的觀點

正如前面已經強調過的，你的文獻探討應當寫成一篇對已探討回顧過的研究有特定觀點的文章形式。這個觀點就如你的碩士論文的論述（文章其餘部分的聲明或主張）。

你的觀點並不需要詳盡或詳細的表達出來（儘管它可以）。在範例 10.3.1 中，文獻探討者簡略指出他們的觀點（社經地位、認知－情感因素和健康可能是互有關聯）。這在文獻探討之初就已告知讀者，這個支配一切的觀點引導了文獻的闡明和整合。

當然，只有當你已閱讀並思考文獻的內容將它視為一個整體之後，你才應該決定你的觀點。換句話說，這個指南指出你什麼時候應該表達你的觀點（文獻探討之初），而不是你什麼時候應該發展一個觀點。

---

2 DePaulo, B. M. et al. (2003). Cues to deception. *Psychological Bulletin, 129,* 74-118.

範例 10.3.1[3]

論述路徑的初期摘要：

社經地位與認知－情感因素的關聯並未呈現在近期列舉的文獻中（但可參閱 Kohn、Dohrenwend 和 Mirotznik 1998 年有關社經地位與心理疾患的文獻）。因此，我們更詳細的分析此研究。根據我們的文獻探討和批判性分析，我們提出了一個理解路徑的框架，可能藉此連結社經地位、認知－情感因素與健康。最後，我們總結，建議未來的研究可以多強調論文中所提出的中介假說。

>>> 指南 4：目標是一個明確和連貫的文章，避免注解

迄今為止已多次強調，有效的文獻探討應以書面形式寫成一篇文章。也許新手學術作者最常提出的單一問題，是他們在文獻探討中放棄使用注解的困難。

注解是文章內容簡短的摘要。在文獻探討的內容中，將幾個注解串在一起，可能說明在某一個主題中可以獲得的研究有哪些，但它無法為讀者組織材料。一個有效的文獻探討是組織出一個論點。作者需要描述每個研究之間的相互關係。什麼是相對優勢和相對劣勢？差距在哪裡，它們為什麼存在？所有的這些細節和更多內容需要，支持作者寫這篇文獻探討的目的。第八章中描述的詳細大綱，描寫了論述的路徑，但作者可以自行決定，是否將此轉化為散文式的報告，以統整研究文獻中重要的細節，成為一篇

---

3 Gallo, L. C., & Matthews, K. A. (2003). Understanding the association between socioeconomic status and physical health: Do negative emotions play a role? *Psychological Bulletin, 129,* 10-51.

傳遞其觀點的文章。

　　範例 10.4.1 顯示如何將幾篇研究引用在一起，變成一個段落的一部分。該段以主題句開頭，以根據引用文獻的主題句結尾。注意文獻探討者提出的觀點之一是由三篇參考文獻所支持。顯然，該段的組織是主題式的，而非個別作者的報告。

範例 10.4.1[4]

有多種來源的單一段落：

在家庭層面，父母和子女間的關係在哮喘住院的病例中，可能扮演重要角色。兒童哮喘患者與健康兒童相較，已發現有較高比例的臨床上顯著的家庭壓力（Bussing, Burket, & Kelleher, 1996）。家庭凝聚性較強的兒童更有可能控制哮喘（Meijer, Griffioen, van Nierop, & Oppenheimer, 1995）。此外，父母在兒童早期照護的困難，尤其處在高壓力時，已發現可用來預測童年的哮喘發病（Klinnert, Mrazek, & Mrazek,1994; Klinnert et al., 2001; Mrazek et al., 1999）。因此，家庭的壓力，如家庭成員之間的衝突和疾病對家庭關係帶來的衝擊等形式，可能與更經常住院的哮喘兒童有關。

>>> 指南 5：長篇的文獻探討需加上副標題

　　由於長篇文獻探討，特別是那些為碩士論文和博士論文寫的文獻探討，經常處理多個學科領域的文章，建議使用副標題。如果你決定使用副標題，

---

[4] Chen, E., Bloomberg, G. R., Fisher, E. B., & Strunk, R. C. (2003). Predictors of repeat hospitalizations in children with asthma: The role of psychosocial and socioenvironmental factors. *Health Psychology, 22,* 12-18.

有策略的排放它們，以幫助促進你的論述，讓讀者更容易著眼於你的論述。你在第八章準備的主題大綱可以幫助你，決定副標應該放在哪裡，儘管你可能需要改寫一些主題的標題以便作為標示，而不是論述。

>>> 指南 6：使用轉換來幫助你追蹤你的論述

程序的轉換短語可以幫助讀者跟著你的論述。例如，你可以轉換提供給讀者的文字線索來標示討論的進展，像是在段落開頭使用「第一」、「第二」和「第三」，以標示三個相關觀點的發展。當然，任何標準的寫作手冊都會包含普遍正式書寫使用的表達轉換清單。

但是，這些轉換不應過分使用，特別是在短篇的文獻探討，當每個觀點已在相鄰段落說明，可能沒有必要使用這些短語來標示三個相關觀點的發展。另一個問題往往在短篇文獻探討中被發現，即是過度使用 Bem（1995）所稱的「後設意見」，這是指文獻探討本身的意見（而不是被探討的文獻中的意見）[5]。例如，在範例 10.6.1，作者重申該文獻探討的組織（此即後設意見的例子）。本質上產生後設意見沒有什麼錯，你應該避免頻繁重申論述，這會推翻你先前已聲明的論述。

範例 10.6.1

過度使用後設意見的例子：

回想一下，本文處理提問兒童的問題，是如何被用來解釋各種不同的學習風格。同時回想，我們探討有關教室中提問的使用的研究，且達成了一些初步結論。現在，我們會思考兩個基本類型的問題，幼童經常提問，並指出……

---

5 Bem, D. J. (1995). Writing a review article for *Psychological Bulletin. Psychological Bulletin, 118,* 172-177.

>>> 指南 7：如果你的主題橫跨學科，考慮分別從每個學科的研究進行文獻探討

自然會有一些主題是超越學科界限。例如，如果你書寫關於少女糖尿病管理，你會在一些學科領域發現相關資料來源，包括醫療保健、營養和心理學。醫療保健的文獻，例如，可能是處理在胰島素療法上的變項（變項比如胰島素使用的種類，或透過幫浦對比透過注射器來給予胰島素）。另一方面，營養學期刊可能包括管理食物攝取，以尋求更有效的方法來控制胰島素休克發作的替代方法的研究。最後，心理學文獻可能提供少女常見壓力來源的洞察，特別是關於這些壓力如何干擾女孩的決策過程，這些決策過程包括自我監控、營養選擇和價值取向。雖然這些例子是假設的，但很容易看到這樣的文獻探討如何從被區分的三部分而受益，且分別從每一個學科領域去探討其發現。

>>> 指南 8：在文獻探討之末，寫一個結論

你的文獻探討應該為讀者提供一個結論，也就是說，論述的路徑應該以結論作為結束。無論如何，你如何為文獻探討做總結，是取決於你寫此篇文章的理由。如果文獻探討是寫來獨立運行，如學期論文或發表評論文章，結論需要清楚地說明文獻探討的內容，支持了概述裡提出的主張或論點。另一方面，碩士論文、博士論文或呈現原始研究的期刊文章，通常會產生將被提出的研究問題。

如果你的文獻探討是篇幅冗長和複雜的，你應該簡要地總結你論述的主要思路，然後提出你的結論。否則，可能會導致你的讀者為了重建你所提出的例子而停頓下來。較短的文獻探討通常不需要總結，但這個判斷將取決於你提出論述的複雜性。你可能需要從你的指導教授或朋友獲得回饋，來幫助你確定你在結尾時有多需要再做聲明。範例 10.8.1 呈現了長篇文獻探討的簡短摘要和結論部分。在大多數情況下，就長篇的文獻探討而言，

需要更詳細的總結。

範例 10.8.1[6]

位於長篇文獻探討之末的摘要和結論部分：

得自廣泛的心理學學科的證據顯示，身體和社會性的痛苦，是透過共同機制運作的。兩者都是必要的，以促進社會性動物的生存，運作來引導動物遠離威脅和驅近其他同類（對它是有益的）。兩者能引起快速、防禦的行為，且是極端情感上的厭惡。這兩種類型的痛苦有相同的心理關聯和生理途徑。最終，兩者都出現原始類化的威脅—反應機制。

總之，我們認為，這個文獻探討有助於新興的概念：人們的社會和物質世界是緊緊交織在一起的。我們特別強調個人對其他人的情感，可能源於相同的痛苦，以便保持他們身體上的安全。我們還認為，社會痛苦理論有助於強調人類行為中與他人連結的重要作用。我們生活在個人主義的社會，充斥著鼓吹自主性和個性的訊息。然而，正在出現的情景是，人們對彼此是如此重要，社會性的需求深植於我們的生理，我們之所以會有社會痛苦，就是我們深切的需要對方的例證。

>>> 指南 9：論述需流暢富連貫性

學術寫作其中最困難的技巧是：評估自己寫作的連貫性。連貫是指如何將草稿放在一起作為統一的文件。重要的是，你要問自己，文獻探討中各種元素如何彼此連接。這就要求你仔細評估你文件中修辭要素的效用，

---

6 MacDonald, G., & Leary, M. R. (2005). Why does social exclusion hurt? The relationship between social and physical pain. *Psychological Bulletin, 131,* 202-223.

讓讀者了解其結構和它的要素們之間的關係。副標題經常對辨認手稿結構大有幫助。轉換性的表達和其他修辭標記也有助於確定各章節之間的關係，如「在下一個例子」，「在相關的研究」，「反例」和「最近（或相關）的研究」。顯然，還有很多這樣的例子。記住，對你的讀者來說這些修辭是有用的導航工具，特別是如果文獻探討的細節很複雜時。

第 10 章的活動

說明：針對你指導老師指派的每個文獻探討範本，回答下列問題。這些探討的範本列於本書末。

1. 當文獻探討是長篇的，作者有否在開頭附近提供一個文獻探討的概述？請解釋之。
2. 作者是否明確說明在文獻探討中什麼會和不會被包括在內？請解釋之。
3. 文獻探討是明確和一致性的文章嗎？請解釋之。
4. 作者是否避開聲明？請解釋之。
5. 若文獻探討過長，作者是否使用副標題？請解釋之。
6. 作者是否使用「轉換」來協助追查其論點？請解釋之。
7. 若該專題有跨學科，作者是否就每個學科各別地做出文獻探討？
8. 作者有否為最終的文獻探討寫一個結論？
9. 論述的流暢度是否達到一致連貫性？

如何撰寫文獻探討
給社會暨行為科學學生指南

Writing Literature Reviews: A Guide for Students of the Social and Behavioral Sciences

格式、制式化、語言使用的指南

前兩章處理撰寫一篇文獻探討的一般問題。本章則將重點放在更多與格式、制式化和語言使用有關的特殊問題上。這些議題對撰寫一份沒有制式化錯誤的草稿來說，是重要的。

>>> 指南 1：比較初稿與主題大綱

在閱讀第八章之後，你所準備的主題大綱隨即依文獻探討的論證方向而發展。現在你的初稿已完成了，去比較你之前寫的主題大綱是什麼，以便確認已適當的充實論證方向。

>>> 指南 2：檢查你文獻探討的結構是否一致

對於閱讀特別長且複雜的文獻探討之讀者，在內化這些分析和整合的細節時，要能依循草稿的結構。一個主題大綱將牽涉到標準的一致性結構之法則。舉例來說，一個缺點的討論將被一個優點的討論所平衡；一個正面的論證將被一個反面的論證所平衡等等。這些部分讀者的期望源於學術寫作長期的修辭傳統。所以你需要確認你的稿件，去注意你的論述是否有適當的平衡。這可能需要你解釋某個特定一致性的缺失，這個缺失也許沒有明確的被指出，它是一個沒有被研究發現的矛盾特殊論點（參閱第九章中的指南 10 是否可應用到你的文獻探討中）。

>>> 指南 3：很長的句子要避免直接引用

　　過度引用對於社會行為科學的學術寫作者而言，是一個嚴重的問題。在大學寫作課程中，特別強調引用別人文字的正確慣例用法，是可理解的。事實上，使用直接引用在本質上並沒有錯誤。然而，問題肇始於當他們的用法是不適當或帶有偏見的。

　　一個斷章取義的引文，不能充分傳達出原作者原本的意圖。當讀者努力了解文獻中引文的含義，卻會因此而受干擾。去解釋一個引文脈絡中的無關細節，會使讀者對手中的文獻更加混淆。相較之下，套用主要思想的作者通常是更有效、更容易避免無關的細節。

　　最後，一般很少能接受用一個引文做為文獻探討的開始。有些學生對此難以抗拒。切記對讀者來說是很難去體會到：當文獻探討的作者建立適當的脈絡之前，就先呈現引用意欲的作用。

>>> 指南 4：核對格式手冊正確使用引文

　　為了內文引用參考的需要，請先確認你有核對在你的研究領域中為了適當的慣例而使用的格式手冊。例如，《美國心理學會出版手冊》對引文有下列特定的方針：

a. 在你的敘述中，你會用數種方式中的一種去正式的引用一個參考文獻。一個結論的敘述，是呈現某些人的想法，你引用作者的姓和出版年，將它們設置在括弧內並用逗號分開，例如（Doe, 2005）。如果你在文章中使用作者的名字，應立即在名字之後，簡單的在括弧內標示出版年，例如：「Doe（2005）指出……」。

b. 當你在括弧內引用多位作者的名字，用&代替 and 這個字。如果是文章內的引用，則使用 and 這個字。

c. 使用分號去隔開括弧內的多個引用，例如：（Black, 2004; Brown, 2005; Green, 2005）。

d. 當你引用第二手資料，要確定你標示得很清楚，例如：（Doe, as cited in Smith, 2004）。記住只有 Smith（2004）可以被放在參考文獻的清單內。

>>> 指南 5：對於重複出現的字應避免使用同義字

實徵研究文獻的焦點應放在盡可能嚴謹、清楚地呈現、說明及綜合其他學者想法與研究發現。這可能需要重複的詞語描述例行方面的幾項研究。學生們剛開始從事學術著作時，常把這工作任務視為是一份創作寫作練習。這不是！文獻探討應該包括許多研究資料（和其他類型的文獻），讀者應該要能夠迅速內化所有這些部分。因此，重要的是堅持使用傳統的術語，即使它們一再的出現。當作者堅持用傳統的術語時，才是達到清楚明晰的最佳途徑，特別是當提到有關研究的方法學或一些研究的其他技術層面的細節。

一般來說，最好不要使用不同的標籤。例如，如果一項研究涉及兩組參與者，研究人員將他們標示為第一組和第二組，你通常應該避免替換成較富創意的詞組（如「鳳凰隊」或「原始的青少年組」）。另一方面，如果替代的標籤可幫助釐清研究設計（例如，第一組為對照組而第二組為實驗組），使用替代的表達，但在你的討論過程中，詞組要維持一致性。範例 11.5.1 示範了使用同義詞和「創意」句子結構如何混淆了讀者。在文章的不同處，第一組被稱為「鳳凰隊」、「組 I」和「實驗組」，這勢必會引起混亂。範例 11.5.2 則是改進版本，其中作者使用一貫的術語「實驗組」和「控制組」，以確定兩個群組。

範例 11.5.1

辨認術語使用上的不一致：

鳳凰隊（被教導用名稱來正確識別各種動物玩具），被研究人員帶回加以研究兩次，一次是六個月後，又一次是在今年年底。另一組的青少年在六個月後被要求回答一組問題，且只有一次，但他們被教導用顏色來識別動物，而不是名稱。組 I 的成績明顯優於組 II。實驗組成績較好的原因是……

範例 11.5.2

範例 11.5.1 的改良版：

實驗組被教導用顏色來識別動物，並在六個月的時間間隔重新測試兩次。對照組被教導用名稱來識別玩具，在六個月後只做了一次重新測試。實驗組的成績表現優於對照組。實驗組成績表現較優越的原因是……

>>> 指南 6：當你第一次使用首字母縮寫，請詳加說明，並避免使用太多

　　許多首字母縮寫已經成為我們日常生活的詞彙，在編輯的過程中很容易被忽略，一些例子像是學校的縮寫，如加州大學洛杉磯分校（UCLA）和南加州大學（USC）；專業的縮寫如美國心理學會（APA）和現代語言

學會（MLA）；和來自我們日常生活中的縮寫，如聯邦調查局（FBI）、
美國食品暨藥物管理局（FDA）和學業平均成績（GPA）。很明顯的，從
這個指南看起來，找出這些和其他永遠不會被詳加說明的例子是很常見的，
請務必仔細檢查你文件中的縮寫並在第一次使用它們時詳加說明。有時用
縮寫來指稱東西是有幫助的，尤其是它的全名很長，且你需要提到好幾遍
的時候。例如，美國加州州立大學校的學生「畢業論文評量規定」（Grad-
uate Writing Assessment Requirement）通常簡稱為GWAR。通常來說，你應
該避免使用過多的縮寫，特別是那些不是一般常用的，像GWAR。在複雜
的文獻中，使用一些縮寫可能會有所幫助，但使用太多可能會混淆。

>>> 指南 7：避免使用縮寫形式，在正式學術寫作中它們是不適當的

　　縮寫形式是使用語言的一個自然部分。它們是語言簡化的自然過程的
一個例子，解釋所有文字如何緩慢而穩步地跨越時間的變化。許多教師，
甚至一些英語作文教師，允許使用縮寫形式的假設是，它們的使用反映了
接受現代美式英語的不斷變化標準。儘管有這種態度，但是，在正式學術
寫作中使用縮寫形式，幾乎總是不適當的。

>>> 指南 8：自創的術語在使用時，應設置引號

　　有時自創一個術語，用一個或兩個詞來描述東西是有幫助的，否則需
要一個或更多句子。自創的術語頻繁地成為常用用法的一部分，如同現在
常用為動詞的名詞「午餐」（你昨天和珍妮午餐啦？）。然而，在正式寫
作上應該謹慎的使用自創的術語。如果你決定自創一個術語，要設置引號
去表明它在一本標準字典裡不可能被發現的意思。

>>> 指南 9：避免俚語、方言和慣用語

　　切記學術寫作是正式寫作。所以，俚語、方言和慣用語在文獻探討是

不適當的。雖然許多俚語，如「酷」（意思是「好」）和「才不」（ain't）已經成為對話的一部分，但在學術寫作時應該完全避免使用。在方言中，如「事」（thing），「本質」（stuff），應適當的改為非方言性的術語〔例如，「項目」（item），「專題」（feature）和「特徵」（characteristic）〕。同樣的，在慣用語裡，如「上升到了頂峰」和「生存測試」，應改為更正式的表達方式，如「變得突出」或「是成功的」。

>>> 指南 10：在括號的內容中使用拉丁文縮寫；其他地方用英文翻譯

如下所示是有其英文翻譯的拉丁文縮寫，通常用於正式的學術寫作。除此之外，這些縮寫僅限於括號中的內容。例如，在這個句子最後的括號內的拉丁文縮寫是正確的：（即，這是一個正確的例子）（ie., this is a correct example）。如果這不是在括號中，你應該使用英語翻譯：即這也是一個正確例子（that is, this is also a correct example）。此外，注意這些縮寫所需的每一個標點符號。特別注意的是，在 et al. 的 "et" 後面沒有句號。

cf. 比較（compare）　　e.g., 例如（for example）　et al. 等等（and others）

etc. 等等（and so forth）　i.e., 亦即（that is）　　vs. 對，對照（versus, against）

>>> 指南 11：用一般的寫作慣例檢查你的草稿

這裡有一些所有學術原則皆要求的額外寫作慣例。把草稿送給你的老師閱讀之前，檢查你的草稿，以確保你已經應用以下所有項目。

a. 請確保你使用完整的句子。

b. 在寫文獻探討使用第一人稱有時是可以接受的。然而，你應該避免對第一人稱的過分使用。

c. 使用性別歧視的語言在學術寫作中是不適當的。例如，這是不正確的：一直使用男性或女性代詞（他、他的受格、他的對照她、她的

受格、她的），去指稱一個你不能確定其性別的人（如，「老師離開了她的教室……」）。通常，性別歧視的語言可以透過使用複數形式來避免（「老師們離開了教室……」）。如果你必須使用單數形式，請交替使用男性和女性或使用「他或她」。

d. 你在寫作上應該力爭明確。因此，你應該避免間接句子，例如「在史密斯的研究中，發現了它……」，應該改為「史密斯發現了……」。

e. 一般來說，從零到九的數都用國字表示，但第 10 和以上被寫作為阿拉伯數字。這個規則的兩個例外是數字被用在圖表中，以及數字涉及小數或公制單位。

f. 當作編號系列時，用大寫數字或字母表示一個具體的編號系列。例如，這是第十一章指南 11 的項目 f（Item f under Guideline 11 in Chapter 11 中的 I、G、C 是大寫）。

g. 當數字是句子中的第一個詞或詞組，請用國字，如，「七十五個參與者被訪問了……」。有時句子可以被重寫而使數字不在句首。例如：「研究員訪問了 75 個參與者……」。

>>> 指南１２：為文獻探討寫一個簡潔和描述性的標題

文獻探討的標題應該要能定義你調查的學科領域以及告訴讀者你的觀點。然而，它應該也是要精確地描述你所編寫的報告。一般來說，標題不應該只注重於本身的描寫，而是應該幫助讀者採取適當的架構，用以閱讀您的報告。以下建議將幫助你避免出現一些標題中常見的問題。

a. 定義領域，但不完全描述它。特別是冗長和複雜的文獻探討，設法描述你論據的每個方面是不可行的。如果這樣做，其結果將是一個過於冗長而詳細的標題。你的標題應該引導讀者容易了解你的報告。它不應該是迫使讀者為了解讀它而停頓。

b. 明確說明你考慮的傾向、定位或定界。如果你的文獻探討是寫於可

識別的傾向、定位或定界，它可能需要指定出它的主題。例如，如果你對文獻的某些方面要做批判，可以考慮使用片語，如「批判……」或「一個批判的評價……」作為部分的標題。副標題往往可以有效地用於這一目的。例如，「墮胎政策：質性研究的探討」有一個副標題，指出探討所劃定的是質性研究的界限。

c. 避免「令人感到戲謔的」標題。避免雙關語，或者其他非學術的引用來降低標題的可看性。雖然像「音意對照『隱含的』語言」的標題看似聰明，如果你的文獻探討是對閱讀指導的整個語言方法的評論，那它可能會使讀者分散注意力。一個更加清楚表白的標題，例如「閱讀如同語言溝通的自然或不自然產物」，將讓讀者在理解你的論文時有一個更好的開始。

d. 標題保持簡短。標題應該簡短和切要。為了使目錄中的數百個子標題變得容易閱讀，專業作者經常限制提議的標題字數大約為九個。當學期論文或章節標題沒有這樣的字數限制時，盡可能設法保持你的評論標題又簡單又短，仍然是可行的。一個良好的基本原則是大約十個字上下加減三個字的標題。

>>> 指南 13：嘗試寫一份容易閱讀的草稿

你應該將你的初稿看成是論文寫作的過程。同樣地，應該請讀者評論的方法來編排它。因此，它應該是易讀和使用讓讀者容易聯想到你的想法的方式。以下列出確保你的草稿是容易閱讀的一些建議。請求你的指導教授評論這份表單，並增加其他的適當項目。

a. 拼寫檢查、校對、編輯你的原稿。新的文書處理軟體有拼寫檢查功能。在請求任何人讀你的論文之前，使用拼寫檢查功能。然而，這是一個不是很仔細審視原稿的方式，特別是因為拼寫檢查功能會忽略一些你的錯誤，例如，「看」（see）和「海」（sea）拼字都是正確的，但如果你錯誤地將它們中的一個字母打成另一個字母，拼寫

檢查功能不會強調它們為錯誤的。切記你的目標應該是有一篇容易傳達內容、且不會因為粗心的錯誤使讀者分心的正確無誤的論文。

b. 所有頁數加上頁碼。教授除了在頁邊空白寫下注解外，有時還用表格或便條寫下一些評論。頁面若沒有頁碼，會更難以撰寫評論，因為教授無法在便條上提及頁碼。

c. 草稿使用雙行間距。單行間距的文件使讀者難以寫下具體意見或建議替代的措辭。

d. 使用寬邊界。窄的邊界也許節省紙張，但它們縮小了你的指導教授表達意見可使用的空間大小。

e. 使用釘書機或長尾夾固定草稿。你的草稿是你的指導教授將閱讀的許多論文中的一份。用釘書機或長尾夾固定草稿，將使你的草稿易於保持完整。如果你使用一個文件夾或黏合劑固定你的草稿，請確保它能攤平的打開。無法平整打開的塑膠資料夾會使得教授（或編輯）難以在頁面邊緣寫下意見。

f. 註明自己是撰寫者，且包括電話號碼或電子信箱。由於你的草稿是你的指導教授將要閱讀的許多論文中的一份，所以註記自己為撰寫者是重要的。製作含有以你的名字和電話號碼或者電子信箱的一張封面，以防萬一你的教授想要與你聯繫。如果你是以文學探討作為學期論文，一定要說明課程編號和標題以及日期。

g. 確定草稿列印清楚。一般情況下，你應該避免使用有色帶的印表機，除非你確定列印內容是夠黑，且足以讓它能舒適地被閱讀。同樣，如果你遞交你的草稿影本，確定影本是夠黑的，並拷貝一份作為備份！因為學生論文有時會誤置，而且電腦的硬碟有時損壞。

h. 避免「過於可愛」的一面。一般情況下，對於想要強調的文字你應該避免使用彩色字體（用斜體字代替），或是混合不同的字體大小（除了標題，從頭到尾使用同樣的字體大小），這些會使讀者分散注意於論文表面的呈現。

>>>指南 14：謹慎小心避免抄襲

　　如果你不確定如何算構成抄襲，請參考你大學的論文規範。它通常在部分大學的網頁主目錄，而且學生可以從幾個容易取得的其他來源得知。例如，華盛頓大學心理學寫作中心在它的網站 http://depts.washington.edu/psywc/中，列出了有效防止抄襲與學生寫作原則的免費分享資料。在首頁，點擊 "Handouts"，會連接到 PDF 格式資料列表的頁面。在 "About Plagiarism" 標題底下，你會發現一份大學學術委員會編纂的學術責任聲明（Committee on Academic Conduct）（1994）[1]，其中談論了抄襲的六個類型。

(1)使用其他作者的文字而沒有適當的引用；

(2)使用其他作者的概念而沒有適當的引用；

(3)引用來源但複製引用出處精確的文字卻沒有引用的標記；

(4)借用其他作者片語或句子的結構卻沒有標示從何作者而來；

(5)借用其他作者全部或部分的論文或使用別人的大綱來撰寫自己的論文；

(6)使用坊間的論文寫作服務或請朋友為你寫作論文。（p. 23）

　　論文的爭論很容易出現，借用一樣的一個或兩個詞是否構成抄襲是容易引起爭論的，或「概念」是否真正的屬於作者。然而，簡單的標示你的引用來源，便很容易避免抄襲的指責。

>>>指南 15：有需要請尋求協助

　　顯然地，從本章的內容可知，在學術寫作上對正確性和準確性的期待相當高。如果你認為論文的文字上無法達到這些要求，你可能需要別人的

1　Committee on Academic Conduct. (1994). *Bachelor's degree handbook*. University of Washington.

Writing Literature Reviews: A Guide for Students of the Social and Behavioral Sciences

幫助。經常勸告國際學生雇用校對員幫助他們去達到指導教授的期望。多
數大學透過英語系或在其他學科提供寫作課程。一些學校為寫作碩士論文
或博士論文有需求的學生提供研討會，而且許多大學有為學生提供各式各
樣服務的寫作中心。如果你覺得你需要幫助，可以與你的指導教授談論有
關你的大學中可利用的服務。你不應該期望你的指導教授編輯論文的格式
和制式化。

 ## 第 11 章的活動

1. 檢視位於本書末的文獻探討範本的標題
   - 確認文獻探討領域的每個標題是否適用？
   - 文章的標題是否明確表達作者在文獻探討中的觀點？
2. 現在考慮你自己文獻探討的初稿。
   - 將你的初稿和你準備的主題大綱做比較。它們是否相吻合？如果沒有，
     你的草稿在哪裡偏離了大綱？這變化是否影響你文獻探討的「論據」？
   - 在你的文獻探討中發現二個或三個地方是你的討論跳到你的主題大綱的
     下個主要類目。讀者如何知道你改變了一個新的類目（即，你是否使用
     小標題或轉折去表示轉換）？

如何撰寫文獻探討
給社會暨行為科學學生指南

Writing Literature Reviews: A Guide for Students of the Social and Behavioral Sciences

整合回饋和精緻化初稿

目前在寫作初稿的過程中，你已完成了你文獻探討批判的大部分。然而，你的工作尚未完成。現在應該專注在最後的重要步驟——重寫你的探討過程。

初次寫作的人經常在這一階段犯錯，因為他們預期可以非常個人化的採取片斷的公平觀點。在先前的階段中，作為一個作者，你是能夠分析、評價和綜合其他作者的報告的人。現在，你的草稿是你自己和你的讀者分析和評價的主題。這不是一項容易的任務，但是它是在撰寫有效（effective）的文獻探討中重要和必要的下一個步驟。

第一步是伴隨角色互換把原稿放到一邊一段時間，從而在原稿和你這個作家的角色中製造一段距離。其次，提醒自己寫作過程是持續的在作者和意欲的觀眾之間協商。這就是為什麼角色互換是很重要的。你應該從現在起找一位願意閱讀和了解論證的人商量你的初稿。

重整的過程典型地牽涉評價和整合回饋。回饋也許來自指導教授和你的同儕，或者它可以來自你自己試圖去精緻和修正你自己的初稿。如果你寫文獻探討是為了作為學期報告，在寫作過程中，請你的指導教授在關鍵點給予嚴格回饋，或在拜訪辦公室時談論你的想法，如果你的指導教授有意願，可以藉由遞交初稿審查意見。如果它是碩士論文或博士論文，你最早的回饋將是來自你的指導教授，雖然你也可以考慮請同學和同事給予意

見。如果文獻探討是為了供出版使用，你應該從指導教授、同學和同事尋找回饋。

作為一個作者，你應該決定哪些評論是你將要整合的，而哪些是你將要修改的。你從這些各式各樣的來源接受的回饋，將提供你有價值的訊息以改進你的想法。以下指南是設計來幫助你完成這個過程。

>>>指南 1：讀者總是對的

這條指南故意誇張些好引起你對它的注意力，因為它是在重整過程中最重要的一環。如果一個受過教育的讀者不了解你的觀點，傳達便無法運作。所以，你應該慎重考慮改變初稿使其能為讀者所了解。捍衛初稿的原稿，經常獲得反效果。反過來說，你應該設法了解為什麼讀者不了解它。你是否在分析犯了錯？你是否提供不足的背景資料？是否在每一段落中增加更明確的轉變？這些問題和其他類似的問題，應該能引導你與你選擇要提供回饋的讀者進行討論。

>>>指南 2：期望你的指導教授在內容上做審查

及早重整你的原稿內容（content），以獲得你指導教授的回饋，對你是很重要的。如果你的初稿包含了許多格式和制式化錯誤，例如拼錯或誤置標題，你的指導教授會覺得不得不將焦點放在這些問題上而延緩對內容的審查，直到原稿更加容易閱讀為止。

>>>指南 3：首先關注有關你觀點的評論

如前兩個指南的建議，在這個階段你的優先考慮應該是去確認你的想法如你所預期的出現。當然，你最後應該注意關於文體的事，但你的第一要務應該是再確認你傳達了你發展的論證。因此，你需要仔細評估你從所有資源中（你同學和你指導教授）所收到的回饋，因為在這個階段中，你需要關注你的成果，以確信你的報告有效地和正確地傳達你的想法（在下

個章節包括一些關於格式、語言用法和文法的重要事情）。

>>> 指南 4：藉由尋找說明來調解相互矛盾的回饋

你可能遇到不同的意見，這些意見來自審查你初稿文件的那些人。例如，碩士論文或博士論文委員會的口試委員給你矛盾的回饋，這很正常。一名口試委員也許要求你提供關於研究的額外細節，但另一名口試委員也許要你不去強調它。如果你遇到這樣不同的意見，你的責任是從兩個來源尋求進一步說明，以協商爭論的決議。首先，確認不同的觀點並非出於一人的疏於了解你的論證。其次，與兩方討論事情且達到妥協。

>>> 指南 5：用你的格式手冊調解有關格式的評論

確認你已仔細地審查你的寫作工作所要求的論文格式。如果你最早的學術寫作經驗是在一門英語系課程中，你也許被訓練使用現代語文學會（Modern Language Association）出版的格式手冊[1]。許多大學圖書館建議碩士論文和博士論文遵守芝加哥大學格式手冊（University of Chicago style manual）[2]。然而，在社會和行為科學中，最被廣泛使用的是美國心理學會（American Psychological Association）的格式手冊[3]。如果你正準備出版一篇論文，在投稿前，先檢查期刊或出版社特定的格式。最後，許多學術部門和學校將有他們自己所注重的格式。不管你的寫作工作有關哪個格式手冊，切記萬般留意你的作品。當你考慮整合你接受的所有回饋，確信它依照格式手冊的要求。

---

[1] Gibaldi, J. (1998). *MLA style manual and guide to scholarly publishing* (2nd ed.). New York: Modern Language Association of America.

[2] University of Chicago Press. (2003). *The Chicago manual of style* (15th ed.). Chicago: University of Chicago Press.

[3] American Psychological Association. (2001). *Publication manual of the American Psychological Association* (5th ed.). Washington, DC: American Psychological Association.

>>>指南 6：多花一點時間在回饋和重整過程

　　當學生在固定期限內要對主要結構或內容有所修正時，學生經常感到挫折。你要預期必須準備至少改寫一次文獻探討初稿，為此你應該多給自己一點時間。專業作者認為一個文件成為一份定稿前，他們至少要經過三次或更多次地修改初稿。當你無法有相當多初稿時，你應該騰出足夠的時間去輕鬆地反覆自我修改文章。

 # 第 12 章的活動

1. 要求兩個朋友讀你的文獻探討的初稿並評論其內容。再來比較他們的評論。
   - 你的朋友同意哪些論點？
   - 他們不同意哪些論點？兩方的觀點，你將跟隨哪一方？為什麼？
   - 在你的文獻探討中有哪些地方是你的朋友難以理解的。重寫這些段落，讓你的朋友了解你的觀點。

2. 設計五個問題以引導你的指導教授或你的朋友在你的文獻探討中給你回饋。
   - 再讀你的文獻探討初稿，並且假裝你是自己的指導教授，來反詰你自己的問題。
   - 根據你自己的回饋修訂初稿。
   - 反思你為你的指導教授或朋友寫下的五個問題。你會在名單留下哪些問題？你會增加什麼問題？

最後定稿的綜合自編檢核表

最後的完稿無論是內容與制式格式，這兩方面都必須盡可能的要求精確與零錯誤。當你已經謹慎思慮過同儕與指導教授的回饋，以及按照他們的意見校訂原稿後，到此最後階段，你也需要細心的編撰文章。最終的審閱目的只有一個，就是要精準。

下文列出的檢核表細目，是依照指導老師們用來評定學生寫作的主要標準所綜合而得的。當撰寫一篇碩士或博士論文時，大部分的標準是相當具批判性的。不過，在撰寫學期中的學期報告時，你的指導教授或許會放寬部分的標準。

你將會發現多數的檢核表細目已經在前幾章的指南中陳述過。但是許多附加的細目，則涉及一些學生有時會忽略的普遍性問題。你可以與指導教授討論這個檢核表，並依其意見增刪細目。

請牢記，設計這個檢核表格的目的在協助你修訂原稿。最後，你如何仔細的編修你的作品，將會影響它好壞的程度。

在編撰與改寫文章的過程中的堅持

_____ 1. 你是否請指導老師審閱這張檢核表，並且依照其意見增刪一些細目？

_____ 2. 完成最終的草稿後，在進行修訂前，你是否將原稿置放數天（也就是說，從寫作者的角色跳脫至閱讀者的角色時，你是否**遠離**你的研究）？

_____ 3. 你是否請第三人審閱原稿？

_____ 4. 對於檢閱者提出的問題你都處理過了嗎？

_____ 5. 你已經對檢閱者間意見的歧異求得平衡？

主題的重要性與意涵

_____ 6. 無論是從理論或是實務觀點，你的主題重要嗎？

_____ 7. 它是創新的觀點或是發現到文獻上的缺口（也就是說，它提出的問題不是以前提過的）嗎？

_____ 8. 你主題的意涵或重要性，是可以明白顯示及證明的嗎？

_____ 9. 在你的研究領域中，這是適當的主題嗎？

_____ 10. 從研究文獻中，這方面主題是適時的嗎？

_____ 11. 在審閱主題後，原稿的篇名能充分顯示你的研究嗎？

組織與其他全面性思量

_____ 12. 你的審閱包含緒論、討論和結論嗎？

_____ 13. 包含文獻參考清單嗎？

_____ 14. 你文章的長度和組織有遵守以下各方的規定嗎：(1)指導老師，如果是學期報告；(2)委員會主持人，如果是寫碩士或博士論文；(3)你預備投稿的期刊公開體例，如果你的寫作是為了某本刊物？

緒論的效度

_____ 15. 你的緒論充分描述了你閱讀過的文獻範圍和主題的重點嗎？

_____ 16. 緒論中有充分描述整篇研究報告的大綱嗎？

_____ 17. 在文章中，緒論是否沿著立論的軌跡描述？

_____ 18. 如果文章是適當的，緒論是否提出哪些部分被論及哪些部分未被論及？

_____ 19. 如果文章是有意義的，緒論是否有呈現出專題的論點及意見的特色嗎？

參考文獻的近期性與相關性

_____ 20. 你讀過這個主題最近期的文獻了嗎？

_____ 21. 你讀的研究文獻是近期的嗎？

_____ 22. 如果你包含了較舊的文獻，你有包含它們的合理理由嗎？

_____ 23. 你有解釋為何某些發現是權威的嗎？

_____ 24. 你有解釋為何其他發現是薄弱的嗎？

_____ 25. 你在文獻中有發現某些重要的模式或趨勢嗎？

_____ 26. 在你的文稿中有發現或舉證出經典或是標竿性的研究嗎？

_____ 27. 你有具體說明這些經典研究與其後所影響的研究之間的關係嗎？

文獻探討的完整性與正確性

_____ 28. 你的評論包含的範圍是適當的嗎？

_____ 29. 你有注意到解釋文獻的落差嗎？

_____ 30. 你有描述此領域中任何有關的爭議之處嗎？

_____31. 如果第 30 題你回答「是」，你有釐清哪些研究是反對此爭議的嗎？

_____32. 你有檢查文獻中哪些是類似的嗎？

_____33. 你有注意到和解釋研究間的關係，例如哪些先發現？哪些有相似之處？哪些有不同之處？

_____34. 你有指出關鍵字或概念的出處嗎？

_____35. 你的文稿正文中有沒有遺漏之處？

論證的連貫性

_____36. 你論證中的每個研究都能具體的符合你主題的要點嗎？

_____37. 你已經刪除了與本研究無關的參考文獻嗎？

_____38. 在整篇文稿中，你的論證軌跡是明瞭易懂的嗎？

_____39. 你的評論是否有邏輯可循？

_____40. 如果你使用「後設意見」（見第十章，指南 6），它們是重要的嗎？

_____41. 如果你使用副標題，副標題對你的論證有幫助嗎？

_____42. 如果你沒有用副標題，你會用副標題來改良你的論證嗎？

_____43. 你的文稿是否有連貫性？或者額外轉換的聲明來協助澄清其相關程度？

結論的效度

_____44. 你的結論為讀者提供結果討論嗎？

_____45. 你的結論有涉及緒論中所詳列的論點嗎？

參考文獻的正確性

_____46. 你有檢查參考文獻的文體格式嗎（如，哪時用括弧，如何引用多位作者，和如何寫二手資料）？

_____47. 你檢查過文章中每個文獻的引用都已在最後的文獻清單中出現？

_____48. 你已經檢查過最後的文獻清單在正文中都有出現嗎？

_____49. 你已經把沒有引用的參考文獻項目刪去了嗎？

_____50. 你已經檢查過文稿與文獻清單的正確性與一致性了嗎？

_____51. 你已經檢查過文稿與文獻清單的作者名稱的拼寫了嗎？

_____52. 包含在文獻清單中的大多數研究是最近的嗎？

文稿中的制式化和全面正確性

_____53. 你仔細閱讀及編輯文稿了嗎？

_____54. 你檢查過整份文章中的拼寫了嗎？

_____55. 你的頁邊空白合適嗎？

_____56. 你有編頁碼嗎？

_____57. 你的文章是雙行間距嗎？

_____58. 你有寫全名嗎（而且在碩士和博士論文中，你有留下電話號碼或電子信箱）？

格式及語言使用的適合性

_____59. 你仔細審閱過此領域中適合的格式手冊了嗎？

_____60. 你檢查過你的原稿與格式手冊的一致性了嗎？

_____61. 你的文章標題符合格式手冊的要求嗎？

_____ 62. 如果你用的是拉丁文縮寫（i.e., e.g., etc.），它們是括在括弧裡的嗎？且你有檢查所需要的標點符號嗎？

_____ 63. 如果你使用的是較長的引文，它確定是必需的嗎？

_____ 64. 每個引文明顯的對此論證是有所助益的嗎？

_____ 65. 可以將這些引文改寫嗎？

_____ 66. 你避免使用到重要關鍵字和概念的同義字了嗎？

_____ 67. 如果你自創了新字，它有加引號嗎？

_____ 68. 你有避免使用俚語、口語及方言嗎？

_____ 69. 你有避免使用縮寫嗎？

_____ 70. 你註記了某個與論述無關的結論注解嗎？

_____ 71. 你避免使用一系列的注解嗎？

_____ 72. 第一次提到這些縮寫字的時候，它們有全被拼出來嗎？

_____ 73. 如果你用了第一人稱，是合適的嗎？

_____ 74. 你是否避免使用性別歧視的字眼？

_____ 75. 如果文章中用到數字的寫法，你確定寫出了國字零至九嗎？

_____ 76. 如果你使用的名詞後面緊接著數字來代表序列中的某個特別位置，你有把該名詞大寫嗎？

_____ 77. 如果數字放在句首，數字是用國字嗎？

文法的精確

_____ 78. 你檢查過文法的正確性了嗎？

_____ 79. 你的文句是完整的嗎？

_____ 80. 你有避免使用間接句的結構嗎（例如：「在 Galvan 的研究中，發現了它……」）？

_____ 81. 在用詞的時態上是一致的嗎（也就是說，如果你在描述某個研究的發現用的是現在式，你是整篇文章都用現在式，除非你是評論

這些研究上歷史的關係）？

_____ 82. 你檢查過逗號和其他標點符號的使用是適宜的嗎？

_____ 83. 你企圖避免使用完整的文句結構？

_____ 84. 如果你有較長的文句（例如：幾行），你企圖把它們分成兩句或數句嗎？

_____ 85. 如果你有較長的段落（例如：一頁或更長），你企圖把它們分成兩段或數段嗎？

專為非母語的使用者與學生增列編輯步驟

_____ 86. 如果你的英文不是很好，有尋求校對者的協助嗎？

_____ 87. 你有檢查過文章中冠詞（例如：a、an、the）的用法嗎？

_____ 88. 你有檢查過文章中介系詞的用法嗎？

_____ 89. 你檢查過句子中的主詞與動詞是一致的嗎？

_____ 90. 你檢查過文章中解釋慣用語的用法嗎？

指導教授的建議

_____ 91. _____

_____ 92. _____

_____ 93. _____

_____ 94. _____

_____ 95. _____

如何撰寫文獻探討
給社會暨行為科學學生指南

Writing Literature Reviews: A Guide for Students of the Social and Behavioral Sciences

文獻探討範本的討論和評論

MODEL LITERATURE REVIEW A

Maintaining Change Following Eating Disorder Treatment[1]

One of your eating disorder clients is nearing her date of discharge, and she tells you that she is worried about being able to maintain the changes that she worked so hard to make during her admission. She tells you that her family and friends also worry that she may relapse. You suggest that she keep a log of her thoughts and feelings in a journal, use the coping skills she has developed in the program, follow her meal plan, maintain appointments with her therapist, and join a support group in the community. However, deep down you share the uncertainty about her ability to choose non-eating disorder coping strategies when her distress level runs high. You consider keeping her in the program longer, but even if this were feasible, you are aware that this may simply delay the inevitable. Is there anything that you can do to help her with this inherently destabilizing transition? Is there anything that you can say to help her maintain the changes she has made? Is there anything that you can recommend to outpatient practitioners who will provide her with follow-up care?

There is a growing body of research investigating ways to enhance readiness to change eating disorder behaviors (Cockell, Geller, & Linden, 2002, 2003; Geller, Williams, & Srikameswaran, 2001; Treasure & Schmidt, 2001; Vitousek, Watson, & Wilson, 1998), but relatively little attention has been given to an equally important topic—how to promote the maintenance of change once it has been achieved. Learning more about this critical phase of change is important, as relapse rates in eating disorders are reported to range from 33% to 63% (Field et al., 1997; Herzog et al., 1999; Keel & Mitchell, 1997; Olmstead, Kaplan, & Rockert, 1994), and repeated admissions to treatment programs are common (Woodside, Kohn, & Kerr, 1998).

High relapse and readmission rates are understandable when the challenges of treating eating disorders are acknowledged. First, eating disorders have a tremendous impact on physical, psychological, and social systems, all of which need to be considered when working with clients. Accordingly, many physicians welcome collaboration with psychologists and other mental health professionals because they recognize that medical interventions alone do not address the powerful psychological underpinnings of the disorder. Likewise, nonmedical professionals often seek permission to consult with a client's general practitioner, because they recognize that some of the presenting symptoms (e.g., fatigue, sleep disturbance, cognitive impairment, obsessive thinking) can be explained best by malnutrition and that the malnutrition needs to be closely monitored and addressed. The coordination of medical and nonmedical treatment is not always available, however, and as a result, clients receive less than optimal interventions, which may account for poor prognosis.

Second, most individuals with eating disorders present with multiple problems. For instance, many clients report comorbid depressive, anxiety, and/or substance abuse disorders, and some report self-harm and/or suicidal ideation. These individuals may also have rigid interpersonal styles (e.g., passive, dependent, borderline) and defense strategies (e.g., magnification, minimization, displacement of emotions onto the body) that support their eating disorders. At a deeper level, core beliefs (e.g., I am not good enough; something is wrong with me; I never fit in) and difficult life experiences that have contributed to the development of these beliefs need to be addressed. Given these issues, it is not surprising that recovery from an eating disorder takes a great deal of time and commitment (Strober, Freeman, & Morrell, 1997). The unfortunate reality, however, is that intensive treatment programs tend to be time limited, and even when longer periods of treatment are available, clients often have trouble completing the treatment.

Third, individuals with eating disorders tend to be ambivalent about treatment and recovery. This is not surprising given that the eating disorder often represents an individual's best attempt to cope. Many negative consequences may be identified, but the functional value of the eating disorder tends to outweigh the cost. Each person's reasons for engaging in eating disorder behaviors vary, but there seems to be a general theme of avoidance coping. Typical areas of avoidance include thoughts and feelings related to difficult early life experiences, as well as current intra- and interpersonal conflict and distress (Cockell et al., 2003). Thus, recovery requires not only developing new ways of thinking and behaving in relation to eating, shape, and weight, but addressing core issues with new coping strategies. When one takes these various

---

[1] Literature review excerpt from: Cockell, S. J., Zaitsoff, S. L., & Geller, J. (2004). Maintaining change following eating disorder treatment. *Professional Psychology: Research and Practice*, 35, 527–534. Copyright © 2004 by the American Psychological Association. All rights reserved. Reprinted with permission.

factors into consideration, it is not surprising that the
95　process of recovery is often slow and bumpy.

What Supports Recovery?

Although recovery from an eating disorder is an
enormous challenge, many individuals do attain partial
or full recovery. For instance, in one of the more comprehensive assessments of treatment outcome, Strober
100　et al. (1997) found that 76% of individuals were free
of the physical and cognitive-behavioral signs of their
eating disorder at completion of follow-up, some 10 to
15 years after initial assessment for specialized treatment. It is important to note, however, that the process
105　toward both partial and full recovery is protracted.
Although eating disorder symptoms are reduced by the
end of treatment, the probabilities of partial or full
recovery are only 10% and 0%, respectively, 2 years
following hospitalization, and they are 21% and 1%,
110　respectively, at the end of 3 years. At the end of 4
years, recovery rates rise and continue to accelerate
fairly steadily until 6 years follow-up, at which point
they decelerate. Rates then rise again after 8 years and
finally reach a plateau after 10 years (Strober et al.,
115　1997).

While it is well-understood that the course of recovery from an eating disorder is slow, what remains
unclear is an understanding of what factors support a
favorable outcome. A small number of published
120　qualitative studies have assessed factors that assist
clients in their recovery process (Beresin, Gordon, &
Herzog, 1989; Hsu, Crisp, & Callender, 1992; Pettersen & Rosenvinge, 2002; Rorty, Yager, & Rossotto,
1993). Participants in these studies had a past diagno-
125　sis of anorexia nervosa or bulimia nervosa, and assessments were conducted between 1 and 20 years
posttreatment. With the exception of one study (Hsu et
al., 1992), semistructured interviews were audiotaped
and transcribed, and responses were coded according
130　to a categorical system developed by author consensus.
Two general findings emerged from these studies.
First, social support from professionals, family, and
friends was identified as helpful in maintaining recovery behaviors. Having the opportunity to identify and
135　express feelings and to receive empathic, nonjudgmen-
tal responses was said to promote movement toward
health. Connecting with individuals who had recovered was reported to be particularly helpful, as this
contact generated feelings of acceptance and provided
140　hope for the future (Beresin et al., 1989; Pettersen &
Rosenvinge, 2002; Rorty et al., 1993). Second, experiences that increased positive emotions and self-esteem
were identified as helpful in maintaining change. Clients noted that these positive experiences nurtured an
145　identity separate from the eating disorder, which in
turn supported recovery behaviors (Beresin et al.,

1989; Hsu et al., 1992; Pettersen & Rosenvinge, 2002;
Rorty et al., 1993).

150　In the most thorough study to date, 30 women
(17 recovered, 13 partially recovered) who had received treatment for bulimia nervosa participated in
qualitative interviews (Peters & Fallon, 1994). Their
responses were coded according to content, sorted by
155　computer, and analyzed for themes and response patterns. Levels of recovery ranged along three continua
from denial, alienation, and passivity at one end to
reality, connection, and personal power, respectively,
at the other. The continuum from denial to reality re-
160　flected the cognitive and emotional shifts that occur in
response to eating and appearance issues. This included challenging distorted beliefs about nutrition
and evaluating shape and weight more accurately. The
continuum from alienation to connection reflected an
165　improvement in communication and relationships.
This included talking openly about the eating disorder,
being assertive in social situations, and taking on new
interpersonal roles. The continuum from passivity to
personal power reflected an increasing sense of capa-
170　bility to change and control one's future. These findings intuitively fit well with those identified in other
relevant studies. For instance, the ability to connect
with others is likely related to the establishment of
social supports, and personal power is likely related to
175　positive emotions, self-esteem enhancement, and identity development. Moreover, these findings add to the
literature by suggesting how these factors promote
recovery. This focus on the process of change and
maintenance merits further investigation and discus-
180　sion, particularly in the context of generating clinical
practice guidelines for professionals working with
clients who are in the later stages of change (see the
transtheoretical model of change; Prochaska, Di-
Clemente, & Norcross, 1992).

What Hinders Recovery?

We found two published qualitative studies of
185　factors that interfered with recovery. In a study of 40
women who had recovered from bulimia nervosa, a
lack of understanding from partners, friends, or family
and societal insensitivity to eating disorders were identified as barriers to recovery (Rorty et al., 1993). Simi-
190　larly, a study of 13 women who had recovered from
anorexia nervosa also identified lack of social support
as an impediment to recovery (Beresin et al., 1989).
This second study revealed a number of other factors
that interfered with recovery, including the following:
195　(a) spending too much time in therapy focusing on
parent shortcomings and related angry feelings, as
opposed to understanding parent limitations and working toward forgiveness; (b) being told covertly or ex-
plicitly how to appear, feel, or think; (c) comparing
200　oneself to other "skeletons" and competing for the role

of most impaired; and (d) learning bad habits (e.g., water loading before being weighed, purging techniques) from fellow patients. Given the lack of research in this area, replication studies are needed to assess the extent to which these findings generalize to other samples and can be incorporated into professional practice recommendations.

In summary, although few research studies have examined the maintenance of change in eating disorders, a few findings are noteworthy. Three factors are consistently mentioned as helpful in promoting lasting change: (a) social factors, including adopting an assertive style and establishing effective social supports; (b) cognitive factors, including challenging core beliefs about eating, shape, and weight; and (c) affective factors, including enhancing positive emotions, especially a sense of empowerment and hope for the future. The only factor consistently identified as impeding recovery is lack of effective social support. The extent to which these findings apply to clients who have recently completed treatment is not known. However, the answer to this question has great clinical value because the period immediately following discharge has been identified as challenging (Fichter & Quadflieg, 1996; Herzog et al., 1999; Olmstead et al., 1994; Woodside et al., 1998) and a time when individuals are most prone to slips and relapse (Strober et al., 1997). The purpose of this study was to identify factors that help or hinder the maintenance of change and the ongoing promotion of recovery during the critical 6 months immediately following eating disorder treatment. The use of qualitative methodology was selected so that a highly detailed account of clients' phenomenological experiences could be obtained and examined.

References

Beresin, E. V., Gordon, C., & Herzog, D. B. (1989). The process of recovering from anorexia nervosa. *Journal of the American Academy of Psychoanalysis, 17*, 103–130.

Cockell, S. J., Geller, J., & Linden, W. (2002). The development of a decisional balance scale for anorexia nervosa. *European Eating Disorders Review, 10*, 359–375.

Cockell, S. J., Geller, J., & Linden, W. (2003). Decisional balance in anorexia nervosa: Capitalizing on the ambivalence. *European Eating Disorders Review, 11*, 75–89.

Fichter, M. M., & Quadflieg, N. (1996). Course and two-year outcome in anorexic and bulimic adolescents. *Journal of Youth and Adolescence, 25*, 545–562.

Field, A. E., Herzog, D. B., Keller, M. B., West, J., Nussbaum, K., & Colditz, G. A. (1997). Distinguishing recovery from remission in a cohort of bulimic women: How should asymptomatic periods be described? *Journal of Clinical Epidemiology, 50*, 1339–1345.

Geller, J., Williams, K., & Srikameswaran, S. (2001). Clinician stance in the treatment of chronic eating disorders. *European Eating Disorders Review, 9*, 365–373.

Herzog, D. B., Dorer, D. J., Keel, P. K., Selwyn, S. E., Ekeblad, E. R., Flores, A. T. et al. (1999). Recovery and relapse in anorexia and bulimia nervosa: A 7.5 year follow-up study. *Journal of the American Academy of Child and Adolescent Psychiatry, 38*, 829–837.

Hsu, L., Crisp, A. H., & Callender, J. S. (1992). Recovery in anorexia nervosa: The patient's perspective. *International Journal of Eating Disorders, 11*, 341–350.

Keel, P. K., & Mitchell, J. E. (1997). Outcome in bulimia nervosa. *American Journal of Psychiatry, 154*, 313–321.

Olmstead, M. P., Kaplan, A. S., & Rockert, W. (1994). Rate and prediction of relapse in bulimia nervosa. *American Journal of Psychiatry, 151*, 738–743.

Peters, L., & Fallon, P. (1994). The journey of recovery: Dimensions of change. In P. Fallon, M. Katzman, & S. Wooley (Eds.), *Feminist perspectives on eating disorders* (pp. 339–354). New York: Guilford Press.

Pettersen, G., & Rosenvinge, J. H. (2002). Improvement and recovery from eating disorders: A patient perspective. *Eating Disorders: The Journal of Treatment and Prevention, 10*, 61–71.

Prochaska, J. O., DiClemente, C. C., & Norcross, J. C. (1992). In search of how people change. *American Psychologist, 47*, 1102–1114.

Rorty, M., Yager, J., & Rossotto, E. (1993). Why and how do women recover from bulimia nervosa? The subjective appraisals of forty women recovered for a year or more. *International Journal of Eating Disorders, 14*, 249–260.

Strober, M., Freeman, R., & Morrell, W. (1997). The long-term course of severe anorexia nervosa in adolescence: Survival analysis of recovery, relapse, and outcome predictors over 10–15 years in a prospective study. *International Journal of Eating Disorders, 22*, 339–360.

Treasure, J., & Schmidt, U. (2001). Ready, willing and able to change: Motivational aspects of the assessment and treatment of eating disorders. *European Eating Disorders Review, 9*, 4–18.

Vitousek, K. B., Watson, S., & Wilson, G. T. (1998). Enhancing motivation for change in treatment-resistant eating disorders. *Clinical Psychology Review, 18*, 391–420.

Woodside, D. B., Kohn, M., & Kerr, A. (1998). Patterns of relapse and recovery following intensive treatment for eating disorders: A qualitative description. *Eating Disorders: The Journal of Treatment and Prevention, 6*, 231–239.

About the authors: Sarah J. Cockell received her PhD in clinical psychology in 2001 from the University of British Columbia. She is currently the coordinator of the Quest Program at the St. Paul's Hospital Eating Disorders Program in Vancouver, as well as working in private practice. Her current research interests are ambivalence about change, relapse prevention, eating disorders, and quality of life. Shannon L. Zaitsoff received her MA in child clinical psychology from the University of Windsor in Ontario. She is currently working on her PhD. Her current area of research is readiness and motivation for change in adolescents with eating disorders. Josie Geller received her PhD in clinical psychology from the University of British Columbia in 1996. She is currently the director of research at the St. Paul's Hospital Eating Disorders Program and an associate professor in the Department of Psychiatry at the University of British Columbia. Her current research interests are motivational interviewing, clinician stance, eating disorders, and HIV.

Acknowledgment: This research was supported by a grant from the British Columbia Health Research Foundation.

Address correspondence to: Sarah J. Cockell, c/o Eating Disorders Program, St. Paul's Hospital, 1081 Burrard Street, Vancouver, British Columbia, Canada, V6Z 1Y6. E-mail: scockell@ providencehealth.bc.ca

MODEL LITERATURE REVIEW B

Office versus Home-Based Family Therapy for Runaway, Alcohol-Abusing Adolescents: Examination of Factors Associated with Treatment Attendance[1]

Even when substance-abusing individuals contact a treatment system, early drop-out is a significant problem. Lawendowski (1998) suggested that adolescents tend to be more ambivalent and resistant to change. Indeed, Szapocznik, Perez-Vidal, Brickman, Foote, Santisteban, Hervis, and Kurtines (1988), in a study of treatment engagement, found that 62% of youth between the ages of 12 and 21 years refused to attend treatment sessions. Several studies have examined the relationship between age and dropout rates directly and some found evidence that, along the age continuum of substance abusers, youth is linked to higher treatment dropout rates (Ball, Lange, Meyers, & Friedman, 1988; Feigelman, 1987).

The general consensus is that runaway youth are difficult to engage and maintain in therapy (Morrissette, 1992; Smart & Ogborne, 1994) and are "difficult to work with" (Kufeldt & Nimmo, 1987). Given that treatment attendance is often a complicating factor for successful treatment outcome (Institute of Medicine, 1990), and that few studies have examined predictors of treatment attendance among runaway youth and their families, further research in this area is needed to help guide treatment providers. This paper examines factors associated with treatment attendance among alcohol-abusing runaway youth and their families utilizing a home-based versus office-based family therapy intervention.

Runaway youth are beset with many problems, including physical and sexual abuse, high levels of alcohol and drug use, depression, teen pregnancy, and frequent prostitution (Johnson, Aschkenasy, Herbers, & Gillenwater, 1996; Zimet, Sobo, Zimmerman, Jackson, Mortimer, Yanda, & Lazebnik, 1995). The alcohol abuse rate of runaway and homeless youths is estimated to range from 70% to 85% (Rotheram-Borus, Selfridge, Koopman, Haignere, Meyer-Bahlburg, & Ehrhardt, 1989; Shaffer & Caton, 1984; Yates, MacKenzie, Pennbridge, & Cohen, 1988), and the level of alcohol involvement in runaways is at least double that of school youths (Forst & Crim, 1994). Limited evidence suggests that rates of alcohol abuse are similar to rates reported among homeless adults (Robertson, 1989). Runaway and homeless youth use alcohol at a younger age and experience greater impaired social functioning owing to alcohol use compared to nonhomeless adolescents (Kipke, Montgomery, & MacKenzie, 1993). Even given their severe alcohol abuse and related problem behaviors, one study determined that only 15% of this population of youth had ever received treatment for alcohol problems (Robertson, 1989).

Research suggests that family disturbance is highly correlated to the act of running away; hence, family therapy is identified as an important treatment to evaluate with this population. Engaging parents in counseling is almost always advisable given their involvement in precipitating the running-away behavior (Rohr & James, 1994), an obvious role in reunification with their child. In fact, Teare, Furst, Peterson, and Authier (1992) found that in their sample of shelter youths, those not reunified with their family had higher levels of hopelessness, suicide ideation, and reported more family problems than those reunified. Youths' perceptions of family dysfunction were significantly associated with reunification and those not reunified were at greater risk of suicide, had more overall dissatisfaction with life, and more generalized negative expectations about the future.

Post and McCoard (1994) found that during a crisis, runaway youths and families may be more amenable than usual to counseling, and the need for intervention is intense, with the timing (when they have sought help at a shelter) critical. These researchers also noted that runaways who go to shelters, unlike many, are asking for help. Their reported greatest needs concerned living arrangements, family relationships, and communication with their parents.

Reviews of formal clinical trials of family-based treatments consistently found that more drug-abusing adolescents enter, engage in, and remain in family therapy longer than in other modalities (Liddle & Dakof, 1995; Waldron, 1997). However, few studies have directly compared family therapy models, making conclusions about the superiority of one approach over another difficult. Moreover, researchers have noted

---

[1] Literature review excerpt from: Slesnick, N., & Prestopnik, J. L. (2004). Office versus home-based family therapy for runaway, alcohol-abusing adolescents: Examination of factors associated with treatment attendance. *Alcoholism Treatment Quarterly, 22,* 3–19. Copyright © 2004 by The Haworth Press, Inc. All rights reserved. Reprinted with permission.

limited variation in theoretical orientation across models (Stanton & Shadish, 1997). For example, the vast majority of family-based interventions (i.e., traditional 145 approaches) for substance abuse problems focus on family interaction patterns and parenting behaviors as major targets of change. The two approaches examined in this paper include the office-based Functional Family Therapy (FFT) and Ecologically Based Family 150 Therapy (EBFT), which is conducted in the home.

Functional Family Therapy (FFT; Barton & Alexander, 1981; Alexander & Parsons, 1982) has a family systems conceptual base. Similar to other systems models, problems with alcohol and drugs are 155 viewed as behaviors which occur in the context of and have meaning for family relationships. FFT has received considerable research attention during the past 30 years. It was initially developed and empirically supported for crisis intervention with juvenile offend- 160 ers, including runaway adolescents and their families (Alexander, 1971). Alexander and his colleagues conducted several treatment outcome studies examining the effectiveness of FFT with runaway and status delinquents in reducing out-of-home placement, improv- 165 ing parent–child process, and reducing negativity using a 12-week format (Alexander, 1971; Alexander & Parsons, 1973; Barton, Alexander, Waldron, Turner, & Warburton, 1985). In these studies, FFT made significantly more improvements in adolescent and family functioning compared to individual therapy, a client-centered family therapy approach and a control group with minimal attention from probation officers.

EBFT is a multisystemic, home-based treatment based on the recognition that substance use and other related problem behaviors derive commonly from many sources of influence and occur in the context of multiple systems. It is based largely on family systems (Haley, 1976; Minuchin, 1974) conceptualizations of behavior, and behavior change. EBFT posits that behavior problems can be maintained by problematic transactions within any given system or between some combination of pertinent systems, including the intrapersonal system of the individual adolescent, the interpersonal systems of the family and peers, and the extra-personal systems of the shelter, juvenile justice system, school, and the community.

In-home therapy has been successful with families assessed as disorganized, chaotic, and with few resources (Henggeler, Borduin, Melton, Mann, Smith, Hall, Cone, & Fucci, 1991). Henggeler et al. (1991) noted that home-based interventions are particularly successful in facilitating treatment engagement of multiproblem youth. That is, working with the family in their home and in their neighborhood allows the assessment of multiple ecological influences impacting the adolescent and family. In-home sessions also allow the intervention to be perceived as a natural process

and enhances treatment engagement and acceptability (Henggeler et al., 1991; Joanning, Thomas, Quinn, & Millen, 1992; Kazdin, Stolar, & Marciano, 1995). A high percentage of missed or canceled office-based appointments occurs because a family does not have reliable transportation or because the meeting time conflicts with a parent's work schedule (Henggeler & Borduin, 1995). These authors note that a therapist's time is often used most efficiently when sessions are conducted in the family's home, as it is much easier for unmotivated families to ignore an appointment at a clinic than to ignore the therapist who knocks at their door at the scheduled time.

It is expected that treatment engagement and overall attendance will be significantly higher for families assigned to the home-based intervention, as it removes many barriers for chaotic and disadvantaged families that otherwise would preclude their attendance in the session, as noted by Henggeler et al. (1991). Thus, based upon the theoretical model of home-based therapy, we expected that lower income, more family chaos, and more adolescent problem behaviors (externalizing behaviors and substance use) would predict higher treatment attendance for the home-based compared to the office-based intervention.

References

Alexander, J. F. (1971). *Evaluation summary: Family groups treatment program.* Report to Juvenile Court, District 1, State of Utah, Salt Lake City.

Alexander, J. F., & Parsons, B. V. (1973). Short-term behavioral intervention with delinquent families: Impact on family process and recidivism. *Journal of Abnormal Psychology, 81,* 219–225.

Alexander, J. F., & Parsons, B. V. (1982). *Functional family therapy: Principles and procedures.* Carmel, CA: Brooks/Cole.

Ball, J. C., Lange, W. R., Meyers, C. P., & Friedman, S. R. (1988). Reducing the risk of AIDS through methadone maintenance treatment. *Journal of Health and Social Behavior, 29,* 214–226.

Barton, C., & Alexander, J. F. (1981). Functional family therapy. In A. S. Gurman & D. P. Kniskern (Eds.), *Handbook of family therapy* (pp. 403–443). New York: Brunner/Mazel.

Barton, C., Alexander, J. F., Waldron, H., Turner, C. W., & Warburton, J. (1985). Generalizing treatment effects of Functional Family Therapy: Three replications. *American Journal of Family Therapy, 17,* 335–347.

Feigelman, W. (1987). Day-care treatment for multiple drug abusing adolescents: Social factors linked with completing treatment. *Journal of Psychoactive Drugs, 19,* 335–344.

Forst, M. L., & Crim, D. (1994). A substance use profile of delinquent and homeless youths. *Journal of Drug Education, 24,* 219–231.

Haley, J. (1976). *Problem-solving therapy.* San Francisco: Jossey-Bass.

Henggeler, S. W., & Borduin, C. M. (1995). Multisystemic treatment of serious juvenile offenders and their families. In I. M. Scwartz and P. AuClaire (Eds.), *Home-based services for troubled children.* Lincoln: University of Nebraska Press.

Henggeler, S. W., Borduin, C. M., Melton, G. B., Mann, B. J., Smith L. A., Hall, J. A., Cone, L., & Fucci, B. R. (1991). Effects of multisystemic therapy on drug use and abuse in serious juvenile offenders: A progress report from two outcome studies. *Family Dynamics of Addiction Quarterly, 1,* 40–51.

Institute of Medicine (1990). *Treating drug problems (Vol. 1.).* Washington, DC: National Academy Press.

Joanning, H., Thomas, F., Quinn, W., & Millen, R. (1992). Treating adolescent drug abuse: A comparison of family systems therapy, group therapy, and family drug education. *Journal of Marital and Family Therapy, 18,* 345–356.

Johnson, T. P., Aschkenasy, J. R., Herbers, M. R., & Gillenwater, S. A. (1996). Self-reported risk factors for AIDS among homeless youth. *AIDS Education and Prevention, 8,* 308–322.

Kazdin, A. E., Stolar, M. J., Marciano, P. L. (1995). Risk factors for dropping out of treatment among white and black families. *Journal of Family Psy-*

chology: JFP: Journal of the Division of Family Psychology of the American Psychological Association (Division 43), 9, 402–416.

Kipke, M., Montgomery, S., & MacKenzie, R. (1993) Substance use among youth seen at a community-based health clinic. *Journal of Adolescent Health, 14*, 289–294.

Kufeldt, K., & Nimmo, M. (1987). Youth on the street: Abuse and neglect in the eighties. *Child Abuse and Neglect, 11*, 531–543.

Lawendowski, L. A. (1998). A motivational intervention for adolescent smokers. *Preventive Medicine, 27*, A39.

Liddle, H. A., & Dakof, G. A. (1995). Family-based treatment for adolescent drug use: State of the science. *NIDA Research Monograph, 156*, 218–254.

Minuchin, S. (1974). *Families and family therapy.* Cambridge: Harvard University Press.

Morrissette, P. (1992). Engagement strategies with reluctant homeless young people. *Psychotherapy, 29*, 447–451.

Post, P., & McCoard, D. (1994). Needs and self-concept of runaway adolescents. *The School Counselor, 41*, 212–219.

Robertson, M. (1989). *Homeless youth in Hollywood: Patterns of alcohol use.* A report of the National Institute on Alcohol Abuse and Alcoholism. Berkeley, CA: Alcohol Research Group, School of Public Health, University of Southern California.

Rohr, M. E., & James, R. (1994). Runaways: Some suggestions for prevention, coordinating services, and expediting the reentry process. *The School Counselor, 42*, 40–47.

Rotheram-Borus, M. J., Selfridge, C., Koopman, C., Haignere, C., Meyer-Bahlburg, H. F. L., & Ehrhardt, A. (1989). The relationship of knowledge and attitudes towards AIDS to safe sex practices among runaway and gay adolescents. In *Abstracts: V International Conference on AIDS.* Ottawa, Ontario, Canada: International Development Research Centre, p. 728. *Runaway and homeless youth and programs that serve them.* Washington, DC

Shaffer, D., & Caton, C. L. M. (1984). *Runaway and homeless youth in New York City.* A report to the Ittleson Foundation, New York City.

Smart, R. G., & Ogborne, A. C. (1994). Street youth in substance abuse treatment: Characteristics and treatment compliance. *Adolescence, 29*, 733–745.

Stanton, M. D., & Shadish, W. R. (1997). Outcome, attrition, and family-couples treatment for drug abuse: A meta-analysis and review of the controlled, comparative studies. *Psychological Bulletin, 122*, 170–191.

Szapocznik, J., Perez-Vidal, A., Brickman, A. L., Foote, F. H., Santisteban, D. A., Hervis, O. E., & Kurtines, W. M. (1988). Engaging adolescent drug abusers and their families into treatment: A strategic structural systems approach. *Journal of Consulting and Clinical Psychology, 56*, 552–557.

Teare, J. F., Furst, D. W., Peterson, R. W., & Authier, K. (1992). Family reunification following shelter placement: Child, family, and program correlates. *American Journal of Orthopsychiatry, 62*, 142–146.

Waldron, H. B. (1997). Adolescent substance abuse and family therapy outcome: A review of randomized trials (pp. 199–234). In T. H. Ollendick & R. J. Prinz (Eds.), *Advances in clinical child psychology* (Vol. 19). New York: Plenum.

Yates, G. L., MacKenzie, R., Pennbridge, J., & Cohen, E. (1988). A risk profile comparison of runaway and non-runaway youth. *American Journal of Public Health, 78*, 820–821.

Zimet, G. D., Sobo, E. J., Zimmerman, T., Jackson, J., Mortimer, J., Yanda, C. P., & Lazebnik, R. (1995). Sexual behavior, drug use, and AIDS knowledge among Midwestern runaways. *Youth and Society, 26*, 450–462.

About the authors: Natasha Slesnick and Jillian Prestopnik are affiliated with The University of New Mexico, Center on Alcoholism, Substance Abuse and Addictions (CASAA).

Acknowledgment: This work was supported by a NIAAA and CSAT grant (R01 AA 12173).

Address correspondence to: Natasha Slesnick, The University of New Mexico, Center on Alcoholism, Substance Abuse and Addictions, 2650 Yale SE, Suite 200, Albuquerque, NM 87106. E-mail: tash@unm.edu

MODEL LITERATURE REVIEW C

Distinguishing Features of Emerging Adulthood: The Role of Self-Classification As an Adult[1]

Until the late 1990s, researchers (e.g., Greene, Wheatley, & Aldava, 1992; Hogan & Astone, 1986) have specified events such as marriage, completion of education, and starting a career as markers of adulthood. However, recent research (e.g., Arnett, 1997), which employs self-report formats, reveals that those individuals who are actually in the process of making the transition to adulthood do not consider marriage and other events as important markers or criteria for adulthood. Instead, these studies of 18- to 25-year-olds have found that young people use more internal and individualistic qualities as their criteria for adulthood, which include taking responsibility for one's actions, independent decision making, and financial independence from parents. Besides having these criteria for adulthood, 18- to 25-year-olds (a) are becoming increasingly devoted to individualistic-oriented, rather than other-oriented, goals; (b) are experimenting with work, relationships, and worldviews; (c) lack specific transitional roles that prepare them for adult roles; (d) are entering into increasingly intimate, nonmarital relationships; and (e) are engaging in relatively high rates of risky behaviors, such as unprotected intercourse, illegal drug use, and driving while drunk (see Arnett, 2000). Given the length and changing nature of this part of young people's lives, Arnett (2000) has argued that this is a new and distinct developmental period that he has labeled emerging adulthood.

One of the most convincing pieces of evidence that emerging adulthood is a unique period in development is the ambivalence that emerging adults have about their own status as adults. When asked whether they have reached adulthood, young people between the ages of 18 and 25 tend to respond with "in some respects yes, in some respects no" (e.g., Arnett, 1997, 2001; Nelson, 2003). This reflects the transitional nature of this time of their lives; they know that they have left adolescence, but at the same time they do not yet feel that they have taken on adult roles. It is not until the late 20s and early 30s that a clear majority of people consider themselves to be adults (Arnett, 2000).

However, there are some 18- to 25-year-old individuals who do consider themselves to be adults (e.g., Arnett, 1997, 1998, 2001; Nelson, 2003). Although they are clearly the minority within this age group,

they represent a unique group that is worthy of investigation. They stand out because they perceive themselves as adults at an age when the majority of their peers do not. This finding gives rise to the question of how they differ from their peers. Furthermore, it is unclear whether they have different criteria that they use to define themselves as adults. If these individuals are employing different criteria, it would be interesting to know what those criteria are. If these individuals are using the same criteria, it would be important to know if they indeed believe that they have achieved those criteria. Finally, questions exist as to whether these self-perceived adults differ from their emerging-adult peers in attitudes and behaviors that are characteristic of this developmental period (e.g., identity issues, risk-taking behaviors). Thus, this study sought to identify a subset of 18- to 25-year-old perceived adults and compare them to their emerging-adult peers to see whether they (a) use the same criteria for adulthood, (b) believe that they have achieved those criteria, and (c) are different on three significant emerging-adulthood issues (identity issues, risk-taking behaviors, and depression).

Defining Features of Emerging Adulthood
Criteria for Adulthood

The first question that may be asked of those 18- to 25-year-old individuals who consider themselves to be adults is whether they use the same criteria for adult status as their emerging-adult peers. As previously noted, recent research done primarily in the United States reveals that emerging adults do not consider marriage and other events as important markers or criteria for adulthood. Instead, young people use more internal and individualistic qualities as criteria for adulthood, which include taking responsibility for one's actions, independent decision making, and financial independence from parents (Arnett, 1997, 1998, 2001; Greene et al., 1992), (including in various cultural subgroups within the United States such as ethnic minority groups [Arnett, 2001] and religious subgroups) (Nelson, 2003). Taken together, studies of young people predominantly from individualistic cultures suggest that the theme of independence (e.g., financial independence, independent decision making) is a general feature in the process of becoming adults.

---

[1] Literature review excerpt from: Nelson, L. J., & Barry, C. M. (2005). Distinguishing features of emerging adulthood: The role of self-classification as an adult. *Journal of Adolescent Research*, 20, 242–262. Copyright © 2005 by Sage Publications. All rights reserved. Reprinted with permission.

However, although investigators have repeatedly found these criteria to be mentioned as the measuring sticks for adulthood, most of the respondents in these past studies who have listed these current standards as their criteria for adulthood have been individuals who did not yet perceive themselves as adults (i.e., they perceived themselves as emerging adults). In other words, no study has systematically compared those young people who consider themselves to be adults with those who do not. It would be important to compare these groups to determine whether they use the same criteria for adulthood. Thus, the first purpose of the current study was to explore whether self-perceived adults (ages 18 to 25 years) differed from their emerging-adult peers on the criteria that they use to determine adult status. Given that these criteria have emerged repeatedly across studies as the important factors for determining the transition to adulthood, it was believed that there would be no differences between the groups in the criteria that they use to measure adult status.

Assuming adulthood criteria do not differ as a function of perceived adult status, the next question that arises is whether self-perceived adults believe that they have achieved those criteria. No study has actually examined the extent to which the current criteria for adulthood differentiate self-perceived adults from self-perceived emerging adults. Thus, the second purpose of this study was to examine whether self-perceived adults believe that they have achieved those criteria to a greater extent than have their emerging-adult peers. Given the consistent findings that these are the criteria that young people use to measure adulthood (e. g., Arnett, 1998), it was hypothesized that these individuals would perceive themselves as having reached these criteria to a greater extent than would their peers.

Identity Distinctions

Many theorists and researchers have identified identity formation as a defining feature of the transition to adulthood (see Schwartz, 2001, for a review). For example, Erikson (1950) believed that adolescents go through a period of exploration (possibly lasting into the early 20s; Erikson, 1968) during which they attempt to answer the following question: Who am I, and what is my place in society? After a period of exploration, those who successfully self-chose values and vocational goals achieve identity synthesis, whereas those who are unable to develop a working set of ideals on which to base their identity as adults remain in a state of identity confusion.

Based on Erikson's work, Marcia (1966, 1980, 1988) grouped individuals into four categories that are reflective of the progress they have made toward forming a mature identity. These categories are based on an individual's level of exploration and commitment to a specific set of goals, values, and beliefs, including identity achievement (a period of exploration followed by a commitment), identity moratorium (active exploration without much commitment), identity foreclosure (commitment with little exploration), and identity diffusion (lack of both exploration and commitment). In general, emerging adulthood tends to be characterized as a state of moratorium, extensive exploration with little commitment.

Additional work in this area has extended and expanded on the foundational work of Erikson (1950, 1968) and Marcia (1966, 1980, 1988), including (a) work focusing more specifically on the process of exploration (Grotevant, 1987); (b) conceptualizations of identity styles based on how individuals make decisions on a daily basis (Berzonsky, 1989); (c) the importance of individual skills and abilities in making decisions that influence identity (Kurtines, Azmitia, & Alvarez, 1992); and (d) the capital, or resources, that a person's identity gives him or her (Côté, 1997). Taken together, these perspectives underscore the processes involved in and the importance of acquiring a mature identity going into adulthood.

Exploration during this period of time tends to occur in multiple domains. For example, Côté (1996) identified three domain clusters including psychological (e.g., career choice), interactional (e.g., dating), and social-structural (e.g., politics, morality). Given that emerging adults, especially those in higher education, have few societal roles, responsibilities, and expectations placed on them during these years, they have an extended period of time to explore and try on various possible selves in each of these domains. First, explorations in work can be seen in emerging adults' tendencies to change majors, increasingly attend graduate school (often in fields different from undergraduate paths), participate in short-term volunteer jobs (e.g., Americorps, Peace Corps), and travel to various places in the country or the world as part of work or educational experiences (Arnett, 2000). Second, explorations in love can be observed in that romantic relationships during these years tend to last longer than in adolescence (but still tend not to be long-term relationships or include marriage), are likely to include sexual intercourse, and may include cohabitation (Michael, Gagnon, Laumann, & Kolata, 1995). Finally, research shows that emerging adults explore worldviews (Arnett, 1997; Pascarella & Terenzini, 1991) and religious beliefs (Arnett & Jensen, 2002; Hoge, Johnson, & Luidens, 1993), with many often changing from the views in which they were raised (Perry, 1970/1999).

Given the importance of identity exploration during emerging adulthood, the third purpose of this study was to compare perceived adults and perceived emerg-

ing adults in the extent to which they were exploring their identity. Specifically, the two groups were com-
200 pared in their progress toward identity resolution of values and beliefs, career, romantic partner, and an overall sense of self. Because identity exploration is such a focus of emerging adulthood, it was expected that those individuals who feel a sense of instability in
205 regard to who they are would be less likely to consider themselves to be adults. Hence, it was expected that compared to perceived emerging adults, perceived adults would have a stronger sense of their identity with respect to their values or beliefs, career, romantic
210 partner, and overall sense of self.

Depression

Because emerging adulthood is a time of experimentation and exploration, for some, it may also be a time of instability and uncertainty. The lack of roles and responsibilities, coupled with the search for iden-
215 tity, may lead to a sense of ambivalence. Such instability and ambivalence may give rise to depression. Indeed, studies have found that depression is a growing problem across college campuses in the United States (O'Conner, 2001). Whether this is because of in-
220 creased reporting of the problem or changing aspects of the age period is unclear, but it is possible that heightened instability and exploration may be related to depression for some individuals.

According to adolescents, some of the perceived
225 causes of their depression include psychological harm to the self by others, separation from someone close, conflict with someone close, loneliness, and feelings of incompetence (see Harter, 1999). Based on these potential causes of depression, there are several rea-
230 sons why depression may be an issue of concern during emerging adulthood, including those attending a university. First, by definition, emerging adulthood is a time during which young people are trying to separate themselves from their parents. Although an impor-
235 tant process, this renegotiation of the parent–child relationship can be a painful process, too. Furthermore, as emerging adults explore their identity, they often move in and out (i.e., separation) of romantic relationships (Michael et al., 1995). Hence, separation is a recurring
240 theme of this time period, and the attachment literature (Bowlby, 1973) has documented that separation typically fosters depression. Furthermore, separation could very well lead to loneliness, which also could contribute to the possibility of depression (Harter, 1999). Fi-
245 nally, as emerging adults attempt new things and try out possible identities, questions about one's own competence and failures are likely to occur, as seen in research that shows that feelings of incompetence are typical during periods of transition (Wigfield, Eccles,
250 MacIver, Reuman, & Midgley, 1991).

Taken together, there are several aspects of emerging adulthood (e.g., separation, loneliness, exploration, and failure) that lend themselves to the possibility of depression during this time period. Hence,
255 another purpose of this study was to compare perceived adults and perceived emerging adults in levels of depression. It was expected that perceived adults would be experiencing less depression because they are experiencing less instability and ambivalence in
260 their lives compared to their emerging-adult peers.

Behavioral Distinctions

In addition to differences in identity development and depression that set emerging adults apart from others, there are numerous behavioral characteristics of emerging adults that distinguish them from adoles-
265 cents and young adults. As described earlier, romantic relationships (nonmarital) tend to include sexual intercourse and often cohabitation (Michael et al., 1995). Furthermore, emerging adulthood (rather than adolescence) is the peak period for several risk behaviors,
270 including unprotected sex; most types of substance use, including binge drinking; and risky driving behaviors, such as driving at high speeds or while intoxicated (Arnett, 1992; Bachman, Johnston, O'Malley, & Schulenberg, 1996). Parental monitoring decreases
275 during emerging adulthood, which may be one reason why risk behavior is consistently higher for emerging adults than for adolescents (Arnett, 1998; Bachman et al., 1996). However, research shows that parenting (Barnes & Farrell, 1992; Bogenschneider, Wu, Raf-
280 faelli, & Tsay, 1998), peers (Berndt, 1996), school environment (Kasen, Cohen, & Brook, 1998), religiosity (Wallace & Williams, 1997), and individual factors such as aggression (Donovan, Umlauf, & Salzberg, 1988) all contribute to risk behaviors in adolescence
285 and emerging adulthood.

Regardless of the reasons why risk behaviors are common during emerging adulthood, they are important features of this developmental period. An interesting finding was that cessation of risk behaviors does
290 not rank at the top of the criteria necessary for adulthood. Therefore, given the prevalence of risk behaviors for 18- to 25-year-olds and the relative lack of importance placed on the elimination of risk behaviors to become an adult, it would be useful to know
295 whether perceived adults and emerging adults can be distinguished by their behavior. Because researchers to date have not examined this issue, the final purpose of this study was to examine whether 18- to 25-year-olds who consider themselves to be adults engage in less
300 risk behaviors than do their emerging-adult peers. It was hypothesized that perceived adults would engage in fewer risk behaviors than would emerging adults because perceived maturity of adulthood would be reflected in perceived maturity of behavior.

305　　　　In summary, emerging adulthood (i.e., 18 to 25 years of age) is a new and distinct developmental period defined by ambivalence concerning adult status, individualistic criteria for adulthood, identity exploration, and frequent participation in risk behaviors.
310　Given these unique features that occur between 18 and 25 years of age, it now may be considered atypical to consider oneself an adult during this period of the life span. Thus, there is a need to examine those individuals who do consider themselves to be adults during a
315　time period when it is not expected of them to do so. Therefore, the purpose of this study was to (a) attempt to identify individuals who consider themselves adults at an age when it is developmentally atypical to do so; (b) explore whether they differ from their emerging-
320　adult peers on the criteria that they use for adult status; (c) examine whether they believe they have achieved those criteria; and (d) compare them to their emerging-adult peers on identity development, depression, and risk behaviors (e.g., substance use, drunk driving). It
325　was expected that compared to emerging adults, perceived adults would (a) have the same criteria for adulthood; (b) perceive themselves as having reached those criteria (to a greater extent than their emerging-adult peers); and (c) achieve greater identity formation,
330　experience less depression, and engage in fewer risk behaviors.

References

Arnett. J. J. (1992). Reckless behavior in adolescence: A developmental perspective. *Developmental Review, 12*, 339–373.
Arnett, J. J. (1997). Young people's conceptions of the transition to adulthood. *Youth & Society, 29*, 1–23.
Arnett, J. J. (1998). Learning to stand alone: The contemporary American transition to adulthood in cultural and historical context. *Human Development, 41*, 295–315.
Arnett, J. J. (2000). Emerging adulthood: A theory of development from the late teens through the twenties. *American Psychologist, 55*, 469–480.
Arnett, J. J. (2001). Conceptions of the transition to adulthood: Perspectives from adolescence to midlife. *Journal of Adult Development, 8*, 133–143.
Arnett, J. J. (2001). Conceptions of the transition to adulthood among emerging adults in American ethnic groups. *Journal of Adult Development, 8*, 133–143.
Arnett, J. J., & Jensen, L. A. (2002). A congregation of one: Individualized religious beliefs among emerging adults. *Journal of Adolescent Research, 17*, 451–467.
Bachman, J. G., Johnston, L. D., O'Malley, P., & Schulenberg, J. (1996). Transitions in drug use during late adolescence and young adulthood. In J. A. Graber, J. Brooks-Gunn, & A. C. Petersen (Eds.), *Transitions through adolescence: Interpersonal domains and context.* Mahwah, NJ: Lawrence Erlbaum.
Barnes, G. M., & Farrell, M. P. (1992). Parental support and control as predictors of adolescent drinking, delinquency, and related problem behaviors. *Journal of Marriage and the Family, 54*, 763–776.
Berndt, T. J. (1996). Exploring the effects of friendship quality on social development. In W. M. Bukowski, A. G. Newcomb, & W. W. Hartup (Eds.), *The company they keep.* Cambridge, UK: Cambridge University Press.
Berzonsky, M. D. (1989). Identity style: Conceptualization and measurement. *Journal of Adolescent Research, 4*, 267–281.
Bogenschneider, K., Wu, M., Raffaelli, M., & Tsay, J. C. (1998). Parent influences on adolescent peer orientation and substance use: The interface of parenting practices and values. *Child Development, 69*, 1672–1688.
Bowlby, J. (1973). *Attachment and loss: Separation* (Vol. 2). New York: Basic Books.
Côté, J. E. (1996). An empirical test of the identity capital model. *Journal of Adolescence, 20*, 421–37.
Donovan, D. M., Umlauf, R. L., & Salzberg, P. M. (1988). Derivation of personality subtypes among high risk drivers. *Alcohol, Drugs, and Driving, 4*, 233–244.
Erikson, E. H. (1950). *Childhood and society.* New York: Norton.
Erikson, E. H. (1968). *Identity: Youth and crisis.* New York: Norton.
Greene, A. L., Wheatley, S. M., & Aldava, J. F., IV. (1992). Stages on life's way: Adolescents' implicit theories of the life course. *Journal of Adolescent Research, 7*, 364–381.
Grotevant, H. D. (1987). Toward a process model of identity formation. *Journal of Adolescent Research, 2*, 203–222.
Harter, S. (1999). *The construction of the self.* New York: Guilford.
Hogan, D. P., & Astone, N. M. (1986). The transition to adulthood. *American Sociological Review, 12*, 109–130.
Hoge, D. R., Johnson, B., & Luidens, D. A. (1993). Determinants of church involvement of young adults who grew up in Presbyterian churches. *Journal of the Scientific Study of Religion, 32*, 242–255.
Kasen, S., Cohen, P., & Brook, J. S. (1998). Adolescent school experiences, and dropout, adolescent pregnancy, and young adult deviant behavior. *Journal of Adolescent Research, 13*, 49–72.
Kurtines, W. M., Azmitia, M., & Alvarez, M. (1992). Science, values, and rationality: Philosophy of science from a co-constructivist perspective. In W. M. Kurtines, M. Azmitia, & J. L. Gewirtz (Eds.), *The role of values in psychology and human development* (pp. 3–29). New York: John Wiley.
Marcia, J. E. (1966). Development and validation of ego identity status. *Journal of Personality and Social Psychology, 5*, 551–558.
Marcia, J. E. (1980). Identity in adolescence. In J. Adelson (Ed.), *Handbook of adolescent psychology.* New York: John Wiley.
Marcia, J. E. (1988). Common processes underlying ego identity, cognitive or moral development, and individuation. In D. K. Lapsley & F. C. Power (Eds.), *Self ego, and identity: Integrative approaches* (pp. 211–266). New York/Berlin: Springer-Verlag.
Michael, R. T., Gagnon, J. H., Laumann, E. O., & Kolata, G. (1995). *Sex in America: A definitive survey.* New York: Warner Brooks.
Nelson, L. J. (2003). Rites of passage in emerging adulthood: Perspectives of young Mormons. *New Directions in Child and Adolescent Development, 100*, 33–49.
O'Conner, E. M. (2001). Student mental health: Secondary education no more. *Monitor on Psychology, 32*, 44–47.
Pascarella, E., & Terenzini, P. (1991). *How college affects students: Findings and insights from twenty years of research.* San Francisco: Jossey-Bass.
Perry, W. G. (1999). *Forms of ethical and intellectual development in the college years: A scheme.* San Francisco: Jossey-Bass. (Original work published 1970)
Schwartz, S. J. (2001). The evolution of Eriksonian and neo-Eriksonian identity theory and research: A review and integration. *Identity: An International Journal of Theory and Research, 1*, 7–58.
Wallace, J. M., & Williams, D. R. (1997). Religion and adolescent health-compromising behavior. In J. Schulenberg, J. L. Maggs, & K. Hurrelmann (Eds.), *Health risks and developmental transitions in adolescence* (pp. 444–468). New York: Cambridge University Press.
Wigfield, A., Eccles, J., Mac Iver, D., Reuman, D., & Midgley, C. (1991). Transitions at early adolescence: Changes in children's domain-specific self-perceptions and general self-esteem across the transition to junior high school. *Developmental Psychology, 26*, 552–565.

About the authors: *Larry J. Nelson* is an assistant professor of marriage, family, and human development in the School of Family Life at Brigham Young University. He received his Ph.D. in 2000 from the University of Maryland, College Park. His major research interests are in social and self-development during early childhood and emerging adulthood. *Carolyn McNamara Barry* is an assistant professor of psychology at Loyola College in Maryland. She received her Ph.D. in 2001 from the University of Maryland, College Park. Her major research interests are in social and self-development during adolescence and emerging adulthood.

Acknowledgments: The authors express appreciation to the human development and psychology instructors at the University of Maryland, College Park, for their assistance. We also extend our gratitude for the grant support of the College of Family, Home, and Social Sciences and the Family Studies Center at Brigham Young University.

Address correspondence to: Larry J. Nelson, Ph.D., Marriage, Family, and Human Development, School of Family Life, 924 SWKT, Brigham Young University, Provo, UT 84602. E-mail: larry_nelson@byu.edu

MODEL LITERATURE REVIEW D

Mental Health Professionals' Contact with Family Members of People with Psychiatric Disabilities[1]

Background Literature

Studies drawn from the mental health practice literature called for increased contact with families of mental health consumers as avenues of improved consumer mental health status, decreased treatment costs, and increased family member coping skills (DeChillo, 1993; Falloon, McGill, Boyd, & Pederson, 1987; Hogarty et al., 1991; Lefley, 1994). Werrbach, Jenson, and Bubar (2002) reported that training mental health professionals in family strengths assessment and collaborative practice reduced parent and professional tensions and increased communication between the groups. Family inclusive interventions were developed and studied (i.e., family support groups, psychoeducation, collaboration, consultation, education, and involvement; Heller, Roccoforte, Hsieh, Cook, & Pickett, 1997; St-Onge & Morin, 1998). Family psychoeducation, consisting of a series of meetings with families to discuss mental illness, mental health treatment, community resources, and coping with stressors, showed particular promise. According to Falloon's (1998) research, 20 of 22 controlled studies, including 14 studies that used random assignment, demonstrated that adding family psychoeducation to mental health programs for people with psychiatric disabilities resulted in decreased consumer mental illness symptoms. Falloon (1998) offered further review of the outcomes of family psychoeducation in the mental health literature: "Major exacerbations of psychotic symptoms and admissions to hospitals are more than halved, social disability is reduced, and with increased employment rates, burdens on family caregivers are lowered, and their health improved" (Appendix, p. 1).

Family inclusive interventions incorporate a number of theoretical assumptions. Family members are viewed from a competence paradigm (Marsh, 1994). Competent family members are presumed to be potential sources of social and instrumental support for mental health consumers who are served by a biopsychosocial and cultural model of mental health treatment (Lefley, 1996; Spaniol & Zipple, 2000). At the same time, family members of people with serious mental illnesses are subject to the same stressors as those of individuals with serious physical illnesses; they may experience grief and loss as well as stress,

coping, and adaptation responses (Hatfield, 1990). It is assumed that family inclusive interventions are part of effective mental health practice because they support and strengthen family caregivers of people with psychiatric disabilities. Families are strengthened by acquiring knowledge about mental illness, mental health treatment, community resources, and coping strategies. In turn, the process may offer positive outcomes for consumers because stronger social or family support networks may be associated with improved mental health.

Despite two decades of mental health literature recommending family contact and demonstrated positive outcomes reported within studies of family inclusive interventions, little is known about professionals' reported contact with families within today's community-based mental health practice. Several studies found that family relationship information was not collected by mental health agencies (Nicholson, 1994) or available within mental health agencies' family therapy billing records (Dixon et al., 1999). The studies discussed herein include the majority of the published mental health literature about mental health professionals' reported frequency of contact, patterns of contact, facilitators of contact, and barriers of contact with families of people with psychiatric disabilities.

Frequency of Contact

An early study by Smets (1982) found that a majority of staff in a psychiatric hospital reported spending 0 to 1 hour per week with family members. Bernheim and Switalski (1988) indicated that 82% of 350 community- and hospital-based mental health professionals reported spending less than 2 hours per week with family members. St-Onge and Morin (1998) surveyed 266 mental health professionals working in six community and hospital mental health treatment facilities; respondents reported spending about 1 hour per week engaged in interactions with family members (38.5%) or never contacting family members within the last 6 months (34.6%). Wright (1997) found that most of 184 mental health professionals reported a low total family involvement score ($M = 1.44$, $SD = 1.09$). Wright (1997) reported that this family involvement score meant mental health professionals "not very of-

---

[1] Literature review excerpt from: Riebschleger, J. (2005). Mental health professionals' contact with family members of people with psychiatric disabilities. *Families in Society: The Journal of Contemporary Social Services, 86*, 9–16. Copyright © 2005 by the Alliance for Children and Families. All rights reserved. Reprinted with permission.

ten to sometimes" interacted with family members of mental health consumers within a 6-month time period (e.g., listening to families, advocating for families). Dixon, Lucksted, Stewart, and Delhanty (2000) surveyed 36 community mental health center therapists who reported at least one past year contact with a family member for 61% of the mental health consumers they served.

Patterns of Contact

Questions about mental health professionals' reported patterns of contact with family members include the following:

- Who contacts whom?
- What is the most frequent contact mode?
- Which family roles are most involved in the contact interactions?
- What activities take place during the interactions between mental health professionals and family members?

Bernheim and Switalski (1988) reported that mental health professionals' contact with family members primarily consisted of "brief, informal chats and telephone calls" usually initiated by family members or mental health consumers. According to Dixon et al. (2000), 36 mental health professionals said that telephone contact with families was the most frequent mode of communication (87%); family members were most likely to be mothers (26%), siblings (13%), or other (34%). According to Atkinson and Coia (1995), parents and spouses are most likely to serve as primary supports and caregivers for people with serious mental illness. In addition, they noted that primary caregivers tend to be female.

Bernheim and Switalski (1988) asked mental health professionals to describe the types of interactive activities that should take place with family members of mental health consumers (e.g., involving family members in treatment planning, teaching family members coping skills, and getting information about consumers from family members). Wright (1997) built on the work of Bernheim and Switalski (1988); their research asked how frequently mental health professionals reported actually engaging in these specific activities with family members of mental health consumers. In the Wright study (1997), mental health professionals responded "less than sometimes" to the following items: (a) helping families understand the consumer's psychiatric illness, (b) encouraging family members to support the consumer emotionally, (c) helping family members "to set appropriate limits," (d) informing families of the consumer's progress, and (e) encouraging families to accept the consumer's independence. According to Wright (1997), mental health professionals' least frequently reported activities (less than not

very often) were conducting family therapy and advocating to help families obtain needed services. Dixon et al. (2000) found that therapists said their interactions with family members most frequently consisted of helping family members in solving a problem related to the consumer's behavior, providing the family members with emotional support, obtaining information about the consumer for assessment, providing education or information to the family members, and dealing with a crisis situation.

Facilitators of Contact

What factors may facilitate mental health professionals' contact with family members? Using ordinary least squares regression, Wright (1997) found that job and organizational factors were the strongest predictors of family involvement (i.e., working day or evening shifts, working as a therapist or social worker, working with consumers who had more severe psychiatric disabilities, and perceptions that the mental health treatment unit was "functioning more smoothly"). Dixon et al. (2000) reported that contact with families occurred most frequently during mental health consumer psychiatric crises; increased interactions with families were statistically associated with serving younger consumers, a consumer diagnosis of schizophrenia, and mental health services in the form of community outreach teams. Farhall et al. (1998) reported that mental health professionals who participated in an extended training program about family issues increased their contact with consumers' families. DeChillo (1993) developed a Collaboration with Families Scale with data drawn from a sample of 102 family members who had experienced at least one in-person meeting with a social worker. DeChillo (1993) found that increased collaboration among family members and mental health professionals was predicted by a higher number of in-person meetings.

Barriers to Contact

What factors may serve as barriers to family contact? According to Bernheim and Switalski (1988), mental health professionals responded that "sometimes to always" the largest barrier to working with families was lack of time (95%). In Dixon et al.'s (1999) report, mental health professionals listed barriers to the implementation of multifamily group psychoeducation in community-based treatment settings. The most frequent barriers included intense work pressure (95%), uncertainty about financing the interventions (71%), agency bureaucracy (68%), skepticism about the intervention (60%), and confidentiality concerns (45%). In a smaller study, Dixon et al. (2000) found the most frequently reported barrier to contact with families was that the therapist "perceived it would be of no benefit."

References

American Psychiatric Association. (1994). *Diagnostic and statistical manual of mental disorders* (4th ed.). Washington, DC: Author.

Atkinson, J. M., & Coia, D. A. (1995). *Families coping with schizophrenia.* New York: Wiley.

Bernheim, K. F., & Switalski, T. (1988). Mental health staff and patient's relatives: How they view each other. *Hospital and Community Psychiatry, 39,* 63–68.

DeChillo, N. (1993). Collaboration between social workers and families of patients with mental illness. *Families in Society, 74,* 104–115.

Dixon, L., Lucksted, A., Stewart, B., & Delhanty, J. (2000). Therapists' contacts with family members of persons with severe mental illness in a community treatment program. *Psychiatric Services, 51,* 1449–1451.

Dixon, L., Lyles, A., Scott, J., Lehman, A., Postrado, L., Goldman, H., & McGlynn, E. (1999). Services to families of adults with schizophrenia: From treatment recommendations to dissemination. *Psychiatric Services, 50,* 233–238.

Fallon, I. R. H. (1998). Cognitive-behavioural interventions for patients with functional psychoses and their caregivers. In *Families as partners in care* (pp. 1–14). Toronto: World Fellowship for Schizophrenia and Allied Disorders.

Fallon, I. R. H., McGill, C. W., Boyd, J. L., & Pederson, J. (1987). Family management in the prevention of morbidity of schizophrenia: Social outcome of a two-year longitudinal study. *Psychological Medicine, 17,* 59–66.

Farhall, J., Webster, B., Hocking, B., Leggatt, M., Riess, C., & Young, J. (1998). Training to enhance partnerships between mental health professionals and family caregivers: A comparative study. *Psychiatric Services, 49,* 1488–1490.

Hatfield, A. B. (1990). *Family education in mental illness.* New York: Guilford.

Heller, T., Roccoforte, J. A., Hsieh, K., Cook, J. A., & Pickett, S. A. (1997). Benefits of support groups for families of adults with severe mental illness. *American Journal of Orthopsychiatry, 67,* 187–198.

Hogarty, G. E., Anderson, C. M., Reiss, D. I., Kornblith, S. J., Greenwald, D. P., Ulrich, R. F., & Carter, M. (1991). Family psychoeducation, social skills training, and maintenance chemotherapy in the aftercare treatment of schizophrenia: II. Two-year effects of a controlled study on relapse and adjustment. *Archives of General Psychiatry, 48,* 340–347.

Lefley, H. P. (1994). Interventions with families: What have we learned? In A. B. Hatfield (Ed.), *Family interventions in mental illness* (Vol. 62, pp. 89–98). San Francisco: Jossey-Bass.

Lefley, H. P. (1996). Family caregiving in mental illness. In D. E. Biegel & R. Schulz (Series Eds.), *Family caregiver application series* (Vol. 7). Thousand Oaks, CA: Sage.

Marsh, D. T. (1994). Services for families: New modes, models, and interventions strategies. In J. A. Talbott (Series Ed.) & H. P. Lefley & M. Wasow (Vol. Eds.), *Chronic mental illness: Volume 2: Helping families cope with mental illness* (pp. 39–62). Chur, Switzerland: Harwood Academic.

Nicholson, J. (1994). Only sixteen states ask if you're a parent. *OMH News, 6,* 16.

Smets, A. C. (1982). Family and staff attitudes toward family involvement in the treatment of hospitalized chronic patients. *Hospital and Community Psychiatry, 33,* 573–575.

Spaniol, L., & Zipple, A. M. (2000). Changing family roles. In L. Spaniol, A. M. Zipple, D. T. Marsh, & L. Y. Finley (Eds.), *The role of the family in psychiatric rehabilitation* (pp. 29–42). Boston: Center for Psychiatric Rehabilitation, Boston University.

St-Onge, M., & Morin, G. (1998). *La collaboration entre le personnel clinique et les familles de personnes d'âge adulte ayant des incapacitiés: Rapport final.* Quebéc: Institut de réadaption en déficience physique de Quebéc and École de service social, Université Laval.

Werrbach, G. B., Jenson, C. E., & Bubar, K. (2002). Collaborative agency training for parent employees and professionals in a new agency addressing children's mental health. *Families in Society, 83,* 457–464.

Wright, E. R. (1997). The impact of organizational factors on mental health professionals' involvement with families. *Psychiatric Services, 48,* 921–927.

About the author: Joanne Riebschleger, Ph.D., ACSW, is assistant professor, School of Social Work, Michigan State University.

Address correspondence to: Joanne Riebschleger, Michigan State University, School of Social Work, 254 Baker Hall, East Lansing, MI 48824-1118. E-mail: riebsch1@msu.edu

MODEL LITERATURE REVIEW E

The Well-Being of Immigrant Latino Youth: A Framework to Inform Practice[1]

According to the 2000 census, the Latino population living in the United States increased by 58% over 10 years, growing from 22.4 million in 1990 to 35.3 million in 2000 (Schmidley, 2001). As their presence
5 in the United States grows, Latinos are relocating in many areas of the country that have not been traditional destinations for new Latino immigrants, such as the South and the Midwest. As a result, health and social service providers, in both traditional and new
10 receiving communities, are working with increasing numbers of Latino clients. To better serve these clients, helping professionals will need to develop an understanding of the risk and protective factors for Latino youth. In particular because the largest percent-
15 age of Latinos living in the United States are immigrants or children of immigrants (Hernandez, 1997; Suarez-Orozco & Suarez-Orozco, 2001), service providers will need to understand the risk and protective factors associated with migration and acculturation.
20 Research suggests that Latino youth face multiple threats to their well-being, including substance use, poor school functioning, and early adult role-taking. These risks may be particularly acute for children who immigrate later in childhood, especially during adoles-
25 cence (Portes & Rumbaut, 2001). Despite these risks, additional research suggests that new immigrant Latino families possess certain cultural attitudes and norms that are protective against the many risks that accompany immigration.
30 In this article, we summarize findings regarding the well-being of Latino youth on domains important to functioning later in life. The summary is followed by a discussion of the psychosocial risks that threaten the successful adaptation of Latino youth in immigrant
35 families and the protective factors that facilitate their adaptation. We argue that the understanding of risk and resiliency among Latino youth can be improved if it is embedded in an ecological framework that more fully accounts for the challenges of immigration.
40 Based on this argument, a framework is proposed to guide helping professionals in assessing the needs of Latino youth.

Status of Latino Youth

Mental Health

Few investigations of the incidence and preva-
45 lence of specific mental health diagnoses for Latino youth exist. Most current research compares several ethnic groups on specific diagnostic categories or other measures of well-being. In a multistage probability sample, Shrout et al. (1992) found limited differences between Puerto Rican and mainland Hispanics on a
50 variety of diagnoses. Kleykamp and Tienda (in press) found limited well-being differences between Latino and white youth in a nationally representative sample. In a study of 3,962 ethnic minority youth receiving outpatient mental health services in San Diego, Yeh,
55 McCabe, Hurlburt, Hough, Hazen, Culver, Garland, and Landsverk (2002) found that Latinos were more likely to receive diagnoses of adjustment disorders, anxiety disorders, and psychotic disorders compared with non-Hispanic whites. The study sample was also
60 less likely to be diagnosed with attention deficit disorder. Latino females appear to be at particular risk for depressive symptoms and suicidal behavior. The Commonwealth Fund reported that 27% of Latina girls enrolled in Grades 5 through 12 experienced depres-
65 sive symptoms in the past 2 weeks; this percentage is higher than that for all other groups except Asian girls (Schoen et al., 1997). In 1999, more than 25% of Latina girls reported seriously considering suicide and nearly 1 in 5 Latina girls between the ages of 12 and
70 21 attempted suicide one or more times in the past 12 months (Centers for Disease Control [CDC], 2002). This percentage for Latina girls was more than double those reported by any other ethnic or racial group regardless of gender. However, more than 25% of Latino
75 boys also reported feeling sad or hopeless almost every day for 2 weeks or longer in the past 12 months (CDC, 2002). Findings suggest that Hispanic adults and children living in New York City have developed higher rates of posttraumatic stress disorder symptoms in re-
80 sponse to the World Trade Center disaster than members of other groups; the reasons for these findings are unclear (Galea et al., 2002).

Although detailed findings on Latino mental health are only now beginning to appear in the litera-
85 ture, other research indicates that these youth are en-

gaged in behaviors and situations that either put them at increased risk for mental health difficulties or are often co-occurring with mental disturbance. In particular, a comparison of documentation of elevated rates of aggressive behavior, hate crimes based on race, school failure, and child sexual abuse between Latino youth and other groups may indicate the presence of un-measured mental health concerns (CDC, 2002; Kaufman et al., 2001; Tienda & Kleykamp, 2000).

Substance Use

Substance abuse of both illicit drugs and alcohol is problematic among Latino youth. Alcohol consumption is thought to act as a gateway to illicit substance use for Latino youth perhaps because its use is culturally accepted (Gil & Vasquez, 1996; Warheit, Vega, Khoury, Gil, & Elfenbein, 1996). For 1999, CDC reported that the percentage of Latino adolescents who had used marijuana, cocaine, heroin, and methamphetamines during their lifetime was higher than for either African Americans or non-Latino whites. In addition, the 1999 CDC report also noted that Latinos had the highest lifetime percentage of students who had injected illegal drugs (CDC, 2002). King, Gaines, Lambert, Summerfelt, and Bickman (2000) confirm that substance abuse disorders in adolescents are often comorbid with mental health diagnoses and are often missed by clinicians.

School Functioning and Early Adult Role-Taking

It is important to note that much of the existing data come from Latino youth who are attending school. Indeed, when one considers Freud's classic definition of mental health, "the ability to work and to love," adequate school functioning represents a full half of Freud's equation among adolescents (Erikson, 1950). In more practical terms, completion of high school predicts improved life chances. Many factors influence school functioning, including individual, family, and institutional characteristics, all of which have been linked to school performance among Latino youth (Fernandez & Velez, 1989; Kao & Tienda, 1995; Ogbu; 1987; Rumberger; 1995; Rumberger & Thomas, 2000; Velez, 1989). However, current data suggest that many Latino youth are falling below grade-level work or dropping out of school (CDC, 2002; U.S. Census Bureau, 1999). The National Center for Education Statistics (1995) reported that 38.2% of young adult Latinos did not have a high school diploma.

Furthermore, accelerated role-taking may be a particularly relevant variable for Latino youth and school success. Early childbearing is commonly correlated with school dropout (Leadbeater, 1996). Given that Latinas are less likely to use contraception before pregnancy or to terminate a pregnancy (Erickson, 1998), teen childbearing, and hence the early adoption of adult roles, likely relates to decreased educational attainment. For Latino boys, family monetary needs may push them into the workforce earlier than their non-Latino counterparts, again interfering with school performance.

Taken together, the literature suggests that, regardless of the presence of considerable cultural strengths, Latino youth are suffering. However, the context of the struggle is missing. These studies do not take into account the immigration experience of the child and family, the role of immigrant generation, acculturation levels, and family functioning. Without that context, practitioners and policymakers are poorly informed about which Latino youth are having difficulties and how the potential protective factors of Latino families interact with contextual risks. The potential results are inadequately informed theoretical or intervention models and inadequate clinical assessments.

Risk Factors for Latino Youth

The Migration Experience: Leaving Home and Entering the United States

Children and families immigrate for many reasons and in many ways. Some come to escape poverty or to expand their economic prospects; others come looking for sanctuary from violence; some come as whole families; others send a parent first with children following months or even years later. The reasons one immigrates and the events that happen during that process may shape both a parent's and a child's experience of entering a new country. In their studies of immigrant children, Suarez-Orozco and Suarez-Orozco (2001) along with Portes and Rumbaut (2001) have documented the stress inherent in immigration. Family separations and reunifications, traumatization before and during the journey, changing socioeconomic status, and changes in family rules and roles conspire to make the immigration process a threat to the well-being of both parents and children (Portes & Rumbaut, 2001; Suarez-Orozco & Suarez-Orozco, 2001).

In addition, parents and youth may experience immigration differently. For example, a parent may make the decision to immigrate and be grateful for the chance to work, no matter how hard, in a new land. For the parent in this example, immigration is a chosen stressor. Adolescents, in contrast, may not have participated in the decision to immigrate. When they are confronted with making new friends, planning for their adult life, and learning to operate in the world outside of home in a radically different culture and in another language, their appraisals may be much less positive than those of their parents. The voluntariness or degree of voluntary choice of a stressor is theorized to be related to how one copes with that stressor (Boss, 1988;

Rumbaut, 1991). Thus, those who have had immigra- 245 tion imposed on them may be less likely to adapt positively than those for whom immigration was a choice. In addition, Suarez-Orozco and Suarez-Orozco (1995) discuss a dual frame of reference, in which one's current circumstances, no matter how dire, are viewed 250 positively compared with the difficult situations that prompted emigration from one's home country. This dual frame of reference may help parents who made the decision to immigrate endure their adjustment to life in a new country. 255

Conceptually and practically, it may be advantageous to extend the dual frame of reference concept to consider multiple frames of reference that may exist within families. For example, children and parents may view the same set of circumstances as positive or 260 negative depending on their experience of both the current circumstances in the host country and past circumstances. Children and youth may be protected in their countries of origin from physical poverty or danger in a way that adults cannot be, creating a sense in 265 children that what they gave up is not worth the hardships they endure as new immigrants.

On arrival in the new country, another group of factors is influential. The support found in coethnic communities and the attitudes of the native culture 270 toward immigrants can create either powerful barriers or opportunities for success (Portes & Rumbaut, 2001; Zayas, Kaplan, Turner, Romano, & Gonzales-Ramos, 2000). Furthermore, work opportunities, the availability of adequate and affordable housing, and the general 275 level of community wealth and support services create a climate that encourages either successful or less successful adaptation by new immigrants (Portes & Rumbaut, 2001).

Acculturation and Assimilation

The experience of immigration is, by definition, 280 one of change. Immigrants leave their native land hoping for a better life in a new place. Yet learning a new language, navigating new systems, reestablishing social connections, and incorporating new norms require a substantial adjustment. Beginning in the 1920s, 285 scholars began examining the process of assimilation (Alba & Nee, 1997). Before 1965, classic assimilation theorists proposed that adaptation to the United States was a gradual but inevitable process by which ethnic immigrants abandoned the culture of their homelands 290 and adopted the cultural and behavioral patterns of the United States (Gordon, 1964). Thus, one was fully assimilated when he or she had given up her or his cultural identity, lost distinctive characteristics, and no longer differed significantly from European Ameri- 295 cans.

Assimilation studies have challenged the classic assimilation perspective with findings that associate

high levels of assimilation with outcomes that diverge from European American norms (Zhou, 1997). Some first- and second-generation children may have better health, education, and employment outcomes than their white or ethnic native counterparts, whereas others may have significantly worse outcomes (Gans, 1992; Perlmann & Waldinger, 1996; Portes, 1995; Zhou, 1999).

Currently, the term *acculturation* is defined as a process of assuming the values, language, and cultural practices of the new culture (Castro, Coe, Gutierres, & Saenz, 1996). Assimilation has traditionally been seen as the endpoint of this process. However, some literature has challenged acculturation and assimilation as positive goals for immigrants. Rather, both high and low levels of acculturation have been seen as risks for a variety of problematic behaviors, including substance abuse and mental health difficulties (Al-Issa & Tousignant, 1997; Delgado, 1998; Caetano & Clark, 2003; Szapocznik & Kurtines, 1980; Szapocznik, Kurtines, & Fernandez, 1980). In addition, the process of acculturation is assumed to be fraught with stress and anxiety, a scenario ripe for producing mental health symptoms. *Acculturation strain* is a term commonly used to describe the emotional difficulties experienced as immigrants adapt to their new environment (Gil & Vega, 1999). Combined with previous stressful experiences and recent life events, acculturation strain has been shown to impact depressive symptoms and other manifestations of distress (Cervantes & Castro, 1985; Miranda & Umhoefer, 1998).

Family Functioning and Attitudes

Caregivers, usually parents, must adapt to their own life changes while trying to help their children adapt and adjust. In this situation, the caregiver's mental and emotional health may be negatively affected. A number of scholars have hypothesized and documented the relationship between family functioning in Latino families and stresses associated with immigration and acculturation. In the United States, intergenerational stress is assumed to be normative. However, this experience can be exacerbated in immigrating families in which adolescent rebellion is unanticipated and compounded by children exposed to norms and expectations that are different from those in their home country (Szapocznik & Williams, 2000). Intergenerational conflict has been demonstrated to increase family stress in immigrant families (Szapocznik & Kurtines, 1980; Szapocznik, Santisteban, Kurtines, Perez-Vidal, & Harvis, 1984, 1986; Zayas, 1987). Younger family members who may have more exposure to the host culture through school and other social outlets may adopt norms and values that conflict with those of their elders, creating strained family relationships (Gil

Writing Literature Reviews: A Guide for Students of the Social and Behavioral Sciences

& Vega, 1996; Gil et al., 1994; Szapocznik & Williams, 2000).

300   The link between caregiver mental health and child well-being is well-documented for both native and immigrant populations (Lovejoy, Graczyk, O'Hare, & Neuman, 2000). Parental depression and related symptoms of anxiety may affect youth in a

305 variety of ways. Genetic transmission or living with a depressed parent may predispose children to develop depressive symptoms of their own. The parent–child relationship may be further affected by less positive interactions because of the parent's depressive symp-

310 toms (Lovejoy et al., 2000). Combined with acculturative stress or symptoms that may follow traumatic events before, during, or after immigration, depressive and related symptoms in parents may be a particularly important issue when considering well-being among

315 new immigrant Latino youth.

School Context and Discrimination

    Outside of the family, the school is the most important institutional environment in the socialization and adaptation of immigrant children. Within schools, immigrant youth become intensively exposed to the

320 native culture, experience discrimination from students or teachers, and as a result will form beliefs about what society and persons outside of their family expect from them. Investigations show that school characteristics, such as school size and student–teacher ratios,

325 predict half of the variance in student turnover regardless of ethnicity (Rumberger; 1995; Rumberger & Thomas, 2000). Teacher support and perceived meaningfulness of school have been related to student grades and level of educational investment (Bowen &

330 Bowen, 1998a, 1998b). For Latino youth, the percentage of Latino students in the school also appears to be a salient predictor of academic success or failure (Rumberger & Thomas, 2000). In areas that have not traditionally incorporated significant numbers of im-

335 migrants, school policies and procedures concerning language use or classroom placement may place new immigrant students at academic risk.

    Schools are often a place where students experienced discrimination (Phinney & Tarver, 1988). For

340 new immigrant youth coming to the United States from a country that is much more racially homogenous, seeing themselves as an ethnic minority may be a new and deeply troubling experience (Romero & Roberts, 2003). Unlike racial groups who have experi-

345 enced discrimination across generations, new immigrant parents may not have the strategies for coping with racism that parents in other minority groups use to help their children cope. Research suggests that incorporating an externally imposed identity as an ethnic

350 minority with limited support for understanding and

coping with this task may pose risks to well-being (Smokowski, Chapman, & Bacallao, 2004).

Protective Factors in Latino Families

    Three themes have emerged consistently as important to parenting and adolescent development

355 among Latinos in the United States: respect, familism, and biculturalism (Harwood, Leyendecker, Carlson, Asencio, & Miller, 2002; Buriel, 1993; Vega, 1990).

Respect

    Respeto, in Latino families, refers to teaching children courtesy and decorum in various social con-

360 texts with people of a particular age, sex, and social status. Among adolescents, emphasis on respect in Latino families is associated with greater deference to parental authority and more cooperative behavior (Flanagan, 1996; Fuligni, 1997; Knight, Cota, &

365 Bernal, 1993), cooperative behavior being that which enhances family relationships and precludes risk-taking that might be detrimental to health.

Familism

    Familism, or *familismo,* refers to "feelings of loyalty, reciprocity, and solidarity towards members of

370 the family, as well as the notion of the family as an extension of self" (Cortes, 1995, p. 249). Familism has been associated with larger and more cohesive social networks composed of extended family systems (Miller & Harwood, 2001; Gamble & Dalla, 1997). It

375 has also been associated with a normative emphasis on family solidarity and support that is reflected in a less child-centered approach to everyday activities, more frequent contact between family members, more positive attitudes toward parents by their children, and

380 greater levels of satisfaction with family life (Fuligni et al., 1999; Leyendecker et al., 2000; Suarez-Orozco & Suarez-Orozco, 1995; Zayas & Solari, 1994). Finally, this strong sense of family orientation, obligation, and cohesion appears to improve the physical

385 health, emotional health, and educational well-being of adolescent youth (Bird et al., 2001; Dumka, Roosa, & Jackson, 1997; Hill, Bush, & Roosa, 2003).

Biculturalism

    The majority of immigrants successfully navigate becoming a part of a new culture. LaFromboise,

390 Coleman, and Gerton (1993) propose a curvilinear relationship between acculturation levels and problem behavior and symptoms. They posit that the ability to interact positively with the dominant culture while retaining one's cultural identity promotes optimal

395 functioning. Both high and low levels of acculturation are thus undesirable. A middle level of acculturation, in which one is able to interact comfortably with and enjoy aspects of the host culture yet retain one's cultural identity, appears optimal in terms of promoting

400 general well-being. This ability to move comfortably between two cultures is referred to as biculturalism. Individuals who are bicultural are believed to have less stress and anxiety because they are not choosing between competing cultural loyalties; rather, they are
405 able to embrace both depending on the situations in which they find themselves (LaFromboise et al., 1993).

References

Alba, R., & Nee, V. (1997). Rethinking assimilation theory for a new era of immigration. *International Migration Journal*, *31*, 826–873.

Al-Issa, I., & Tousignant, M. (Eds.). (1997). *Ethnicity, immigration, and psychopathology*. New York: Plenum.

Bird, H., Canino, G. J., Davies, M., Zhang, H., Ramirez. R., & Lahey, B. B. (2001). Prevalence and correlates of antisocial behaviors among three ethnic groups. *Journal of Abnormal Child Psychology*, *29*, 465–478.

Boss, P. (1988). *Family stress management*. Newbury Park, CA: Sage.

Bowen, N. K., & Bowen, G. L. (1998a). The effects of home microsystem risk factors and school microsystem protective factors on student academic performance and affective investment in schooling. *Social Work in Education*, *20*, 219–231.

Bowen, N. K., & Bowen, G. L. (1998b). The mediating role of educational meaning in the relationship between home academic culture and academic performance. *Family Relations*, *47*, 45–51.

Buriel, R. (1993). Childrearing orientations in Mexican American families: The influence of generation and sociocultural factors. *Journal of Marriage and the Family*, *55*, 987–1000.

Caetano, R., & Clark, L. (2003). Acculturation, alcohol consumption, smoking, & drug use among Hispanics. In K. M. Chum, P. B. Organizta, & G. Marin (Eds.) *Acculturation: Advances in theory, measurement and applied research* (pp. 223–239). Washington, DC: American Psychological Association.

Castro, F. G., Coe, K., Gutierres, S., & Saenz, D. (1996). Designing health promotion programs for Latinos. In P. M. Kato, & T. Mann (Eds.). *Handbook of diversity issues in health psychology* (pp. 319–346). New York: Plenum.

Cervantes, R. C., & Castro, F. G. (1985). Stress, coping, and Mexican-American mental health: A systematic review. *Hispanic Journal of Behavioral Sciences*, *7*, 1–73.

Cortes, D. E. (1995). Variations in familism in two generations of Puerto Ricans. *Hispanic Journal of Behavioral Sciences*, *17*, 249–255.

Delgado, M. (Ed.). (1998). *Alcohol use/abuse among Latinos: Issues and examples of culturally competent service*. New York: Haworth.

Dumka, L. E., Roosa, M. W., & Jackson, K. M. (1997). Risk, conflict, mothers' parenting, and children's adjustment in low-income Mexican immigrant and Mexican American families. *Journal of Marriage and the Family*, *59*, 309–323.

Erickson, P. I. (1998). *Latina adolescent childbearing in East Los Angeles*. Austin: University of Texas Press.

Erikson, E. (1950). *Childhood and society*. New York: Norton.

Fernandez, R. R., & Velez, W. (1989). *Who stays? Who leaves? Findings from the ASPIRA five cities high school drop out study* (Working Paper No. 89-1). Washington, DC: ASPIRA.

Flannagan, D. (1996). Mothers' and kindergarteners' talk about interpersonal relationships. *Merrill-Palmer Quarterly*, *42*, 519–536.

Fuligni, A. I. (1999). Authority, autonomy, and parent–adolescent conflict and cohesion: A study of adolescents from Mexican, Chinese, Filipino, and European family backgrounds. *Developmental Psychology*, *34*, 782–792.

Galea, S., Ahern, I., Resnick, H., Kilpatrick, D., Bucuvalas, M., Gold, I., & Vlahov, D. (2002). Psychological sequelae of the September 11 terrorist attacks in New York City. *New England Journal of Medicine*, *346*, 982–987.

Gamble, W. C., & Dalla, R. L. (1997). Young children's perceptions of their social world in single- and two-parent Euro- and Mexican-American families. *Journal of Social and Personal Relationships*, *14*, 357–372.

Gans, H. J. (1992). Second-generation decline: Scenarios for the economics and the futures of the post-1965 American immigrants. *Ethnic Racial Studies*, *15*, 173–192.

Gil, A. G., & Vega, W. A. (1996). Two different worlds: Acculturation stress and adaptation among Cuban and Nicaraguan families. *Journal of Social and Personal Relationships*, *13*, 435–456.

Gil, R. M., & Vasquez, C. (1996). *The Maria paradox*. New York: Putnam.

Gordon, H. J. (1964). *Assimilation in American life: The role of race, religion, and national origins*. New York: Oxford University Press.

Harwood, R., Leyendecker, B., Carlson, V., Asencio, M., & Miller, A. (2002). Parenting among Latino families in the U.S. In M. H. Bornstein (Ed.). *Handbook of parenting: Social conditions and applied parenting* (2nd ed., pp. 21–46). Mahwah, NJ: Erlbaum.

Hernandez, D. (1997). Child development and the social demography of childhood. *Child Development*, *68*, 149–169.

Hill, N. E., Bush, K. R., & Roosa, M. W. (2003). Parenting and family socialization strategies and children's mental health: low-income Mexican-American and Euro-American mothers and children. *Child Development*, *74*, 189–204.

Kao, G., & Tienda, M. (1995). Optimism and achievement: The educational performance of immigrant youth. *Social Science Quarterly*, *76*, 1–19.

Kaufman, P., Chen, X., Choy, S. P., Peter, K., Ruddy, S. A., Miller, A. K. et al. (2001). *Indicators of school crime and safety: 2001* (NCES 2002-113NCI-190075). Washington, DC: U.S. Department of Education and Justice.

King, R. D., Gaines, L. S., Lambert, E. W., Summerfelt, T., & Bickman, L. (2000). The co-occurrence of psychiatric and substance use diagnoses in adolescents in different service systems: Frequency, recognition, cost, and outcomes. *Journal of Behavioral Health Services and Research*, *27*, 417–430.

Knight, G. P., Cota, M. K., & Bernal, M. E. (1993). The socialization of cooperative, competitive, and individualistic preferences among Mexican American children: The mediating role of ethnic identity. *Hispanic Journal of Behavioral Sciences*, *15*, 291–309.

LaFromboise, T., Coleman, H. L., & Gerton, J. (1993). Psychological impact of biculturalism: Evidence and theory. *Psychological Bulletin*, *114*, 395–412.

Leadbeater, B. I. (1996). School outcomes for minority-group adolescent mothers at 28 to 36 months postpartum: A longitudinal follow-up. *Journal of Research on Adolescence*, *6*, 629–648.

Lovejoy, M. C., Graczyk, P. A., O'Hare, E., & Neuman, G. (2000). Maternal depression and parenting behavior: A meta-analytic review. *Clinical Psychology Review*, *20*, 561–592.

Leyendecker, B., Lamb, M. E., Scholmerich, A., & Fracasso, M. P. (1995). The social worlds of 8- and 12-month-old infants: Early experiences in two subcultural contexts. *Social Development*, *4*, 194–208.

Miller, A. M., & Harwood, R. L. (2001). Long-term socialization goals and the construction of infants' social networks among middle-class Anglo and Puerto Rican mothers. *International Journal of Behavioral Development*, *25*, 450–457.

Miranda, A., & Umhoefer, D. (1998). Depression and social interest differences between Latinos in dissimilar acculturation stages. *Journal of Mental Health Counseling*, *20*, 159–171.

National Center for Education Statistics. (1995). *Trends among high school seniors, 1972–1992*. Washington, DC: U.S. Government Printing Office.

Ogbu, J. U. (1987). Variability in minority school performance: A problem in search of an explanation. *Anthropology and Education Quarterly*, *18*, 312–334.

Perlmann, J., & Waldinger, R. (1996). *Second generation decline? Immigrant children past and present: A reconsideration*. Paper presented at the Conference on Becoming American/American Becoming: International Migration to the United States. Sanibel Island, FL.

Phinney, J. S., & Tarver, S. (1988). Ethnic identity search and commitment in black and white eighth graders. *Journal of Early Adolescence*, *8*, 265–277.

Portes, A. (1995). Children of immigrants: Segmented assimilation and its determinants. In A. Portes (Ed.), *The economic sociology of immigration* (pp. 248–279). New York: Russell Sage Foundation.

Portes, A., & Rumbaut, R. G. (2001). *Ethnicities: Children of immigrants in America*. Berkeley: University of California Press.

Romero, A. J., & Roberts, R. E. (2003). Stress within a bicultural context for adolescents of Mexican descent. *Cultural Diversity and Ethnic Minority Psychology*, *9*, 171–184.

Rumbaut, R. (1991). Migration, adaptation, and mental health: The experience of Southeast Asian refugees in the United States. In H. Alderman (ED.). *Refugee Policy: Canada and the United States* (pp. 383–427). Toronto, Ontario, Canada: York Lanes.

Rumberger, R. W. (1995). Dropping out of middle school: A multilevel analysis of students and schools. *American Educational Research Journal*, *32*, 583–625.

Rumberger, R. W., & Thomas, S. L. (2000). The distribution of dropout and turnover rates among urban and suburban high schools. *Sociology of Education*, *73*, 39–67.

Schmidley, D. A. (2001). Profile of the foreign-born population of the United States. *U.S. Census Bureau current population reports* (Series p 23–206). Washington, DC: U.S. Government Printing Office.

Schoen, C., Davis, K., Collins, K. S., Greenberg, L., Des Roches, C., & Abrams, M. (1997). The Commonwealth Fund Survey of the health of adolescent girls. *Women's Health*. Retrieved December 21, 2004, from http://www.cmwf.org/publications/publications_show.htm?doc_id=221230

如何撰寫文獻探討
給社會暨行為科學學生指南

Shrout, P. E., Canino, G. J., Bird, H. R., Rubio-Stipec, M., Bravo, M., & Burnam, M. A. (1992). Mental health status among Puerto Ricans, Mexican Americans, and non-Hispanic whites. *American Journal of Community Psychology, 20,* 729–753.

Smokowski, P., Chapman, M. V., & Bacallao, M. (2004). *Discrimination and mental health in new immigrant youth.* Manuscript submitted for publication.

Suarez-Orozco, C., & Suarez-Orozco, M. M. (1995). *Transformations: Migration, family life, and achievement motivation among Latino adolescents.* Stanford. CA: Stanford University Press.

Suarez-Orozco, C., & Suarez-Orozco, M. M. (2001). *Children of immigration.* Cambridge. MA: Harvard University Press.

Szapocznik, J., & Kurtines, W. (1980). Acculturation, biculturalism and adjustment among Cuban Americans. In A. Padilla (Ed.). *Acculturation: Theory, models, and some new findings* (pp. 139–159). Boulder. CO: Praeger.

Szapocznik, J., Kurtines, W., & Fernandez, T. (1980). Biculturalism involvement and adjustment in Hispanic American youths. *International Journal of Intercultural Relations, 4,* 353–365.

Szapocznik, J., Santisteban, D., Kurtines, W., Perez-Vidal, A., & Harvis, O. (1984). Bicultural effectiveness training: A treatment intervention for enhancing intercultural adjustment in Cuban American families. *Hispanic Journal of Behavioral Sciences,* 6, 317–344.

Szapocznik, J., Santisteban, D., Kurtines, W., Perez-Vidal, A., & Harvis, O. (1986). Bicultural Effectiveness Training (BET): An experimental test of an intervention modality for families experiencing intergenerational/intercultural conflict. *Hispanic Journal of Behavioral Sciences, 4,* 303–330.

Szapocznik, J., & Williams, R. A. (2000). Brief strategic family therapy: Twenty-five years of interplay among theory, research and practice in adolescent behavior problems and drug abuse. *Clinical Child and Family Psychology Review, 3,* 117–134.

Tienda, M., & Kleykamp, M. (2000). *Physical and mental health status of Hispanic adolescent girls: A comparative perspective.* Office of Population Research, Princeton University.

U.S. Census Bureau. (1999). *School enrollment in the United States: Social and economic characteristics of students.* Available from http://www.census.gov

Vega, W. (1990). Hispanic families in the 1980s: A decade of research. *Journal of Marriage and the Family, 52,* 1015–1024.

Velez, W. (1989). High school attrition among Hispanic and non-Hispanic white youths. *Sociology of Education, 62,* 119–133.

Yeh, M., McCabe, L., Hurlburt, M., Hough, R., Hazen, A. L., Culver, S., Garland, A., & Landsverk, J. (2002). Referral sources, diagnoses, and service types of youth in public outpatient mental health care: A focus on ethnic minorities. *Journal of Behavioral Health Services and Research, 29,* 45–60.

Zayas, L. H. (1987). Toward an understanding of suicide risks in young Hispanic females. *Journal of Adolescent Research, 2,* 1–11.

Zayas, L. H., Kaplan, C., Turner, S., Romano, K., & Gonzales-Ramos, G. (2000). Understanding suicide attempts by adolescent Hispanic females. *Social Work, 45,* 53–63.

Zayas, L. H., & Solari, F. (1994). Early childhood socialization in Hispanic families: Context, culture, and practice implications. *Professional Psychology: Research and Practice, 25,* 200–234.

Zhou, M. (1997). Growing up American: The challenge confronting immigrant children and children of immigrants. *Annual Review of Sociology, 23,* 63–95.

Zhou, M. (1999). Segmented assimilation: Issues, controversies, and recent research on the new second generation. In C. Hirschman, P. Kasinitz, & J. Dewind (Eds.). *The handbook of international migration: The American experience* (pp. 196–211). New York: Russell Sage Foundation.

About the authors: *Mimi V. Chapman,* MSW, Ph.D., is assistant professor, School of Social Work, The University of North Carolina at Chapel Hill. *Krista M. Perreira,* Ph.D., is assistant professor, Department of Public Policy, The University of North Carolina at Chapel Hill.

Address correspondence to: Mimi V. Chapman, The University of North Carolina at Chapel Hill, 307 Pittsboro St., #3550, Chapel Hill, NC 27599-3550. E-mail: mimi@email.unc.edu

MODEL LITERATURE REVIEW F

Early Intervention in Autism[1]

ABSTRACT. We now know that professionals can diagnose children with autism when they are as young as 2 years of age (Lord, 1995). Screening and the role of the pediatrician have become even more critical as we have recognized the stability of early diagnosis over time and the importance of early intervention. At this point, experts working with children with autism agree that early intervention is critical. There is professional consensus about certain crucial aspects of treatment (intensity, family involvement, focus on generalization) and empirical evidence for certain intervention strategies. However, there are many programs developed for children with autism that differ in philosophy and a lack of research comparing the various intervention programs. Most of the programs for children with autism that exist are designed for children of preschool age, and not all are widely known or available. While outcome data are published for some of these programs, empirical studies comparing intervention programs are lacking. In this review, existing intervention programs and empirical studies on these programs will be reviewed, with a particular emphasis on the birth to 3 age group.

Background

Autism is a developmental disorder that was first described by Leo Kanner in 1943, in a classic article that included case studies of 11 children. Since that time, the diagnostic criteria have evolved based on continued observations and research, resulting in the current criteria in the *Diagnostic and Statistical Manual of Mental Disorders, Fourth Edition or DSM-IV* (American Psychiatric Association, 1994) and the *International Classification of Diseases or ICD-10* (World Health Organization, 1993). At the present time, *autistic disorder* is defined in terms of qualitative impairments in social interaction and communication, and restricted, repetitive, and stereotyped patterns of behaviors, interests, and activities, with impairments in one of these areas prior to the age of 3 years.

In addition to autistic disorder, there are 4 other specific diagnoses included within the autistic spectrum disorders (ASD) category, which is a term now preferred by most parents and professional organizations (Filipek et al., 2000; Lord & McGee, 2001). Included among them are 2 disorders that are defined by a regression in skills: Rett syndrome and childhood disintegrative disorder. These will not be the focus of this article. Recently, a specific gene has been linked with Rett syndrome (Cheadle et al., 2000). Childhood disintegrative disorder is a very rare disorder, with reported prevalence rates of 0.6 per 100,000 (Chakrabarti & Fombonne, 2001). This disorder involves a period of normal development in the first 2 years of life, followed by a regression in a number of skill areas prior to the age of 4 years, resulting in autistic symptoms.

The other 2 ASD diagnoses are Asperger's disorder and pervasive developmental disorder—not otherwise specified (PDD-NOS). Asperger's disorder, like autistic disorder, includes qualitative impairments in reciprocal social interactions, and restricted, repetitive, and stereotyped patterns of behaviors, interests, and activities. However, unlike autistic disorder, it does not require qualitative impairments in communication. In addition, this diagnosis requires that there is no clinically significant language delay prior to 3 years of age, no cognitive delays, and that the criteria for another specific PDD have not been met. If children who have ever met criteria for autistic disorder are ruled out, the diagnosis of Asperger's disorder is very rare (Miller & Ozonoff, 1997). Nevertheless, the diagnosis of Asperger's disorder is often used for milder cases of high-functioning autism. The final diagnosis within this general category is PDD-NOS. This disorder is characterized by qualitative impairments in social interaction, accompanied by either qualitative impairments in communication or restricted, repetitive, and stereotyped patterns of behaviors, interests, and activities. There is still controversy about this diagnosis, including whether it is "almost autism" or "atypical autism" (Towbin, 1997).

Recent epidemiological studies have reported rates of ASDs as high as 66 per 10,000 (Fombonne, 2002), which is a surprising increase over rates reported in the past. Early identification has increased in importance, as many studies have found that children with ASDs who receive services prior to 48 months of age make greater improvements than those who enter programs after 48 months of age (Harris & Weiss, 1998; Sheinkopf & Siegel, 1998).

Over the past 10 to 15 years, there has been evidence that children with ASDs can be reliably diagnosed as young as 2 years of age (Lord, 1995). One of the largest errors in diagnoses of 2-year-olds referred for autism is underdiagnosing children on the basis of

[1] Literature review excerpt from: Corsello, C. M. (2005). Early intervention in autism. *Infants & Young Children, 18*, 74–85.

Table 1
Intervention Studies

Method	Authors	Subjects/groups	Age, mo	Outcome measure	Findings
TEACCH home program	Ozonoff & Cathcart (1998)	11 TEACCH 11 control	31–69	PEP-R	TEACCH had significant gains in PEP-R scores when compared with controls
Discrete trial	Lovaas (1987)	19 for 40 h 19 for 10 h 21 no treatment	$M = 32$ $M = 35$	IQ score Educational placement Educational support	Intense intervention group: 47% in regular education 31 point IQ gain
Discrete trial	McEachin, Smith, & Lovaas (1993)	19 for 40 h 19 for 10 h	$M = 32$ $M = 35$	IQ score Adaptive behavior score	Intense intervention group: IQ higher Vineland score higher
Discrete trial	Smith, Groen, & Wynn (2000)	15 for 30 h 13 for 5 h by parents, 15 h special cases	18–42	IQ Language Behavioral measure Adaptive measure Class placement	27% in regular education 16 point gain Little difference in behavior Little difference in adaptive scores
Discrete trial & incidental teaching	Luiselli, Cannon, Ellis, & Sisson (2000)	8 younger than 3 y 8 older than 3 y	$M = 2.63$ y $M = 3.98$ y	ELAP or LAP	Duration of treatment was only predictor of change
Applied behavior analysis	Harris & Handleman (2000)	27 subjects No control group	31–65	Class placement	IQ and age predicted class placement
Incidental teaching	McGee, Morrier, & Daly (1999)	28 subjects No control group	29	Verbal sample Peer proximity	82% using meaningful words 71% improved in peer proximity
LEAP	Strain & Hoyson (2000)	6 subjects No control group	30–53	Class placement LAP CARS	Improvements in all areas

* PEP-R, Psychoeducational Profile—Revised; *M*, mean; ELAP, Early Learning Accomplishment Profile; LAP, Learning Accomplishment Profile; IQ, intelligence quotient; LEAP, Lifeskills and Education for Students with Autism and other Pervasive Developmental Disorders; CARS, Childhood Autism Rating Scale; mo, months; h, hours; and y, years.

clinical impression when their scores on standardized measures are consistent with a diagnosis of autism (Lord & Risi, 1998). Possible contributors to this bias are the variability in behaviors of 2-year-olds who have ASDs (Lord, 1995) and the lack of repetitive behaviors in autism that are often present in 3-year-olds, but may not be present in 2-year-olds with autism (Cox et al., 1999; Lord, 1995; Stone et al., 1999).

In this review, early intervention programs and empirical studies available on each of the programs (Table 1) will be reviewed, with a specific focus on the birth to 3 age group. When reviewing empirical support and programs, it is important to differentiate program outcome studies, which are designed to determine if a program is having the desired effect, from controlled empirical studies, which are designed to determine if the program or specific aspects of the program are clearly responsible for the changes observed.

When reviewing research on intervention for children with ASDs, there are several important considerations. These include the age groups included in the study, the control group, the control condition, and the outcome measures (Table 1). When reviewing programs, there are several components to cover, including method of intervention, the format, the setting, who implements the program, and whether it is child- or adult-directed (Table 2). Within this review, we will first focus on issues relevant to early intervention, followed by a review of programs and empirical support for programs, and suggested next steps with regard to intervention with very young children.

Interventions

Over the years, there have been many treatments developed for children with autism, evolving from different philosophies. These include behavioral interventions, developmental interventions, and cognitive–behavioral interventions. While each program is based on a different philosophy and uses unique intervention strategies, there is also considerable overlap in components of the programs.

Two aspects of intervention that are common to most intervention programs designed for ASDs and have empirical support include the intensity of the program and the age at which children should begin intervention. Dawson and Osterling (1997), based on a

Table 2
Intervention Programs

Method	Authors/program	H/wk	Format	Setting	Implementer	Adult- or child-directed
Incidental teaching	Walden Infant Toddler Program	30+	Group 1 to 1	Childcare center Home	Parents Educational staff	Child
Social pragmatic developmental approach	Wetherby & Prizant	Variable	1 to 1	Home	Parent Therapist Teacher	Child
Structured teaching	TEACCH	Variable	Group	Classroom Home	Parents School staff	Adult
Discrete trial	Lovaas (1987)	40	1 to 1	Home	Student therapists Trained consultants	Adult
Discrete trial	Douglass Developmental Disabilities Center	35–45	1 to 1 Small group	Class Home	School staff Parents Student therapists	Adult
Pivotal response intervention	Koegel, Koegel, & Harrows (1999)	Variable	1 to 1 Group	Inclusive setting	Highly skilled specialists Family Consultants	Child
				Home Preschool	School staff	
Behavioral and inclusion	LEAP*	15	Group	Integrated classroom	Teacher	Adult and child
Developmental	Greenspan	Variable	1 to 1	Home	Parents Educational staff	Child
Developmental	Denver Model	22	Group	Classroom	Trained staff	Child

* LEAP indicates Lifeskills and Education for Students with Autism and other Pervasive Developmental Disorders

review of programs for children with autism, report that most programs involve 15 to 25 hours of intervention a week. There is also empirical evidence that chil-
120 dren who enter programs at younger ages make greater gains than those who enter programs at older ages (Harris & Handleman, 2000; Sheinkopf & Siegel, 1998). These studies generally compare children who are older than 4 or 5 years with those who are younger
125 than 4 or 5 years. One study comparing children younger than 3 years with those older than 3 years did not find age differences in improvement (Luiselli, Cannon, Ellis, & Sisson, 2000), which may suggest that 4 years of age is young enough to lead to signifi-
130 cant gains. A potentially complicating factor is that children tend to make intelligence quotient (IQ) gains regardless of intervention at the younger ages (Gabriels, Hill, Pierce, Rogers & Wehner, 2001; Lord & Schopler, 1989). This also leads to difficulties in inter-
135 preting changes in IQ scores, which are often used as an outcome measure.

Most early intervention programs are designed for preschool-aged children, although they may include younger children in their programs as well. It is
140 only more recently that we have been able to identify children with autism as young as 2 years of age. There

are a few programs that are specifically designed for children between birth and 3 years of age. We will first
145 cover the programs designed specifically for the birth to 3 age group, followed by widely available preschool programs, and finally preschool programs that are less widely available.

Early Intervention Programs
Designed for Toddlers
Walden Toddler Program

The Walden Toddler Program (McGee, Morrier, & Daly, 2001) is a program designed specifically for
150 toddlers with autism. The program is based on a typical daycare model, with a focus on using incidental teaching and social inclusion. Incidental teaching is a method of applied behavior analysis (ABA) that uses behavioral principles within natural learning contexts.
155 The environment includes toys and activities that are appealing to young children, and the adult expands on requests and activities that the child initiates. The program is very structured and works on individual goals within planned activities. The program includes typical
160 toddlers and toddlers with autism, between the ages of 15 and 36 months. There are no controlled empirical studies of this program, but program evaluation data found that 82% of the toddlers used meaningful words

when they left the program and 71% of the children
165 showed improvements in their proximity to other children.

Social Pragmatic Communication Approach

Amy Wetherby (Wetherby & Prizant, 1999) has also developed strategies for teaching communication to young children with ASDs, based on a pragmatic
170 communication developmental approach. She has not developed a comprehensive intervention program; however, she has focused her intervention strategies on social pragmatic communication development for children younger than 3 years. Within this approach,
175 the importance of teaching in naturalistic contexts, using a facilitative rather than a directive style, providing opportunities for communication, and consistently and contingently reinforcing communication attempts are emphasized (Wetherby & Prizant, 1999). Other
180 strategies used in teaching communication to young children include incorporating environmental supports to create a predictable environment and teaching peers to initiate and respond to children with ASDs.

Comprehensive Programs

There are many comprehensive programs for
185 children with ASDs; among the most widely known are the Developmental Intervention Model or Greenspan approach (Greenspan & Wieder, 1997), the TEACCH Model (Marcus, Lansing, Andrews, & Schopler, 1978; Mesibov, 1997; Schopler, Mesibov, &
190 Baker, 1982), the UCLA Young Autism Project (Lovaas, 1987), the LEAP (Lifeskills and Education for Students with Autism and other Pervasive Developmental Disorders) Program, and the Denver Model. Most of these programs have been developed for chil-
195 dren of preschool age or older. The Walden Toddler Program is an exception, as it was designed specifically for toddlers. Most of the research on the available models is descriptive rather than based on empirical studies. Currently, there is no empirical evidence that
200 one program is superior to another.

There are many common elements of these programs, although they differ considerably in philosophy. All of these programs include young children (mean ages between 30 and 47 months), active family
205 involvement, and are intensive in hours (12–36 hours a week). In addition, in most of the model programs, staff is well-trained and experienced in working with children with autism and the physical environment is supportive. It is important to note, however, that level
210 of experience and training can vary considerably, particularly when adapting or incorporating model programs into the public domain. All of the programs focus on developmental skills and goals, and contain ongoing objective assessment of progress. The pro-
215 grams also use teaching strategies designed for the generalization and maintenance of skills, individual-

ized intervention plans based on a child's strengths and needs, and planned transitions from preschool to school age. While there are many similarities, each
220 program also has a different emphasis and defining features. Each of the programs will be reviewed below.

The TEACCH Program

The TEACCH program is a statewide, community-based intervention program that emphasizes environmental organization and visual supports, individu-
225 alization of goals, and the teaching of independence and developmental skills. The setting in which the program is implemented varies, depending on the abilities and needs of each child (self-contained classroom, included classroom, home). Teaching strategies
230 are designed to be meaningful to the child with autism, and are therefore taught within the natural environment and within context. The TEACCH program views ASDs as lifelong. From the beginning, it emphasizes skills that are important for future independ-
235 ence. One of the strengths of the TEACCH program is a focus on the lifespan and community-based intervention. One of the weaknesses is the lack of empirical studies of the program.

While the TEACCH program has been in exis-
240 tence for more than 30 years, there are relatively few empirical studies of the program. Two studies, comparing TEACCH interventions with only public education intervention, found significant differences in scores on the Psychoeducational Profile – Revised on
245 follow-up testing (Ozonoff & Cathcart, 1998; Panerai, Ferrante, & Zingale, 2002). Only one of these studies focused on younger children (Ozonoff & Cathcart, 1998) and compared a TEACCH home program, involving 10 sessions, in addition to services provided
250 by the public school, to solely public school services for children between 2 and 6 years of age. Children in the TEACCH group had significantly higher scores on the PEP-R than the children in the control group following 4 months of intervention. The groups in this
255 study were small, but were matched on age, PEP-R pretest scores, and severity of autism and not randomly assigned.

Applied Behavioral Analysis Programs

One of the most widely known and sought-after types of intervention is applied behavior analysis
260 (ABA). Parents and professionals frequently associate the name Ivar Lovaas and the discrete trial format of instruction with ABA intervention. The popularity of the Lovaas intervention is partly the result of his 1987 study (Lovaas, 1987) and Catherine Maurice's (Mau-
265 rice, 1993) book, both of which provide accounts of remarkable improvements and use the term "normal functioning" in the best outcome group of children with autism who received discrete trial intervention.

In reality, discrete trials and the Lovaas method 325
270 is only one specific type of ABA intervention. Applied
behavior analysis includes a number of other intervention strategies and programs that are based on behavioral principles. Many treatment studies are based on
behavioral interventions, which is the case not only in 330
275 autism but also in psychology in general.

The UCLA Young Autism Project uses the
Lovaas method of intervention, specifically discrete
trial intervention, implemented in a one-to-one setting
by trained ABA therapists, supervised by trained pro- 335
280 fessionals. The focus of the first year is on imitation,
interaction, play, and response to basic requests. In the
second year, the focus shifts to continued work on
language, descriptions of emotions, and preacademic
skills. To teach generalization, the children practice 340
285 the skills in other situations and with other people,
once they have mastered them in a one-to-one setting.

The UCLA Young Autism Project has been empirically studied, and the most commonly cited article
is Lovaas' article (Lovaas, 1987). At the time treat- 345
290 ment began, the children had a mean age of 35 months
in the experimental group and 41 months in the control
group. The experimental group received one-to-one
intervention 40 hours a week, and the control group
received intervention 10 hours a week for 2 to 3 years. 350
295 It was this article that started the belief that autistic
children required intervention at least 40 hours a week.
Lovaas (1987) used the term "normal functioning" in
this article (p. 9), and he used IQ and class placement
as outcome variables in this study. Understandably, 355
300 parents have been quite influenced by this study. In a
follow-up study of the children, between 9 and 19
years of age, the experimental group continued to have
significantly higher IQs and Vineland scores than the
control group (McEachin, Smith, & Lovaas, 1993). 360
305 There have been numerous criticisms of this
study, including nonrandom selection of groups (the
age restriction was lower for children without language and children had to achieve a certain mental age
to be included), nonrandom assignment to groups, and 365
310 a large discrepancy between the number of hours of
intervention between the control and experimental
groups. However, it was one of the first empirical
studies of an intervention program for children with
autism. 370
315 More recently, another study on the Lovaas
method of intervention has been published and addresses some of the concerns of the original article
(Smith, Groen, & Wynn, 2000). In this study, the experimental group received approximately 25 hours a 375
320 week of intervention while the control group received
5 hours a week of parent training. In the parent-
training condition, the parents were asked to work with
the children 5 hours a week at home, and they were
enrolled in special education classrooms for 10 to 15 380

hours a week. The children with ASDs in this study
had IQ scores between 35 and 75, and an age range of
18 to 42 months at the time of enrollment in the program.

As in the Lovaas study, the experimental group
had higher IQs than the control group on follow-up. At
the time of follow-up, between the ages of 7 and 8
years, 27% of the children in the experimental group
were in regular education and had made a 16-point IQ
gain. There were little differences in Child Behavior
Checklist (CBCL) scores and Vineland scores between
the 2 groups. The outcome was not as impressive as in
Lovaas' original study, as only 27% of the children in
this study were defined as best outcome (IQ > 85 and
in regular education without support) as opposed to
47% in the McEachin (McEachin et al., 1993) study.
The average IQ gain was half that reported in the
McEachin study, and the behavior and adaptive skills
ratings were still reported as problematic in the experimental group in the Smith et al. study. Clearly,
children made gains in this program, but not the same
degree of progress described in the original Lovaas
and McEachin studies. The Smith study, with better
controls and design, suggests that children improve
more than they would with early education and focused parent support or education, but do not recover
when they receive approximately 25 hours a week of
intensive one-to-one ABA intervention.

Another model ABA program is the Douglass
Developmental Center at Rutgers in New Jersey. This
program has different levels, starting with a one-to-one
format for the youngest children, then moving to a
small classroom with a 2:1 ratio and then to a class
with typical peers, using a model similar to the LEAP
program, which is described later in this article. A follow-up study of the children in the program reported
that age and IQ predicted outcome (Harris & Handleman, 2000). Approximately 33% of the children had
average IQs upon discharge from the program. It is
important to note that 22% of the children (6 out of 27)
had IQ changes from the range of mental retardation to
average. Of these 6 children, 4 (67%) were between 3
and 4 years of age and 2 (33%) were between 4 and 5
years of age at the time they started the program. Upon
exit from the program, 3 of these children were in special education, 2 were in integrated classrooms with
support, and 1 child was fully included without support.

More recently, embedded trials, pivotal response
training, and incidental teaching have emerged from
the ABA literature. These techniques are less well-
known and less widely available at the present time,
but hold some promise for intervention for very young
children with autism. Contemporary ABA strategies
include naturalistic teaching methods, such as natural
language paradigms (Koegel, O'Dell, & Koegel,

1987), incidental teaching (Hart, 1985; McGee, Krantz, & McClannahan, 1985; McGee, Morrier, & Daly, 1999), time delay and milieu intervention (Charlop, Schriebman, & Thibodeau, 1985; Charlop & Trasowech, 1991; Hwang & Hughes, 2000; Kaiser, 1993; Kaiser, Yoder, & Keetz, 1992), and pivotal response training or teaching core behaviors, with the idea that they will lead to changes in other behaviors and skills (Koegel, 1995; Koegel, Camarata, Koegel, Ben-Tall, & Smith, 1998). These methodologies have commonalities, including teaching within natural contexts (during play, snack, work, within the classroom, at home), the use of natural reinforcers (reinforcing children for requesting by giving them what they are asking for), and systematic trials that are initiated by the child (the child makes the initial attempt).

Contemporary behavioral approaches have resulted in good outcomes for teaching language content, including single word vocabulary, describing objects and pictures, responding to questions, and increasing the intelligibility of speech (Goldstein, 1999; Koegel et al., 1998; Krantz, Zalewski, Hall, Fenski, & McClannahan, 1981). McGee and colleagues (1999) also reported good outcomes through natural reinforcers of vocalization, speech shaping, and incidental teaching. Contemporary behavioral approaches have also been applied with some success to teach broader communication skills, such as functional communication, that may lead to decreases in challenging behaviors (Horner et al., 1990; Horner, Carr, Strain, Todd, & Reed, 2000; Koegel, Koegel, & Surratt, 1992). Spontaneous language is more difficult to teach and requires a number of naturalistic as well as developmental methods of instruction (Watson, Lord, Schaffer, & Schopler, 1989). Children who use more spontaneous language earlier in treatment have more favorable language outcomes.

Very few intervention strategies have demonstrated success using behavioral interventions in teaching skills, such as joint attention and symbolic abilities, that focus on what are considered core deficits to children with autism. However, there are a few studies that documented some success in teaching symbolic play skills through pivotal response training (Stahmer, 1995; Thorp, Stahmer, & Schreibman, 1995). Other studies that have demonstrated some improvements in these skills include increase in gaze to regulate social interactions, joint attention, shared positive affect, and the use of conventional gestures. Recently, there has also been documentation that naturalistic teaching of communication skills leads to improvements in joint attention in children with autism (Buffington, Krantz, McClannahan, & Poulson, 1998; Hwang & Hughes, 2000; Pierce & Schreibman, 1995).

The LEAP Program

There is an emphasis on including peers in intervention programs because children with autism have difficulty generalizing skills learned with adults to interactions with peers (Bartak & Rutter, 1973). Including typical peers is an essential component of both the LEAP program and the Walden Toddler Program. The LEAP program includes 10 typical children and 6 children with autism between the ages of 3 and 5 years in each classroom. The children are in class for 15 hours a week. The classroom is structured and incorporates incidental teaching and other ABA methods of intervention. Interventions are both child- and adult-directed. Peers are considered to be an essential element of the program (Harris & Handleman, 1994). Peer-mediated techniques for increasing interactions involve teaching peers to be "play organizers." These strategies have been shown to be effective in increasing social interactions, which have generalized to some extent and been maintained over time (Goldstein, Kaczmarek, Pennington, & Shafer, 1992; Hoyson, Jamison, & Strain, 1984; Strain, Kerr, & Ragland, 1979; Strain, Shores, & Timm, 1977).

Developmental Interventions

Developmental intervention is a specific term used to describe a philosophy and specific strategies for working with children with autism. One common feature of developmental interventions is that they are child-directed. In developmental interventions, the environment is organized to encourage or facilitate communicative and social interactions. The child initiates and the adult responds. There is limited empirical support for developmental approaches, but there is some support for language outcomes using such strategies (Hwang & Hughes, 2000; Lewy & Dawson, 1992; Rogers & Lewis, 1989) and many case studies (Greenspan & Wieder, 1997) using these approaches. Rogers and Lewis (1989) have documented improvements in symbolic play as a result of structured, development-based programs, and Lewy and Dawson (1992) also demonstrated improvements in gaze, turn taking, object use, and joint attention with a child-directed imitation strategy.

There are some limitations to developmental interventions. Because the intervention approach is child-directed, it requires that the child engage in behaviors to which the adult can respond. Many children with autism do not explore the environment in the way that typical children might. They may become stuck on certain activities or not play with the toys present in their environment. Developmental methods require considerable effort and skill on the part of the teacher or therapist, as she or he must know what child behaviors to respond to as well as how to respond. When the child engages in behaviors that the therapist can re-

The Greenspan Model

490   One of the most well-known developmental approaches is the Greenspan approach, also known as the Developmental Individual Difference (DIR) Model (Greenspan & Wieder, 1997). The Greenspan model is described as a "relationship-based model," in which

495 the goal is to help the child develop interpersonal connections that will lead to the mastery of cognitive and developmental skills, including (1) attention and focus, (2) engaging and relating, (3) nonverbal gesturing, (4) affect cuing, (5) complex problem solving, (6) sym-

500 bolic communication, and (7) abstract and logical thinking. The program is based on following the child's lead and looking for opportunities to "close the circle of communication" or respond in a way that leads to expanding a skill or interaction. Within this

505 model, it is recommended that a child spend at least 4 hours a day in spontaneous play interactions with an adult, at least 2 hours a day in semistructured skill building activities with an adult, and at least 1 hour a day in sensory-motor play activities. The Greenspan

510 program is supplemented by time in an inclusive preschool program, speech and occupational therapy.

    The DIR method of intervention is highly dependent on the skills of the parent or professional implementing the program. It requires that the adult rec-

515 ognizes when and how to respond to a child's actions and behaviors, which can make it difficult to implement the program in the community. This differs from many behavioral approaches, which have a prescribed pattern of responses and adult-initiated teaching trials.

520 There are currently no controlled studies of this program.

The Denver Model

    The Denver model (Rogers & Lewis, 1989) is also based on a developmental model of intervention. This program is delivered within a classroom setting

525 that is on a 12-month calendar and meets 4 to 5 hours a day, 5 days a week. The focus is on positive affect, pragmatic communication, and interpersonal interactions within a structured and predictable environment. Almost all activities and therapies are conducted

530 within a play situation. Goals of the program include using positive affect to increase a child's motivation and interest in an activity or person, using reactive language strategies to facilitate communication, and teaching mental representation.

535   There is outcome data available on the program, based on 31 children between 2 and 6 years of age with ASDs. Children demonstrated significant developmental improvements in cognition, language, social/emotional development, perceptual/fine motor

540 development, and gross motor development after 6 to 8 months in the program, after accounting for expected developmental progress. While only 53% of the children had functional speech when they entered the program, 73% had functional speech at follow-up.

545

550

555

560

565

570

575

580

Conclusion

    The available evidence from a variety of programs and studies suggests that early intervention leads to better outcomes. As we have seen, a number of studies have demonstrated that children make greater gains when they enter a program at a younger age. It is important to keep in mind that most of the empirical support for the difference in gains is comparing children younger than 4 or 5 years to children older than 4–5 years of age. The preschool years are still considered "early" when it comes to early intervention.

    There are many strategies for working with children with autism and not all of them are equally known or available. Most of the empirical studies have been conducted on ABA interventions. While there is evidence that certain strategies can be effective for teaching specific skills to children with autism, there is not currently evidence that one program is better than any other. Furthermore, most of the programs are developed for children aged 3 and older, and many interventionists are currently attempting to adapt their programs to better meet the needs of the 0 to 3 age group. This leads to complications when recommending intervention programs to parents of young children with autism. At this time, there is a great deal of interest in the common elements in the programs when making recommendations, including parent involvement, intensity, a predictable environment, incorporating the child's interests, actively engaging the child, and focusing on individualized developmental goals. It is important that professionals and parents are informed about the progress they can expect for their child, as well as remain aware that most research does not support a "cure" or "recovery" from autism. At this point, most of the programs focus on children of preschool age, and there is still much to learn about intervention for the birth to 3 age group.

References

American Psychiatric Association. (1994). *Diagnostic and statistical manual of mental disorders* (4th ed.) Washington, DC: Author.

Bartak, L., & Rutter, M. (1973). Special educational treatment of autistic children: A comparative study: I. Design of study and characteristics of units. *Journal of Child Psychology and Psychiatry and Allied Disciplines, 14,* 161–179.

Buffington, D. M., Krantz, P. J., McClannahan, L. E., & Poulson, C. L. (1998). Procedures for teaching appropriate gestural communication skills to children with autism. *Journal of Autism and Developmental Disorders, 28,* 535–545.

Chakrabarti, S., & Fombonne, E. (2001). Pervasive developmental disorders in preschool children. *JAMA, Special Issue, 285,* 3093–3099.

Charlop, M. H., Schreibman, L., & Thibodeau, M. G. (1985). Increasing spontaneous verbal responding in autistic children using a time delay procedure. *Journal of Applied Behavior Analysis, 18,* 155–166.

Charlop, M. H., & Trasowech, J. E. (1991). Increasing autistic children's daily spontaneous speech. *Journal of Applied Behavior Analysis, 24,* 747–761.

Cheadle, J. P., Gill, H., Fleming, N., Maynard, J., Kerr, A., Leonard, H., et al. (2000). Long-read sequence analysis of the MECP2 gene in Rett syndrome patients: Correlation of disease severity with mutation type and location. *Human Molecular Genetics, 9*, 1119–1129.

Cox, A., Klein, K., Charman, T., Baird, G., Baron-Cohen, S., Swettenham, J., et al. (1999). Autism spectrum disorders at 20 and 42 months of age: Stability of clinical and ADI-R diagnosis. *Journal of Child Psychology and Psychiatry and Allied Disciplines, 40*, 719–732.

Dawson, G., & Osterling, J. (1997). Early intervention in autism. In M. J. Guralnick (Ed.), *The effectiveness of early intervention* (pp. 307–326). Baltimore: Brookes.

Filipek, P. A., Accardo, P. J., Ashwal, S., Baranek, G. T., Cook, E. H., Jr., Dawson, G., et al. (2000). Practice parameter: Screening and diagnosis of autism: Report of the Quality Standards Subcommittee of the American Academy of Neurology and the Child Neurology Society. *Neurology, 55*, 468–479.

Fombonne, E. (2002). Epidemiological trends in rates of autism. *Molecular Psychiatry, 7*, S4–S6.

Gabriels, R. L., Hill, D. E., Pierce, R. A., Rogers, S. J., & Wehner, B. (2001). Predictors of treatment outcome in young children with autism: A retrospective study. *Autism, 5*, 407–429.

Goldstein, H. (1999). *Communication intervention for children with autism: A review of treatment efficacy.* Paper presented at the First Workshop of the Committee on Educational Interventions for Children with Autism, National Research Council, Department of Communication Sciences, Florida State University; December 13–14, 1999; Tallahassee, FL.

Goldstein, H., Kaczmarek, L., Pennington, R., & Shafer, K. (1992). Peer-mediated intervention: Attending to, commenting on, and acknowledging the behavior of preschoolers with autism. *Journal of Applied Behavior Analysis, 25*, 289–305.

Greenspan, S., & Wieder, S. (1997). Developmental patterns and outcomes in infants and children with disorders in relating and communicating: A chart review of 200 cases of children with autism spectrum diagnoses. *Journal of Developmental and Learning Disorders, 1*, 87–141.

Harris, S. L., & Handleman, J. S. (2000). Age and IQ at intake as predictors of placement for young children with autism: A four- to six-year follow-up. *Journal of Autism and Developmental Disorders, 30*, 137–142.

Harris, S. L., & Handleman, J. S. (Eds.). (1994). *Preschool education programs for children with autism.* Austin, TX: Pro-Ed.

Harris, S. L., & Weiss, M. J. (1998). *Right from the start: Behavioral intervention for young children with autism.* Bethesda, MD: Woodbine House.

Hart, B. (1985). Naturalistic language training strategies. In S. F. Warren & A. Rogers-Warren (Eds.), *Teaching functional language* (pp. 63–88). Baltimore: University Park Press.

Horner, R. H., Carr, E. G., Strain, P. S., Todd, A. W., & Reed, H. K. (2000). *Problem behavior interventions for young children with autism: A research synthesis.* Paper presented at the Second Workshop of the Committee on Educational Interventions for Children with Autism, National Research Council, Department of Special Education, University of Oregon; April 12, 2000; Eugene, OR.

Horner, R. H., Dunlap, G., Koegel, R. L., Carr, E. G., Sailor, W., Anderson, J. A., et al. (1990). Toward a technology of "nonaversive" behavioral support. *Journal of the Association for Persons with Severe Handicaps, 15*, 125–132.

Hoyson, M., Jamison, B., & Strain, P. S. (1984). Individualized group instruction of normally developing and autistic-like children: The LEAP curriculum model. *Journal of the Division for Early Childhood, 8*, 157–172.

Hwang, B., & Hughes, C. (2000). Increasing early social-communicative skills of preverbal preschool children with autism through social interactive training. *Journal of the Association for Persons with Severe Handicaps, 25*, 18–28.

Kaiser, A. (1993). Functional language. In M. Snell (Ed.), *Instruction of students with severe disabilities* (pp. 347–379). New York: Macmillan Publishing Co.

Kaiser, A. P., Yoder, P. J., & Keetz, A. (1992). Evaluating milieu teaching. In S. F. Warren & J. Reichle (Eds.), *Causes and effects in communication and language intervention* (Vol. 1 ed., pp. 9–47). Baltimore: Paul H. Brookes.

Koegel, L. K. (1995). Communication and language intervention. In *Teaching children with autism: Strategies for initiating positive interactions and improving learning opportunities* (pp. 17–32). Baltimore: Paul H. Brookes.

Koegel, R. L., Camarata, S., Koegel, L. K., Ben-Tall, A., & Smith, A. E. (1998). Increasing speech intelligibility in children with autism. *Journal of Autism and Developmental Disorders, 28*, 241–251.

Koegel, R. L., Koegel, L. K., & Surratt, A. (1992). Language intervention and disruptive behavior in preschool children with autism. *Journal of Autism and Developmental Disorders, 22*, 141–153.

Koegel, R. L., O'Dell, M. C., & Koegel, L. K. (1987). A natural language teaching paradigm for nonverbal autistic children. *Journal of Autism and Developmental Disorders, 17*, 187–200.

Krantz, P. J., Zalewski, S., Hall, L., Fenski, E., & McClannahan, L. E. (1981). Teaching complex language to autistic children. *Analysis & Intervention in Developmental Disabilities, 1*, 259–297.

Lewy, A. L., & Dawson, G. (1992). Social stimulation and joint attention in young autistic children. *Journal of Abnormal Child Psychology, 20*, 555–566.

Lord, C. (1995). Follow-up of two-year-olds referred for possible autism. *Journal of Child Psychology and Psychiatry and Allied Disciplines, 36*, 1365–1382.

Lord, C., & McGee, J. P. (2001). *Educating children with autism.* Washington, DC: National Academy Press.

Lord, C., & Risi, S. (1998). Frameworks and methods in diagnosing autism spectrum disorders. *Mental Retardation and Developmental Disabilities Research Reviews: Special Issue: Autism, 4*, 90–96.

Lord, C., & Schopler, E. (1989). The role of age at assessment, developmental level, and test in the stability of intelligence scores in young autistic children. *Journal of Autism and Developmental Disorders, 19*, 483–499.

Lovaas, O. I. (1987). Behavioral treatment and normal educational and intellectual functioning in young autistic children. *Journal of Consulting and Clinical Psychology, 55*, 3–9.

Luiselli, J. K, Cannon, B. O., Ellis, J. T., & Sisson, R. W. (2000). Home-based behavioral interventions for young children with autism/pervasive developmental disorder: A preliminary evaluation of outcome in relation to child age and intensity of service delivery. *Autism, 4*, 389–398.

Marcus, L. M., Lansing, M., Andrews, C. E., & Schopler, E. (1978). Improvement of teaching effectiveness in parents of autistic children. *Journal of the American Academy of Child Psychiatry, 17*, 625–639.

Maurice, C. (1993). *Let me hear your voice: A family's triumph over autism.* New York: Kopf.

McEachin, J. J., Smith, T., & Lovaas, O. I. (1993). Long-term outcome for children with autism who received early intensive behavioral treatment. *American Journal on Mental Retardation , 97*, 359–372.

McGee, G. G., Krantz, P. J., & McClannahan, L. E. (1985). The facilitative effects of incidental teaching on preposition use by autistic children. *Journal of Applied Behavior Analysis, 18*, 17–31.

McGee, G. G., Morrier, M. J., & Daly, T. (1999). An incidental teaching approach to early intervention for toddlers with autism. *Journal of the Association for Persons With Severe Handicaps, 24*, 133–146.

McGee, G. G., Morrier, M. J., & Daly, T. (2001). The Walden Early Childhood Program. In J. Handleman & S. L. Harris (Eds.). *Preschool education programs for children with autism* (2nd ed., pp. 157–190). Austin: Pro-ed.

Mesibov, G. B. (1997). Formal and informal measures on the effectiveness of the TEACCH program. *Autism, 1*, 25–35.

Miller, J. N., & Ozonoff, S. (1997). Did Asperger's cases have Asperger disorder? A research note. *Journal of Child Psychology and Psychiatry and Allied Disciplines, 38*, 247–251.

Ozonoff, S., & Cathcart, K. (1998). Effectiveness of a home program intervention for young children with autism. *Journal of Autism and Developmental Disorders, 28*, 25–32.

Panerai, S., Ferrante, L., & Zingale, M. (2002). Benefits of the Treatment and Education of Autistic and Communication Handicapped Children (TEACCH) programme as compared with a non-specific approach. *Journal of Intellectual Disability Research, 46*, 318–327.

Pierce, K., & Schreibman, L. (1995). Increasing complex social behaviors in children with autism: Effects of peer-implemented pivotal response training. *Journal of Applied Behavior Analysis, 28*, 285–295.

Rogers, S. J., & Lewis, H. (1989). An effective day treatment model for young children with pervasive developmental disorders. *Journal of the American Academy of Child and Adolescent Psychiatry, 28*, 207–214.

Schopler, E., Mesibov, G., & Baker, A. (1982). Evaluation of treatment for autistic children and their parents. *Journal of the American Academy of Child Psychiatry, 21*, 262–267.

Sheinkopf, S. J., & Siegel, B. (1998). Home based behavioral treatment of young children with autism. *Journal of Autism and Developmental Disorders, 28*, 15–23.

Smith, T., Groen, A. D., & Wynn, J. W. (2000). Randomized trial of intensive early intervention for children with pervasive developmental disorder. *American Journal on Mental Retardation, 105*, 269–285.

Stahmer, A. C. (1995). Teaching symbolic play skills to children with autism using pivotal response training. *Journal of Autism and Developmental Disorders, 25*, 123–141.

Stone, W. L., Lee, E. B., Ashford, L., Brissie, J., Hepburn, S. L., Coonrod, E. E., et al. (1999). Can autism be diagnosed accurately in children under 3 years? *Journal of Child Psychology and Psychiatry and Allied Disciplines, 40*, 219–226.

Strain, P. S., Kerr, M. M., & Ragland, E. U. (1979). Effects of peer-mediated social initiations and prompting/reinforcement procedures on the social behavior of autistic children. *Journal of Autism and Developmental Disorders, 9*, 41–54.

Strain, P. S., Shores, R. E., & Timm, M. A. (1977). Effects of peer social initiations on the behavior of withdrawn preschool children. *Journal of Applied Behavior Analysis, 10*, 289–298.

Thorp, D. M., Stahmer, A. C., & Schreibman, L. (1995). Effects of so-ciodramatic play training on children with autism. *Journal of Autism and Developmental Disorders, 25*, 265–282.

Towbin, K. E. (1997). Pervasive developmental disorder not otherwise speci-fied. In D. J. Cohen & F. R. Volkmar (Eds.), *The handbook of autism and other pervasive developmental disorders* (2nd ed., pp. 123–147). New York: Wiley.

Watson, L. R., Lord, C., Schaffer, B., & Schopler, E. (1989). *Teaching spon-taneous communication to autistic and developmentally handicapped chil-dren*. New York: Irvington Publishers Inc.

Wetherby, A. M., & Prizant, B. M. (1999). Enhancing language and commu-nication development in autism: Assessment and intervention guidelines. In D. B. Zager (Ed.), *Autism: Identification, education, and treatment* (2nd ed., pp. 141–174). Mahwah, NJ: Erlbaum.

World Health Organization. (1992). *The ICD 10 Classification of Mental and Behavioral Disorders: Clinical Descriptions and Diagnostic Guidelines*. Geneva, Switzerland: World Health Organization.

About the author: Dr. Christina Corsello is the Associate Director of The University of Michigan Autism & Communications Disor-ders Center. Dr. Corsello is a Licensed Clinical Psychologist and an adjunct clinical instructor in the University of Michigan Psychiatry Department. Dr. Corsello specializes in diagnosis and intervention of children with autism. Dr. Corsello is responsible for the clinical training of psychology graduate students, interns, and postdoctoral students. Dr. Corsello also conducts evaluations and clinical inter-vention programs, collaborates in research, and conducts training seminars nationally and internationally on the leading standardized diagnostic instruments. Dr. Corsello previously worked at The Uni-versity of North Carolina and The University of Chicago.

Address correspondence to: Dr. Christina M. Corsello, UMACC, University of Michigan, 1111 East Catherine Street, Ann Arbor, MI 48109-2054.

MODEL LITERATURE REVIEW G

Effects of Viewing the Television Program *Between the Lions* on the Emergent Literacy Skills of Young Children[1]

One of the most compelling findings from recent evaluations of reading research is that children who have an inadequate start in reading rarely catch up (National Reading Panel, 2000; National Research
5 Council, 1998). For example, in Juel (1988), 88% of children identified as poor readers at the end of first grade were still identified as poor readers at the end of the fourth grade. Reading trajectories are established early and are difficult to change. Johnson and Alling-
10 ton (1991) observed that "remedial reading is gener- ally not very effective in making children more liter- ate" (p. 1001). Therefore, eliminating the need for re- medial reading in the first place may be the most sen- sible alternative. Finding ways that all children can
15 bolster their early literacy experiences, sustain those gains, and become successful, fluent readers is an im- portant challenge that demands attention.

Whitehurst and Lonigan (1998, 2001) proposed that adequate early reading instruction includes oppor-
20 tunities for children to acquire knowledge of two in- terdependent domains of information. First, children need sources of information that directly support their understanding of the meaning of print (i.e., outside-in processes: vocabulary knowledge, conceptual knowl-
25 edge, story schemas, comprehension). Children also need to be able to translate print into sounds and sounds into print (i.e., inside-out: phonemic aware- ness, letter-sound correspondence). Recent interven- tion research designed to provide young children with
30 the necessary early literacy skills to succeed in school has reported that changes in preschool emergent liter- acy environments (see, e.g., Neuman & Roskos, 1997) and teacher-directed (see, e.g., O'Connor, 2000; O'Connor, Jenkins, & Slocum, 1995), parent-led
35 (Whitehurst & Lonigan, 1998), and peer-mediated strategies (Mathes, Howard, Allen, & Fuchs, 1998) help children acquire these skills. However, the ability to widely implement such programs will be difficult and costly, and, as a result, the scale of impact on the
40 nation's population of young children learning to read may be slow and small.

Building on their success teaching preschoolers school readiness skills via television (i.e., *Sesame Street*), the producers of a new television program for
45 young children, in collaboration with leading reading

experts, created a program that incorporated both out- side-in and inside-out emergent literacy processes (Strickland & Rath, 2000). Their goal was to reach all segments of society, especially children who might
50 have little or no access to print resources or few infor- mal literacy opportunities in their homes. The perva- siveness of television (e.g., over 99% of U.S. homes have a television set; *Statistical Abstracts, 2000*) offers a powerful way to address the literacy needs of chil-
55 dren who have "low redundancy of educational oppor- tunity" (Mielke, 1994, p. 126).

Models of Learning from Television

The process of acquiring new information from television is complex, involving attention to and sub- sequent comprehension of program stimuli. When
60 children interact with television, they integrate the various stimuli into meaningful, comprehensible bits of information by attending to important or interesting aspects of the stimuli (Huston & Wright, 1989). Al- though a great deal of knowledge about young children
65 has been gained from past research on traditional print and television, the obvious step of merging print and television to enhance early literacy development is a more recent phenomenon (Linebarger, 2001). Models from the television literature provide the most useful
70 framework for developing testable hypotheses about how print on screen might affect children's attention and learning through television.

Huston, Wright, and their colleagues (Huston & Wright, 1983; Rice, Huston, & Wright, 1982) pro-
75 posed a model of attention to television where percep- tually salient features of the stimulus initially draw a child's attention to the screen. When a child has little experience with television, sounds and unusual visual effects trigger the basic orienting mechanisms of the
80 perceptual system (Miron, Bryant, & Zillman, 2001). These salient features or formal features provide struc- ture and give meaning to the sensory images contained in the programs (Calvert, Huston, Watkins, & Wright, 1982; Campbell, Huston, & Wright, 1987).
85 Comprehension is then improved when formal features are used to denote key moments and critical content for young children's focal attention.

---

[1] Literature review excerpt from: Linebarger, D. L., Kosanic, A. Z., Greenwood, C. R., & Doku, N. S. (2004). Effects of viewing the television program *Between the Lions* on the emergent literacy skills of young children. *Journal of Educational Psychology*, *96*, 297–308. Copyright © 2004 by the American Psychological Association. All rights reserved. Reprinted with permission.

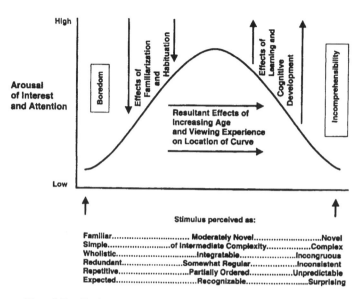

Figure 1. Traveling lens model. Reprinted from "The Forms and Codes of Television: Effects of Children's Attention, Comprehension, and Social Behavior," by M. L. Rice, A. C. Huston, and J. C. Wright, p. 32, in *Television and Behavior: Ten Years of Scientific Progress and Implications for the Eighties*, edited by D. Pearl, L. Bouthilet, and J. Lazar, 1982, Washington, DC: U.S. Government Printing Office. In the public domain.

Huston and Wright (1989; Rice et al., 1982) further elaborated this model of attention (see Figure 1). At
90 various points while viewing a program, children make a series of attentional decisions. These decisions are based on cues of perceptual salience, comprehensibility of the program, and interpretability of the content. This model also predicts that attention is a joint
95 function of the stimulus features, both form and content, and the dispositions of the viewer, including experience with the material, experience with the medium, and general world knowledge. Interest and attention are a function of the stimulus characteristics. A
100 stimulus perceived as "moderately novel, of intermediate complexity, integratable, somewhat regular, partially ordered, and recognizable" (Huston & Wright, 1989, p. 117) should elicit the greatest amounts of interest and attention. When the stimulus characteristics
105 no longer arouse interest or attention because of familiarization and habituation (i.e., familiar, simple, wholistic, redundant, repetitive, and expected), children no longer attend to them. Likewise, if the stimulus characteristics fall at the incomprehensible end of
110 these continua (i.e., novel, complex, incongruous, inconsistent, unpredictable, and surprising), children do not attend because the stimulus is immediately per-

ceived as incomprehensible. High-end stimuli become more familiar and hence more comprehensible with
115 repetition and thus gain attention, whereas the low-end stimuli undergo further habituation with repetition and thus lose attention. The resultant of these two kinds of changes over time is that the high points of interest and attention slowly migrate toward the higher end.
120 With age and viewing experience, the child's focus continually moves toward more cognitively challenging stimuli; hence, the stimuli that are initially incomprehensible "gradually move toward and through the child's focal lens of maximum interest, and then lose
125 attention as they are habituated and become old hat" (Huston & Wright, 1989, p. 118).

Wright (2001) introduced an adjunct theoretical approach where the influence of an early condition, intervention, or other basis for predicting diverging
130 individual differences over time will be greater if it produces differences opposite in direction from the developmental changes expected normatively for that outcome. Conversely, if the antecedent produces differences favoring the developmental direction that is
135 normatively expected, its effects will be attenuated, and harder to detect. (Wright, 2001, p. 1)

For instance, in the literature for television viewing and aggression, interventions that would make boys less aggressive and more prosocial (e.g., educational
140 television) or that would make girls less prosocial or more aggressive (e.g., violent television) would be easier to detect than would an intervention that moves the child in a direction he or she is already progressing toward developmentally.

Application to Literacy

145 These two theoretical models of learning from television suggest that children with little print experience and, subsequently, poor reading skills may find print overly challenging and not attend to it, whereas children who are fluent readers may ignore print be-
150 cause they have habituated to it. When the curricular content of the program falls into the children's focus because it is appropriately interesting and cognitively challenging (i.e., as described in Figure 1), it would be predicted that this group of children would benefit
155 most from the content. Therefore, those children who are most at risk because they have no or very little familiarity with print are not able to benefit initially from exposure to it via television. Only through repeated exposure (either on or off television, or both)
160 would the print stimuli become accessible for these children. Similarly, children who are fluent readers also might not benefit from print exposure because they already have these skills in their repertoire and are progressing along a positive reading trajectory. The
165 group in the middle, emerging readers who are not yet fluent but do have modest levels of print exposure and reading skill, would then be the group evidencing the greatest gains in reading skill development because print is within their traveling lens; however, they may
170 still need significant instruction to attain reading fluency.

Most of the work supporting these models to date has been about comprehension of television content and not about acquisition of literacy skills or the appli-
175 cation of reading risk status to learning associated with viewing television. In addition, descriptions of the children's home media environments and subsequent relations to literacy skill acquisition are a new facet of what is known in the literature. Thus, the purposes of
180 this article are to describe the home media environments of young children, to determine whether watching an educational television series featuring literacy content for young children could improve these children's emergent literacy skills, and to examine
185 whether home media environments and emergent literacy skill improvements varied as a function of reading risk status.

References

Calvert, S. L., Huston, A. C., Watkins, B. A., & Wright, J. C. (1982). The relation between selective attention to television forms and children's comprehension of content. *Child Development, 53*, 601–610.

Campbell, T. A., Huston, A. C., & Wright, J. C. (1987). Form cues and content difficulty as determinants of children's cognitive processing of televised educational messages. *Journal of Experimental Child Psychology, 43*, 311–327.

Huston, A. C., & Wright, J. C. (1983). Children's processing of television: The informative functions of formal features. In J. Bryant & D. R. Anderson (Eds.), *Children's understanding of TV: Research on attention and comprehension* (pp. 37–68). New York: Academic Press.

Huston, A. C., & Wright, J. C. (1989). The forms of television and the child viewer. In G. Comstock (Ed.), *Public communication and behavior* (Vol. 2, pp. 103–158). San Diego, CA: Academic Press.

Johnson, P., & Allington, R. (1991). Remediation. In R. Barr, M. Kamil, P. Mosenthal, & P. D. Pearson (Eds.), *Handbook of reading research* (Vol. 2, pp. 984–1012). New York: Longman.

Juel, C. (1988). Learning to read and write: A longitudinal study of 54 children from first through fourth grades. *Journal of Educational Psychology, 80*, 437–447.

Linebarger, D. L. (2001). Learning to read using television: The effects of captions and narration. *Journal of Educational Psychology, 93*, 288–298.

Mathes, P. G., Howard, J. K., Allen, S. H., & Fuchs, D. (1998). Peer-assisted learning strategies for first-grade readers: Responding to the needs of diverse learners. *Reading Research Quarterly, 33*, 62–94.

Mielke, K. (1994). *Sesame Street* and children in poverty. *Media Studies Journal, 8*, 125–134.

Miron, D., Bryant, J., & Zillman, D. (2001). Creating vigilance for better learning from television. In D. G. Singer & J. L. Singer (Eds.), *Handbook of children and the media* (pp. 153–181). Thousand Oaks, CA: Sage.

National Reading Panel (2000). *Teaching children to read: An evidence-based assessment of the scientific research literature on reading and its implications for reading instruction*. Retrieved February 24, 2004, from http://www.nichd.nih.gov/publications/nrp/smallbook.htm

National Research Council (1998). *Preventing reading difficulties in young children*. Washington, DC: National Academy Press.

Neuman, S., & Roskos, K. (1997). Literacy knowledge in practice: Contexts of participation for young writers and readers. *Reading Research Quarterly, 32*, 10–32.

O'Connor, R. E. (2000). Increasing the intensity of intervention in kindergarten and first grade. *Learning Disabilities Research and Practice, 15*, 43–54.

O'Connor, R. E., Jenkins, J. R., & Slocum, T. A. (1995). Transfer among phonological tasks in kindergarten: Essential instructional content. *Journal of Educational Psychology, 87*, 202–217.

Rice, M. L., Huston, A. C., & Wright, J. C. (1982). The forms and codes of television: Effects of children's attention, comprehension, and social behavior. In D. Pearl, L. Bouthilet, & J. Lazar (Eds.), *Television and behavior: Ten years of scientific progress and implications for the eighties* (pp. 24–38). Washington, DC: U.S. Government Printing Office.

Statistical Abstracts. (2000). Washington, DC: Government Publishing Office.

Strickland, D. S., & Rath, L. K. (2000, August). *Between the Lions*: Public television promotes early literacy. *Reading Online, 4*. Retrieved February 24, 2004, from http://www.readingonline.org/articles/art_index.asp?HREF=/articles/strickland/index.html

Whitehurst, G. J., & Lonigan, C. J. (1998). Child development and emergent literacy. *Child Development, 69*, 848–872.

Whitehurst, G. J., & Lonigan, C. J. (2001). Emergent literacy: Development from prereaders to readers. In S. B. Neuman & D. K. Dickinson (Eds.), *Handbook of early literacy research* (pp. 11–29). New York: Guilford Press.

Wright, J. C. (2001, April). Demographic influences on long-term effects of television: A theoretical approach. In S. M. Fisch (Chair), *Theoretical approaches to the long-term effects of television viewing*. Symposium conducted at the meeting of the Society for Research in Child Development, Minneapolis, MN.

About the authors: *Deborah L. Linebarger*, Annenberg School for Communication, University of Pennsylvania. *Anjelika Z. Kosanic, Charles R. Greenwood*, and *Nii Sai Doku*, Juniper Gardens Children's Project, University of Kansas.

Acknowledgments: We thank Rhett Larsen, Patty Eskrootchi, and Denise Chowning, who collected the data for this project. We are especially thankful to Beth Kirsch, Linda K. Rath, other WGBH Boston staff, and Sirius Thinking, Ltd. staff, who provided valuable assistance and feedback in the completion of this project. Thanks are also extended to those schools, families, and children from the greater Kansas City metropolitan area who kindly volunteered to participate in this study.

Address correspondence to: Deborah L. Linebarger, Annenberg School for Communication, University of Pennsylvania, 3620 Walnut Street, Philadelphia, PA 19104. E-mail: dlinebarger @asc.upenn.edu

附錄 A

ERIC 搜尋實例

1. *Title*: Bright Beginnings for Babies
   Abstract: Notes the importance of positive human interactions and experiences on child development, and describes seven developmental areas crucial to early brain development. Suggests ways to enhance young children's development of emotional intelligence, social skills, motor skills, vision, language acquisition, vocabulary, and thinking skills.

2. *Title*: Diminutivization Supports Gender Acquisition in Russian Children
   Abstract: Gender agreement elicitation was used with Russian children to examine how diminutives common in Russian child-directed speech affect gender learning. Children were shown pictures of familiar and novel animals and asked to describe them after hearing their names, which contained regular morphophonological cues to masculine or feminine gender. Results indicate regularizing features of diminutives....

3. *Title*: Subject Realization and Crosslinguistic Interference in the Bilingual Acquisition of Spanish and English: What Is the Role of the Input?
   Abstract: Investigated whether crosslinguistic interference occurs in the domain of subject realization in Spanish in a bilingual (Spanish–English) acquisition context. Also explored whether the source of the interference is due to child-internal crosslanguage contact between English and Spanish or due to the nature of the language input in a bilingual family.

4. *Title*: Spanish Diminutives in Mother–Child Conversations
   Abstract: Examined gender and age patterns of diminutive use in conversations between Spanish-speaking Peruvian mothers and their 3- and 5-year-old children. Results confirm previous findings concerning both parents' greater use of diminutives with younger children and children's early acquisition of this aspect of morphology. Findings do not support studies on gender differences in parental use of diminut....

5. *Title*: Teaching Children with Autism Self-Initiations As a Pivotal Response
   Abstract: A study assessed whether two children (ages 4–6) with autism could be taught a child-initiated query as a pivotal response to facilitate the use of grammatical morphemes. Children learned the strategy and acquired and generalized the targeted morpheme. Children also showed increases in mean length of utterance and verb acquisition.

6. *Title*: Economy and Word Order Patterns in Bilingual English–Dutch Acquisition
   Abstract: Reports on bilingual acquisition of syntax. Draws on data from a bilingual English–Dutch child whose word order patterns testify to the fact that movement never occurs beyond the target and when deviant word orders are attested they result from lack of raising....

7. *Title*: Let's Change the Subject: Focus Movement in Early Grammar
   Abstract: Reanalyzes what the literature has taken to be children's productions of Gen subjects and argues that Gen subjects do not exist in child English. Suggests that what look like Gen subjects appear only in specific discourse contexts: contexts of contrastive focus or contexts of emphatic focus.

8. *Title*: Partial Constraint Ordering in Child French Syntax
   Abstract: Reanalyzes production data from three French children to make two basic points. Shows that tense and agreement inflection follow independent courses of acquisition (in child French). Using a mechanism of grammatical development based on partial rankings of constraints, analysis successfully models over three stages the frequency with which children use tensed, agreeing, and nonfinite verbs.

9. *Title*: Negative DPs and Elliptical Negation in Child English
   Abstract: Presents a new syntactical analysis of the negative marker "no" in child English. Claims that the majority of "no" constructions in early child English are determiner phrases in which "no" appears as a determiner. The claim is supported on the basis of distributional and morphosyntactic tests, a discourse analysis of children's elliptical negatives, and a comparison of "no" constructions in child....

10. *Title*: Young Children's Acquisition of Wh-Questions: The Role of Structured Input
    Abstract: Examined young children's acquisition of wh-questions. Children heard a wh-question and attempted to repeat it; a "talking bear" answered. The same format was used for two intervention sessions for children in a quasicontrol condition. Suggests very little input—if concentrated and varied and presented so the child attends to it and attempts to parse it—is sufficient for rapid extraction and....

11. *Title*: Lexically Specific Constructions in the Acquisition of Inflection in English
    Abstract: Investigates the acquisition of elements that instantiate the grammatical category of "inflection"—copula "be," auxiliary "be" and 3sg present agreement—in longitudinal transcripts from five children, aged from 1 year and 6 months to 3 years and 5 months in the corpora examined. Aimed to determine whether inflection emerges as a unitary category, as predicted by recent generative accounts, or....

12. *Title*: The Role of Output Speech in Literacy Acquisition: Evidence from Congenital Anarthria
    Abstract: Examines literary acquisition in a congenitally speechless child. Explains that in spite of a complete oral apraxia, the child developed normal intelligence and acquired complete mastery of reading and writing skills. Notes that though both his verbal memory and metaphonological skills were surprisingly preserved, he showed relative impairment in writing nonwords. Discusses the implications of....

13. *Title*: Acquisition of Multiple Languages among Children of Immigrant Families: Parents' Role in the Home-School Language Pendulum
    Abstract: This study examined immigrant parents' role in young children's language learning in various linguistic contexts, focusing on how parents helped their children learn English while maintaining their mother tongue. Findings of questionnaires, observations, and interviews indicated factors supporting children's learning, including parents' interest in the two languages, joint parent–child activities....

14. *Title*: The Status of Functional Categories in Child Second Language Acquisition: Evidence from the Acquisition of CP
    Abstract: Examines the status of the functional categories in child second language (L2) acquisition of English. Results from longitudinally collected data are reported, presenting counterevidence for recent hypotheses on early L2 acquisition that assume the following: (1) structure building approach according to which the acquisition of functional categories follows an implicational sequence of....

15. *Title*: The Role of Writing in Classroom Second Language Acquisition
    Abstract: Argues that writing should play a more prominent role in classroom-based studies of second language acquisition. Contends that an implicit emphasis on spoken language is the result of the historical development of the field of applied linguistics and parent disciplines of structuralist linguistics, linguistic anthropology, and child language development.

16. *Title*: Children's Acquisition of Early Literacy Skills: Examining Family Contributions
    Abstract: Examined the relationship between the family environment and children's language and literacy skills, guided by the three models of: (1) Family as Educator; (2) Resilient Family; and (3) Parent–Child Care Partnership. Found that only the Family as Educator model was significantly related to child language and literacy outcomes.

17. *Title*: Babytalk: Developmental Precursors to Speech
    Abstract: Examines the process of language acquisition as well as scientists' understanding of the intricate process of learning to talk. Specifically addresses: (1) foundations of language; (2) prenatal period; (3) first month after birth; and (4) conversation. Also discusses adult–child activities that stimulate language learning.

18. *Title*: Learning English and Losing Chinese: A Case Study of a Child Adopted from China
    Abstract: Looked at the acquisition of English and the loss of Chinese by a child adopted from China into an English-speaking Canadian family at the age of 17 months. The child's production and comprehension of Chinese were observed from 4 weeks after her arrival. Both acquisition of Chinese and loss of English were remarkably fast. Data suggest that the child's language acquisition was founded on already....

19. *Title*: Getting Started without a System: From Phonetics to Phonology in Bilingual Development
    Abstract: Argues that the question of whether bilinguals initially have one or two phonetic systems is out of place because before the child develops a fairly substantial vocabulary of about 100 words, there is no system at all. This is supported by analyses of early word patterns drawn from three bilingual children.

20. *Title*: The Early Phonological Development of a Farsi–English Bilingual Child
    Abstract: Addresses the issue of whether bilingual children begin phonological acquisition with one phonological system or two. Five hypotheses are suggested for the possible structure of the bilingual child's phonological system. Analyses from a longitudinal study of a Farsi–English bilingual infant supported the hypothesis that the child had acquired two separate phonologies with mutual influence.

21. *Title*: Morphological and Syntactic Transfer in Child L2 Acquisition of the English Dative Alternation
    Abstract: Compares the acquisition of the English to- and for-dative alternation by native-speaking English, Japanese, and Korean children. Investigates whether second language learners (L2) like native language learners overextend the double-object variant and whether L2 learners, like L2 adults, transfer properties of the native language grammar.

22. *Title*: Is There Primacy of Aspect in Child L2 English?
Abstract: Investigates whether the aspect-before-tense hypothesis accounts for the acquisition of tense-aspect morphology in child second language English. Addressed whether early uses of tense-aspect inflections can be analyzed as a spell-out of semantic/aspectual features of verbs. Data are from a longitudinal study of an 8-year-old Russian-speaking child who was learning English in the United States.

23. *Title*: Development of Academic Skills from Preschool through Second Grade: Family and Classroom Predictors of Developmental Trajectories
Abstract: Relates children's experiences with parents and teachers to the acquisition of academic skills from preschool through second grade. Children tended to show better academic skills across time if their parents had more education and reported progressive parenting beliefs. Family background and teacher–child relationships indicated that a closer relationship with the teacher was positively related....

24. *Title*: Implications of Child Errors for the Syntax of Negation in Korean
Abstract: Reviews the existing record pertaining to the acquisition of negation in Korean and juxtaposing it with current research in cross-linguistic child language acquisition.

25. *Title*: Multilanguage Programs. Beginnings Workshop
Abstract: Presents five articles on multilanguage programs in early childhood education: "Bilingualism/Multilingualism and Language Acquisition Theories" (Evienia Papadaki-D'Onofrio); "Training and Supporting Caregivers Who Speak a Language Different from Those in Their Community" (Joan Matsalia and Paula Bowie); "Language Immersion Programs for Young Children" (Francis Wardle); and "Hearing Parents in....

26. *Title*: Determinant of Acquisition Order in Wh-Questions: Re-Evaluating the Role of Caregiver Speech
Abstract: Analyzed naturalistic data from 12 2- to 3-year-old children and their mothers to assess the relative contribution of complexity and input frequency to wh-question acquisition. Results suggest that the relationship between acquisition and complexity may be a by-product of the high correlation between complexity and the frequency with which mothers use particular wh-words and verbs.

27. *Title*: French–English Bilingual Acquisition of Phonology: One Production System or Two?
Abstract: Examines onset, atrophy, and possible interaction of a set of patterns in the speech of a child acquiring French and English. Examines how data bear on the question of whether the bilingual child has two distinct production phonologies from the earliest stage. Tests recent claims consonant harmony patterns.

28. *Title*: The Use and Function of Nonfinite Root Clauses in Swedish Child Language
Abstract: Examines the use and structure of so-called nonfinite root clauses, including root infinitives and root supines, in Swedish child language. Investigation of four Swedish child language corpora shows that children use nonfinite root clauses in a systematic way. Also shows that children's use of root infinitives is closely associated with a particular speech act or speech function called the....

29. *Title*: Tense and Aspect in Early Child Russian
Abstract: Observed child–parent interaction to investigate the early temporal and aspectual morphology in four monolingual Russian-speaking children. Analysis of data obtained in weekly videotaped sessions shows early mastery of all tenses as well as grammatical aspect at an early age.

30. *Title*: Why Is "Is" Easier than "-s"?: Acquisition of Tense/Agreement Morphology by Child Second Language Learners of English
Abstract: This study of first-language-Russian children acquiring English as a second language investigates the reasons behind omission of verbal inflection in second language (L2) acquisition and argues for presence of functional categories in second-language grammar. Shows that child L2 learners, while omitting inflection, almost never produce incorrect tense/agreement morphology.

31. *Title*: Age and Language Skills of Deaf Children in Relation to Theory of Mind Development
Abstract: A study examined theory of mind acquisition in 34 children (ages 5–10) with deafness using four traditional false-belief tasks. Results indicate the age of the child was strongly related to theory of mind development and that the children were delayed by approximately 3 years in this cognitive developmental milestone.

32. *Title*: Promoting Language and Literacy Development through Parent–Child Reading in Hong Kong Preschoolers
Abstract: Evaluated Hong Kong Chinese kindergarten children's literacy development through dialogic reading, typical reading, and control groups. Found that early literacy-related activities in the home have strong effects on literacy growth and language development in Chinese. Concluded that success of the dialogic reading technique contributes to the goal of raising global literacy standards and....

33. *Title*: Approache Pluraliste du Developpement et Etude des Variations Procedurals en Production D'Orthographes Inventees [A Pluralistic Approach to the Development and Study of Procedural Variations in the Production of Invented Spelling]
Abstract: This study used a pluralistic model to examine the procedures used by two preschoolers to achieve written productions using invented orthographies. The model allows children's procedural variations to be taken into consideration by understanding the hierarchy of different processing modes available to children in completing the task and incorporates children's procedural variations at the origin....

34. *Title*: Phonological Neighborhoods in the Developing Lexicon
Abstract: Phonological neighborhood analyses of how children's expressive lexicons, maternal input, and an adult lexicon were conducted. In addition to raw counts and frequency-weighted counts, neighborhood size was calculated as the proportion of the lexicon to which each target word is similar, to normalize for vocabulary size differences. Analyses revealed children's lexicons contain more similar....

35. *Title*: Opposites Attract: The Role of Predicate Dimensionality in Preschool Children's Processing of Negations
Abstract: Three experiments investigated the role of oppositional predicate dimensionally in 4- and 5-year-old children's processing of negation. Children often recalled negated items as affirmations, which suggests that children's use of predicate dimensionally contributes to nonclassical processing.

36. *Title*: Morphosyntactic Constructs in the Development of Spoken and Written Hebrew Text Production
Abstract: Examined the distribution of two Hebrew nominal structures in spoken and written texts of two genres produced by 90 native-speaking participants. Written texts were found to be denser than spoken texts lexically and syntactically as measured by the number of novel N-N compounds and denominal adjectives per clause; in older age groups this difference was found to be more pronounced.

37. *Title*: Early Syntactic Creativity: A Usage-Based Approach
Abstract: Determined the degree to which a sample of one child's creative utterances related to utterances that the child previously produced. Utterances were intelligible, multiword utterances produced by the child in a single hour of interaction with her mother. Results suggest the high degree of creativity in early English child language could be partially based upon entrenched schemas and a small....

38. *Title*: A Connectionist Account of Spanish Determiner Production
Abstract: Investigates phonological cues available to children and explores the possibility that differential frequency in the linguistic input explains the priority given to masculine forms when children are faced with ambiguous novel terms. A connectionist model of determiner production was incrementally trained on a lexicon of determiner-noun phrases taken from parental speech in a longitudinal study.

39. *Title*: Early Words, Multiword Utterances and Maternal Reading Strategies As Predictors of Mastering Word Inflections in Finnish
Abstract: Reports how children's language skills and mothers' book-reading strategies predict mastery of word inflections in a sample of Finnish children. Three theoretical models were tested on the longitudinal data using path analyses. Suggests direct developmental continuity from producing words and multiword utterances on later inflectional growth, but indirect effects of maternal strategies on....

40. *Title*: Outcomes of Early Language Delay: II. Etiology of Transient and Persistent Language Difficulties
Abstract: A study involving 356 twin pairs with early language delay found environmental influences shared by both twins were more substantial than genetic factors. Heritability was significantly higher in those with persisting difficulties but only when assessed in terms of parental concern at 3 years or professional involvement at 4 years.

41. *Title*: Outcomes of Early Language Delay: I. Predicting Persistent and Transient Language Difficulties at 3 and 4 Years
Abstract: Parent-based assessments of vocabulary, grammar, nonverbal ability, and use of language to refer to past and future were obtained for 8,386 twins at age 2. Of the children who had early language delay, 44.1% had persisting language difficulties at 3 years and 40.2% had persisting language difficulties at 4 years.

42. *Title*: Designing an Outcome Study to Monitor the Progress of Students with Autism Spectrum Disorders
Abstract: The Autism Spectrum Disorders Outcome Study is tracking the educational progress of 67 students (ages 2–6) with autism. Initial results, based on the first 16 months of the study, indicate the majority of children have made significant progress in social interaction, expressive speech, and use of language concepts.

43. *Title*: A Developmental Perspective on Language Assessment and Intervention for Children on the Autistic Spectrum
Abstract: This article presents a developmental perspective on language acquisition that can serve as a framework for understanding and treating the language and communication challenges faced by children with

autism. Profiles of five children (ages 3–7) with autism spectrum disorders are discussed to illustrate the application of a Developmental Social–Pragmatic Model.

44. *Title*: Out of the Mouths of Babes: Unlocking the Mysteries of Language and Voice
Abstract: Summarizes three studies that have revolutionized child psychology by teaching us that children are biologically programmed to learn language; children's language development is orderly and pragmatic, but grammatically mysterious; and children's linguistic self-expression reveals some disturbing ways in which they have been socialized. Presents nine ways this information can be useful at camp.

45. *Title*: "Want That" Is Understood Well before "Say That," "Think That," and False Belief: A Test of de Villiers's Linguistic Determinism on German-Speaking Children
Abstract: Two experiments with monolingual German-speaking 2.5- to 4.5-year-olds showed a consistent developmental gap between children's memory/inference of what someone wanted and what someone wrongly said or thought. Correct answers emerged with mastery of the false-belief task. It was concluded that the observed gap constrains de Villiers's linguistic determinism, which claims that acquisition of....

46. *Title*: Beginning to Communicate after Cochlear Implantation: Oral Language Development in a Young Child
Abstract: This longitudinal case study examined the emergence of oral language skills in a child with deafness whose cochlear implant was activated at 20 months. Normal or above-normal rates of development were observed in decreased production of nonwords, increased receptive vocabulary, type-token ratio, regular use of word combinations, and phrase comprehension.

47. *Title*: Parent-Reported Language Skills in Relation to Otitis Media during the First 3 Years of Life
Abstract: A study investigated the degree of association between parent-reported language scores at ages 1, 2, and 3 years, and the cumulative duration of middle-ear effusion (MEE) during the first 3 years in 621 children. At age 3, the cumulative duration of MEE significantly contributed to the variance in parent-reported scores.

48. *Title*: A Prospective Longitudinal Study of Phonological Development in Late Talkers
Abstract: Free play and elicited language samples were obtained monthly for 10 to 12 months from five late-talking children. Analysis indicated that three of the children resolved their late onset of speech by 33 to 35 months of age. Both quantitative factors (e.g., limited phonetic inventory) and qualitative factors (e.g., atypical error patterns) were potential markers of long-term phonological delay.

49. *Title*: Drawing Insight from Pictures: The Development of Concepts of False Drawing and False Belief in Children with Deafness, Normal Hearing, and Autism
Abstract: Three studies examined theory-of-mind concepts among children ages 6–13 years with deafness or autism, and 4-year-olds with normal development. Findings indicated that while the children with deafness or autism scored significantly lower on standard tests of false belief understanding, they scored higher on even the most challenging drawing-based tests.

50. *Title*: Cross-Cultural Similarities in the Predictors of Reading Acquisition
Abstract: Compared reading development among kindergartners in Hong Kong and the United States using measures of word recognition, phonological awareness, speeded naming, visual spatial skill, and processing speed. Found that models of early reading development were similar across cultures. The strongest predictor of reading was phonological awareness. Speed of processing strongly predicted speeded naming....

51. *Title*: Reorganizing the Lexicon by Learning a New Word: Japanese Children's Interpretation of the Meaning of a New Word for a Familiar Artifact
Abstract: Three studies investigated how 3-year-old Japanese children interpret the meaning of a new word associated with a familiar artifact. Findings suggest that children flexibly recruit clues from multiple sources, including shape information and function familiarity, but the clues are weighed in hierarchical order so children can determine the single most plausible solution in a given situation when....

52. *Title*: Understanding Child Bilingual Acquisition Using Parent and Teacher Reports
Abstract: Examined the extent to which years of exposure to a language, amount of language input at home and at school, and amount of exposure to reading and other literacy activities in a language relate to observed bilingual performance in young children as obtained from teacher and parent reports.

53. *Title*: Caregivers' Contingent Comments to 9-Month-Old Infants: Relationships with Later Language
Abstract: Examined the relationship between caregiver input to 9-month-old infants and their subsequent language. Mother–infant dyads were videotaped at ages 9, 12, and 30 months. Language comprehension was measured by parent report and correlated with an independent language measure. Found that the total number of words mothers used when their infants were 9 months predicted vocabulary.

54. *Title*: Minding the Absent: Arguments for the Full Competence Hypothesis
Abstract: Suggests that the systematic omission of functional material by young children, contrary to current

beliefs, argues for the presence of functional structure because in the absence of such structure what is expected is not a systematic omission of functional material but rather its random use.

55. *Title*: Communication Intervention for Infants and Toddlers with Cochlear Implants
Abstract: Discussion of communication intervention with very young children who have cochlear implants examines: (1) the developmental appropriateness of materials and procedures; (2) behavior and compliance issues; (3) the need for less didactic instruction and more incidental learning emphasis; and (4) recognition of the home as the primary venue for language learning. A communication assessment protocol....

56. *Title*: Early Language Stimulation of Down's Syndrome Babies: A Study on the Optimum Age to Begin
Abstract: Examined the marked delay in language acquisition suffered by babies with Down's Syndrome and how early treatment affects the subsequent observed development among 36 subjects in Spain. Found statistically significant differences in language acquisitions in favor of newborns, compared with 90-day-old through 18-month-old infants who experienced early stimulation treatment.

57. *Title*: Measuring Early Language Development in Preschool Children with Autism Spectrum Disorder Using the MacArthur Communicative Development Inventory (Infant Form)
Abstract: Collected data on early language development of preschool children with autism spectrum disorder, using the MacArthur Communicative Development Inventory. The pattern of development of understanding phrases, word comprehension and expression, and production of gestures, was compared to the typical pattern. Implications for assessment and intervention are discussed.

58. *Title*: The Development of Inversion in Wh-Questions: A Reply to Van Valin
Abstract: Responds to a critique of an earlier article. Reexamines the pattern of inversion and universion in Adam's (1973) wh-question data and argues that the Role and Reference grammar explanation put forth cannot account for some of the developmental facts it was designed to explain.

59. *Title*: Genre and Evaluation in Narrative Development
Abstract: Examined Venezuelan children's developing abilities to use evaluative language in fictional and personal narratives. Looks at whether the use of evaluative language varies in fictional and personal narratives, there is a relationship between the use of evaluative language in these two narrative genres, and the role children's age and socioeconomic status.

60. *Title*: Lexical Choice Can Lead to Problems: What False-Belief Tests Tell Us about Greek Alternative Verbs
Abstract: Greek has two verbs of agency that can be used interchangeably to mean "to look for." Examined whether children will obey the principle of contrast to diagnose that one verb is mentalistic and the other is to be construed behaviorally. A study of mothers' verb use confirmed that the verb preferred in home use gave below chance performance on a false-belief test while the less-established verb....

61. *Title*: The Role of Modeling and Request Type on Symbolic Comprehension of Objects and Gestures in Young Children
Abstract: Considered whether modeling and the type of an adult's request influenced children's ability at age 1 year and 8 months and 2 years and 2 months to comprehend gestures and replica objects as symbols for familiar objects. Evaluated whether modeling and type of request influenced children's ability at 1 year and 8 months to understand familiar objects as symbols. Suggests that symbolic....

62. *Title*: Chinese Children's Comprehension of Count-Classifiers and Mass-Classifiers
Abstract: Two experiments were conducted to test Chinese children's comprehension of count-and mass-classifiers. Participants were Chinese-speaking children ages 3 thru 8, plus 16 adults. Results cohere with the linguistic analysis that the count-mass distinction is relevant in Chinese grammar. Results also cohere with the current theory in cognitive development that the ontological constraint reflected in....

63. *Title*: Effects of Lexical Factors on Lexical Access among Typical Language-Learning Children and Children with Word-Finding Difficulties
Abstract: Studied the influence of lexical factors, known to impact lexical access in adults, on the word retrieval of children. Participants included 320 typical and atypical language-learning children, ranging from 7 to 12 years of age. Lexical factors examined included word frequency, age of acquisition, neighborhood density, neighborhood frequency, and stress pattern. Findings indicated that these fact....

64. *Title*: Form Is Easy, Meaning Is Hard: Resolving a Paradox in Early Child Language
Abstract: Offers resolutions to the paradox of infants' ability to abstract patterns over specific items and toddlers' lack of ability to generalize patterns over specific English words/constructions. Argues that contradictions are rooted in differing methodologies and stimuli content. Suggests that the patterns infants extract from linguistic input are not tied to meaning; toddlers do not lose these....

65. *Title*: Why Do Children Learn to Say "Broke"? A Model of Learning the Past Tense without Feedback
Abstract: Presents a hybrid ACT-R model that shows U-shaped learning of the English past tense without direct

feedback, changes in vocabulary, or unrealistically high rates of regular verbs. Illustrates that the model can learn the default rule, even if regular forms are infrequent. Shows that the model can explore the question of why there is a distinction between regular and irregular verbs by examining....

66. *Title*: Seeing the Invisible: Situating L2 Literacy Acquisition in Child–Teacher Interaction
Abstract: Revisits an earlier study on English-as-a Second-Language (ESL) children's emergence into literacy, which was conducted with 5- and 6-year olds at a multilingual K-12 school in Casablanca, Morocco. Discusses the notion of "synchronicity"—a dynamic oneness between teacher and child—as the distinguishing feature of three classrooms where children's literacy development was taking place at an....

67. *Title*: The Play and Language Behavior of Mothers with and without Dyslexia and Its Association to Their Toddlers' Language Development
Abstract: The play and language behavior of mothers with ($n = 49$) and without ($n = 49$) specific reading disabilities were investigated during play with their 14-month-old children. Typically, reading mothers produced significantly more symbolic play and language in play interactions with their children than did the mothers with reading disabilities.

68. *Title*: Normative Scripts for Object Labeling during a Play Activity: Mother–Child and Sibling Conversations in Mexican-Descent Families
Abstract: Patterns of mother and sibling object labeling were observed during play. Subjects were 40 Mexican-descent mothers, their children aged 2–3, and older siblings. Mothers provided names for objects (referential labeling) as often as they mentioned objects within the ongoing activity (labeling in action), while siblings more frequently used referential labeling. Results suggest diverse....

69. *Title*: Moving Beyond Linear Trajectories of Language Shift and Bilingual Language Socialization
Abstract: Mexican-descent families' language socialization experiences and the evolution of their bilingualism were examined through interviews with 63 third-graders and their parents of various immigrant generations and follow-up interviews with 38 families 4–7 years later. Interviews revealed extremely positive attitudes about English, Spanish, bilingualism, and native language maintenance; changing....

70. *Title*: Bibliography of Recent Scholarship in Second Language Writing
Abstract: This bibliography cites and summarizes books, essays, and research reports on second- and foreign-language writing and writing instruction that have become available to its compilers during the period of January 1, 2002 to March 31, 2002.

71. *Title*: Neurolinguistic Aspects of Bilingualism
Abstract: Discusses aphasia, the language deficit resulting from damage to the language centers of the brain, in order to evaluate how research on bilingual and polyglot aphasic individuals has contributed to our knowledge of the representation of language and languages in neurologically intact humans' brains. Examines the literature on treating lateral dominance for language in bilinguals and evaluates....

72. *Title*: /l/ Production in English–Arabic Bilingual Speakers
Abstract: Reports an analysis of /l/ production by English–Arabic bilingual children. Addresses the question of whether the bilingual develops one phonological system or two by calling for a refinement of the notion of system using insights from recent phonetic and sociolinguistic work on variability in speech. English–Arabic bilinguals were studied.

73. *Title*: Phonetic Evidence for Early Language Differentiation: Research Issues and Some Preliminary Data
Abstract: Highlights methodological issues that impact phonetic-phonological data collection and interpretation in studies of early language differentiation. Issues include language context, bilingual versus monolingual mode, and adult listening bias. Presents data from two bilingual children, aged 4 and 2, learning Japanese and English.

74. *Title*: Developing Vowel Systems As a Window to Bilingual Phonology
Abstract: Examines vowel systems of German–Spanish bilingual children to determine whether there is interaction between the two language systems. Given the differences in the vowel systems, which point to a more marked system in the case of German, two predictions are considered: 1) bilingual children will acquire the vowel length contrast in their German productions later than monolingual German-speaking....

75. *Title*: The Role of Markedness in the Acquisition of Complex Prosodic Structures by German–Spanish Bilinguals
Abstract: Addresses bilingual phonological development in the prosodic field by studying the transition from a single metrical foot to the production of one foot preceded by an unstressed syllable or to the production of two consecutive feet. Uses monolingual data to form a baseline comparison with the bilingual data. Establishment of two different constraint hierarchies for the two languages studied....

76. *Title*: Effects of Prelinguistic Milieu Teaching and Parent Responsivity Education on Dyads Involving Children with Intellectual Disabilities
Abstract: This study evaluated the effectiveness of Prelinguistic Milieu Teaching for toddlers ($n = 39$) with

Writing Literature Reviews: A Guide for Students of the Social and Behavioral Sciences

intellectual disabilities and responsivity education for their parents as a means of facilitating children's communication and language production skills. Comparison of parent–child pairs receiving or not receiving the intervention found the intervention facilitated parental responsivity. Effects on....

77. *Title*: Evaluating Attributions of Delay and Confusion in Young Bilinguals: Special Insights from Infants Acquiring a Signed and a Spoken Language
Abstract: Examines whether early simultaneous bilingual language exposure causes children to be language delayed or confused. Cites research suggesting normal and parallel linguistic development occurs in each language in young children and young children's dual language developments are similar to monolingual language acquisition. Research on simultaneous acquisition of French oral and sign language is....

78. *Title*: Developmental Dyslexia as Developmental and Linguistic Variation: Editor's Commentary
Abstract: This commentary reviews forthcoming articles on the scientific study of dyslexia, genetic and neurophysiological aspects of dyslexia, cross-linguistic aspects of literacy development and dyslexia, and theory-based practice. It concludes that educators should continue to strive to promote theory-based research and evidence-based practice to achieve better prevention of and intervention for....

79. *Title*: The Speech and Language of Children Aged 25 Months: Descriptive Data from the Avon Longitudinal Study of Parents and Children
Abstract: The Avon Longitudinal Study of Parents and Children (ALSPAC) provided descriptive data on the speech and language of 25-month-olds. Findings indicated great range in the stage of expressive language development achieved. Girls showed more advanced skills than boys. A clear pattern was identified in use of sound classes. Child verbal comprehension and expressive stage related to pretend play, turn....

80. *Title*: It's Never Too Early
Abstract: Describes a statewide language-development program developed among Maryland's city, county, and regional library systems to help parents prepare their preschoolers for success in school. Discusses child development, the role of libraries, storytelling training, and preschool literacy efforts by the Public Library Association; and lists Web resources.

81. *Title*: Syllable Omission by Two-Year-Old Children
Abstract: A study examined the ability of 10 2-year-olds to produce minimal pairs of novel trisyllabic words with primary stress on the first or second syllables. The syllables contained dissimilar or similar vowel contrasts to determine if segments affected omission. Omission was more frequent for the first syllable of weak-strong-weak word pairs.

82. *Title*: From Ear to Cortex: A Perspective on What Clinicians Need to Understand about Speech Perception and Language Processing
Abstract: This article reviews experiments that have revealed developmental changes in speech perception that accompany improvements in access to phonetic structure. It explains how these perceptual changes appear to be related to other aspects of language development. Evidence is provided that these changes result from adequate language experience in naturalistic contexts.

83. *Title*: Factors Affecting the Development of Speech, Language, and Literacy in Children with Early Cochlear Implantation
Abstract: This study investigated factors contributing to auditory, speech, language, and reading outcomes in 136 children (ages 8–9) with prelingual deafness after 4–6 years of cochlear implants. While child and family characteristics accounted for 20% of outcome variance, the primary rehabilitative factor was educational emphasis on oral–aural communication.

84. *Title*: Changes in Speech Production in a Child with a Cochlear Implant: Acoustic and Kinematic Evidence
Abstract: A method is presented for examining change in motor patterns used to produce linguistic contrasts. In this case study, the method is applied to a child who experienced hearing loss at age 3 and received a multichannel cochlear implant at 7. Post-implant, acoustic durations showed a maturational change.

85. *Title*: In the Beginning Was the Rhyme? A Reflection on Hulme, Hatcher, Nation, Brown, Adams, and Stuart (2002)
Abstract: Describes phonological sensitivity at different grain sizes as a good predictor of reading acquisition in all languages. Presents information on development of phonological sensitivity for syllables, onsets, and rhymes. Illustrates that phoneme-level skills develop fastest in children acquiring orthographically consistent languages with simple syllabic structure. Maintains that for English, both....

86. *Title*: How Much Do We Know about the Importance of Play in Child Development? Review of Research
Abstract: Discusses children's play in conjunction with intellectual development, language, and social benefits. Suggests that play develops personality, encourages personal relations, stimulates creativity, adds to happiness,

and advances learning. Encourages parents and teachers to provide children with richly varied play experiences to promote cognition, language, social/emotional behavior, and….

87.   *Title*: Literacy-Based Planning and Pedagogy That Supports Toddler Language Development
Abstract: Provides an overview of early language and literacy development and influences. Details how teachers can use storybooks to plan toddler curricula, presents criteria for selecting toddler books for curriculum projects, and describes how one book served as the foundation for a curriculum project, focusing on representing ideas and concepts from the book and incorporating activities throughout the….

88.   *Title*: The Lexicon and Phonology: Interactions in Language Acquisition
Abstract: This article highlights the link between lexical and phonological acquisition by considering learning by children beyond the 50-word stage and by applying cognitive models of spoken word processing to development. The effects of lexical and phonological variables on perception, production, and learning are discussed in the context of a two-representation connectionist model.

89.   *Title*: Whole-Word Phonology and Templates: Trap, Bootstrap, or Some of Each?
Abstract: Cognitive mechanisms that may account for the phenomena of whole-word phonology and phonological templates in children are described and strategies for identifying whole-word phonological patterns in normal and disordered phonologies are proposed. Intervention strategies that draw on these same mechanisms as a way to overcome their inappropriate persistence are recommended.

90.   *Title*: Facilitating First Language Development in Young Korean Children through Parent Training in Picture Book Interactions
Abstract: Eleven native-Korean-speaking, Korean-American mothers of children aged 2–4 received 1 hour of training in specific language facilitation techniques around picture-book interactions. A control group received instruction in general emergent literacy development and first-language acquisition. Four weeks later, treatment-group children showed significantly increased language production and….

91.   *Title*: The Relationship between Early Language Delay and Later Difficulties in Literacy
Abstract: Presents diagnostic model of early language delay; examines four longitudinal studies exploring relationship between early language delay and later literacy development. Identifies findings providing strong evidence of continuity between language delay and later reading difficulties and the importance of severity and chronicity of the impairment. Asserts that early language delay is a key risk….

92.   *Title*: Use of the Language Development Survey (LDS) in a National Probability Sample of Children 18 to 35 Months Old
Abstract: Data from 278 children (ages 18–35 months) were used to norm the Language Development Survey (LDS) and the Child Behavioral Checklist. Vocabulary scores increased markedly with age, were higher in girls, and were modestly correlated with socioeconomic level. Correlations between LDS scores and checklist problem scores were low.

93.   *Title*: Play and Language in Children with Autism
Abstract: This article considers the relationship between play and language skills of typical children and children with autism. Evidence for a relationship is reviewed, and it is concluded that if there is a relationship between play and language in children with autism it is weak, if it exists at all.

94.   *Title*: Tracking Preschoolers' Language and Preliteracy Development Using a General Outcome Measurement System: One Education District's Experience
Abstract: This article describes an application of a general outcome measurement system, Individual Growth and Development Indicators, with 68 preschoolers (ages 3–6). Results indicate the measures were easy to use; efficient in administration, scoring, and data interpretation; and provided valuable information for making early childhood education and special education decisions.

95.   *Title*: Child Education and Literacy Learning for Multicultural Societies: The Case of the Brazilian National Curricular References for Child Education (NCRs)
Abstract: Discusses promotion of multicultural child education and literacy learning. Focuses on identity building and language development. Analyzes Brazilian government's "National Curricular References for Child Education." Argues that predominance of a monocultural, cognitive-based approach to child education is detrimental to children whose cultural and linguistic patterns are different from the….

96.   *Title*: Is Chronic Otitis Media Associated with Differences in Parental Input at 12 Months of Age? An Analysis of Joint Attention and Directives
Abstract: Argues that parental input is an important factor often neglected in research that may mediate language outcomes. Investigated how parents interact with their 12-month-old children who suffer from otitis media status. Results indicate that parents of chronically affected children direct attention more often and engage in fewer joint attentional episodes than parents of nonchronically affected….

97. *Title*: The Language Proficiency Profile-2: Assessment of the Global Communication Skills of Deaf Children across Languages and Modalities of Expression
Abstract: Two studies investigated the developmental trends and concurrent validity of the Language Proficiency Profile-2 (LPP-2), a measure of language and communication skills for deaf children. Results indicate that the LPP-2 has good utility not only as a measure of overall language development but also as a predictor of achievement for English language and early reading skills.

98. *Title*: Hearing Status, Language Modality, and Young Children's Communicative and Linguistic Behavior
Abstract: This study compared early pragmatic skill development in 76 children (ages 1–4) with severe or profound hearing loss enrolled in either a simultaneous communication (SC) or oral communication (OC) approach to language learning. Results indicated some advantages of the SC approach, although overall frequency of communication and breadth of vocabulary did not differ between SC and OC groups.

99. *Title*: Assessment of Language Skills in Young Children with Profound Hearing Loss under Two Years of Age
Abstract: The validity of the Diary of Early Language (Di-EL), a parent report technique, was evaluated with nine children with profound hearing loss using cochlear implants or hearing aids. Lexical data, reported by parents using the Di-EL, agreed with results of the MacArthur Communicative Development Inventories and the Rossetti Infant Toddler Language Scale, suggesting the Di-El's validity.

100. *Title*: Play as the Leading Activity of the Preschool Period: Insights from Vygotsky, Leont'ev, and Bakhtin
Abstract: Discusses ideas from Vygotsky, Leont'ev and Bakhtin to show how fantasy play acts as its own zone of proximal development that contributes to the development of symbolic mediation, the appropriation of social roles and symbols, and the preschool child's preparation for elementary school.

101. *Title*: Parental Identification of Early Behavioral Abnormalities in Children with Autistic Disorder
Abstract: Parents of 153 children with autism completed a questionnaire on early childhood behaviors of concern and age of onset. Parents identified the following concerns: gross motor difficulties; social awareness deficits; communication problems; and unusual preoccupations. There was a significant interval between parents first noticing abnormalities and definite diagnosis.

102. *Title*: Genetic Evidence for Bidirectional Effects of Early Lexical and Grammatical Development
Abstract: Two cohorts of same-sex twin pairs were assessed on grammar and vocabulary. Findings indicated that vocabulary and grammar correlated strongly at 2 and 3 years in both cohorts, with a consistently high genetic correlation between vocabulary and grammar at both ages. Findings suggest that the same genetic influences operate for vocabulary and grammar, a finding incompatible with traditional....

103. *Title*: Paradox Lost? No, Paradox Found! Reply to Tomasello and Akhtar (2003)
Abstract: Asserts that the posited paradox between infancy and toddlerhood language was not eliminated by Tomasello and Akhtar's appeal to infants' robust statistical learning abilities. Maintains that scrutiny of their studies supports the resolution that abstracting linguistic form is easy for infants and that toddlers find it difficult to integrate abstract forms with meaning. Claims that intermodal....

104. *Title*: What Paradox? A Response to Naigles (2002)
Abstract: Presents evidence that the supposed paradox in which infants find abstract patterns in speech-like stimuli whereas even some preschoolers struggle to find abstract syntactic patterns within meaningful language is no paradox. Asserts that all research evidence shows that young children's syntactic constructions become abstract in a piecemeal fashion, based on what children have heard in the input....

105. *Title*: Phonological Neighborhood Density Effects in a Rhyme Awareness Task in Five-Year-Old Children
Abstract: Investigates one plausible source of the emergence of phonological awareness—phonological neighborhood density in a group of 5-year-old children, most of whom were pre-readers. Subjects with a high vocabulary age showed neighborhood density effects in a rhyme oddity task, but 5-year-olds with lower vocabulary ages did not.

106. *Title*: Private Speech in Preschool Children: Developmental Stability and Change, Across-Task Constituency and Relations with Classroom Behavior
Abstract: Examined developmental stability and change in children's private speech during the preschool years across-task constituency in children's self-speech, and across-setting relations between private speech in the laboratory and behavior at home and in the classroom. Clear associations were found between children's private speech use in the laboratory and their behavior in the classroom and at home....

107. *Title*: Input and Word Learning: Caregivers' Sensitivity to Lexical Category Distinctions
Abstract: Twenty-four caregivers and their 2- to 4-year-old children took part in a storybook reading task in which caregivers taught children novel labels for familiar objects. Findings indicate parental speech could provide a rich source of information to children in learning how different lexical categories are expressed in their native language.

108. *Title*: The Ability to Learn New Word Meanings from Context by School-Age Children with and without Language Comprehension Difficulties
Abstract: Investigated young children's ability to use narrative contexts to infer the meanings of novel vocabulary terms. Two groups of 15 7- and 8-year-olds participated; children with normally developing reading comprehension skills and children with weak reading comprehension skills. Results are discussed.

109. *Title*: Relative Clause Comprehension Revisited: Commentary on Eisenberg (2002)
Abstract: Eisenberg (2002) presents data from an experiment investigating 3- and 4-year-old children's comprehension of restrictive relative clauses. From the results, she argues that children do not have discourse knowledge of the felicity conditions of relative clauses before acquiring the syntax of relativization. This article evaluates this conclusion on the basis of the methodology used.

110. *Title*: Adult Reformulations of Child Errors as Negative Evidence
Abstract: Examined whether there was negative evidence in adult reformulations of erroneous child utterances, and if so, whether children made use of that evidence. Findings show that adults reformulate erroneous utterances often enough for learning to occur. Children can detect differences between their own utterance and the adult reformulation and make use of that information.

111. *Title*: J's Rhymes: A Longitudinal Case Study of Language Play
Abstract: A longitudinal study of one child documents an invented language game consisting of suffixal reduplication and onset replacement. Argues that this game may more closely resemble adult rhyme.

112. *Title*: The Acquisition of Nuclei: A Longitudinal Analysis of Phonological Vowel Length in Three German-Speaking Children
Abstract: Studies of vowel length acquisition indicate an initial stage in which phonological vowel length is random followed by a stage in which either long vowels or short vowels and codas are produced. To determine whether this sequence of acquisition applies to a group of German-speaking children, monosyllabic and disyllabic words are transcribed and acoustically analyzed. Results are discussed.

113. *Title*: Brief Report: Developmental Change in Theory of Mind Abilities in Children with Autism
Abstract: A longitudinal study investigated developmental change in theory of mind among 57 children (ages 4–14) with autism. Theory of mind tests were administered on an initial visit and one year later. Data indicated significant developmental improvement in theory of mind ability, which was primarily related to the children's language ability.

114. *Title*: Strip Mining for Gold: Research and Policy in Educational Technology—A Response to "Fool's Gold"
Abstract: Responds to a recent critical report on computers in childhood. Highlights include computers, children, and research; social and emotional development; types of software; motivation; social and cognitive interactions; cognitive development; creativity; language and literacy; writing and word processing; mathematics and reasoning; and science and simulations.

115. *Title*: Developmental Profiles of Children Born to Mothers with Intellectual Disability
Abstract: The developmental status of 37 Australian preschool children (ages 5–78 months) born to mothers with intellectual disability was assessed. In all developmental domains, a substantial proportion of the children (between 35% and 57%) showed a delay of at least 3 months. Delays in physical and communication development were most prevalent.

116. *Title*: Do Children with Down's Syndrome Have Difficulty with Argument Structure?
Abstract: The language transcripts of seven children with Down's Syndrome (DS) and seven typically developing children with comparable mean length of utterance levels were compared for verb argument structure. Findings suggest that syntactic difficulties may delay children with DS in overcoming the optional subject phenomena and the lesser number of anomalous arguments shows their inadequate knowledge of....

117. *Title*: Preschoolers Are Sensitive to the Speaker's Knowledge When Learning Proper Names
Abstract: Two experiments examined young children's use of the familiarity principle when learning language. Found that even 2-year-olds successfully identified the referent of a proper name as the individual with whom the speaker was familiar. However, only 5-year-olds reliably succeeded at determining the individual with whom the speaker was familiar based on the speaker's knowledge of an individual's....

118. *Title*: How Children Use Input to Acquire a Lexicon
Abstract: Examined relation of social–pragmatic and data-providing features of input to productive vocabulary of 63 2-year-olds. Found benefits of data provided in mother–child conversation, but no effects of social aspects of those conversations. Properties that benefited lexical development were quantity, lexical richness, and syntactic complexity. Proposed integrated account of role of social and....

119. *Title*: "One Child, Two Languages: A Guide for Preschool Educators of Children Learning English as a Second Language," edited by Patton O. Tabors. Book Review

Abstract: Maintains that Tabor's edited work is the most comprehensive and practical book on the topic available and an essential part of the knowledge base for early care and education professionals. Highlights the book's practical suggestions, concrete examples to illustrate language principles, and recommendations for teachers. Asserts that the content is timely and of critical importance for early....

120. *Title*: The Acquisition of Communication Skills by People with Brain Injury: Some Comparisons with Children with Autism
Abstract: This research identifies the extent to which different contexts modified the language of four people with brain injuries. The four contexts included: their own home, a residential camp, a post-camp period with support, followed by a return home with limited support. Measures demonstrate the success of the enriched camp facility.

121. *Title*: Adjectives Really Do Modify Nouns: The Incremental and Restricted Nature of Early Adjective Acquisition
Abstract: Three experiments introduced 2- and 3-year-olds to novel adjectives either using full noun phrases and describing multiple familiar objects sharing a salient property or describing nouns of vague reference. Found that both groups mapped novel adjectives onto object properties when given taxonomically specific nouns with rich referential and syntactic information, but not when given more general....

122. *Title*: Attention to Novel Objects during Verb Learning
Abstract: Three experiments investigated whether preschoolers attend to actions or objects when learning a novel verb. Findings showed that children learning nouns in the context of novel, moving objects attended exclusively to appearances of objects. Children learning verbs attended equally to appearances and motions. With familiar objects, children attended more to object motions than appearances, similar....

123. *Title*: Children's Command of Quantification
Abstract: Two experiments investigated how child and adult speakers of English and Kannada (Dravidian) interpret scopally ambiguous sentences containing numerally quantified noun phrases and negation. Results showed that 4-year-olds' interpretations were constrained by the surface hierarchical relations (the c-command relations) between sentence elements and not by their linear order.

124. *Title*: Helping Language Grow
Abstract: With early diagnosis and intervention, students with language delays can succeed. This paper presents warning signs and recommends seeking expert help, explaining that supporting such children involves such things as reading to them, using simple but grammatically correct sentences, and following their lead. A sidebar notes areas that may be connected to language delays (e.g., syntax, semantics,....

125. *Title*: Gestural, Signed, and Spoken Modalities in Early Language Development: The Role of Linguistic Input
Abstract: Examined potential effects of early exposure to sign language on the use of communicative gestures by a bilingual hearing child of deaf parents. Data were analyzed to identify types and tokens of communicative gestures, words, signs, and the ways in which they were combined.

126. *Title*: Children's Acquisition of the English Cardinal Number Words: A Special Case of Vocabulary Development
Abstract: To understand the development of number–word construction, students in grades 1, 3, 5, and 7 named and counted from a set of numbers into the billions in two studies. Findings are discussed both in relation to children's growing knowledge of the number system and to vocabulary development.

127. *Title*: The Role of Abstract Syntactic Knowledge in Language Acquisition: A Reply to Tomasello (2000)
Abstract: Argues that Tomasello's (2000) interpretation of young children's conservatism in language production depends on questionable premises. Reviews evidence against the assumptions, showing that children learn item-specific facts about verbs and other lexical items. Asserts that researchers must explore the interactions of lexical and more abstract syntactic knowledge in language acquisition to....

128. *Title*: Phonemic Awareness: A Complex Developmental Process
Abstract: This article uses a developmental model of language (Situational-Discourse-Semantics or SDS), along with a constellation or neuro-network model, to describe the developmental emergence of phonemic awareness. Ten sources of phonemic awareness are profiled along with developmental continuum, providing an integrated view of this complex development.

筆記欄

筆記欄

國家圖書館出版品預行編目（CIP）資料

如何撰寫文獻探討：給社會暨行為科學學生指南／
Jose L. Galvan 著；吳德邦, 馬秀蘭譯.
--初版.--臺北市：心理, 2012.06
面；　公分.--（社會科學研究系列；81220）
譯自：Writing literature reviews：a guide for students
of the social and behavioral sciences

ISBN 978-986-191-483-1（平裝）

1.社會科學 2.行為科學 3.學術研究 4.論文寫作法

501.2   100027720

社會科學研究系列 81220

如何撰寫文獻探討：給社會暨行為科學學生指南

作　　者：Jose L. Galvan
譯　　者：吳德邦、馬秀蘭
執行編輯：李　晶
總 編 輯：林敬堯
發 行 人：洪有義
出 版 者：心理出版社股份有限公司
地　　址：231 新北市新店區光明街 288 號 7 樓
電　　話：(02)29150566
傳　　真：(02)29152928
郵撥帳號：19293172　心理出版社股份有限公司
網　　址：http://www.psy.com.tw
電子信箱：psychoco@ms15.hinet.net
駐美代表：Lisa Wu（lisawu99@optonline.net）
排 版 者：臻圓打字印刷有限公司
印 刷 者：正恒實業有限公司
初版一刷：2012 年 6 月
初版三刷：2017 年 2 月
I S B N：978-986-191-483-1
定　　價：新台幣 250 元